The Politics of Shared Power
Congress and the Executive

Politics and Public Policy Series

Advisory Editor

Robert L. Peabody

Johns Hopkins University

The Politics of Shared Power
Congress and the Executive

Louis Fisher

Congressional Quarterly Press
a division of
CONGRESSIONAL QUARTERLY INC.
1414 22nd Street N.W., Washington, D.C. 20037

Jean L. Woy *Acquisitions Editor*
Sari Horwitz *Project Editor*
Maceo Mayo *Production Supervisor*
Robert O. Redding *Cover Design*
Richard A. Pottern *Art Director*

Printed in the United States of America

Library of Congress Cataloging in Publication Data

Fisher, Louis.
    The politics of shared power.

    Bibliography: p.
    Includes index.
    1. Separation of powers — United States.
2. United States. Congress — Powers and duties.
3. Executive power — United States. I. Title.

JK305.F54   320.4   81-5442
ISBN 0-87187-163-7   AACR2

To my parents,
for staying out of the way,
letting a child
grow

Foreword

The philosophical question of how power is to be distributed among various elements of a government is at least as old as Plato and Aristotle. Many of America's constitutional framers were especially familiar with the writings of Montesquieu and Locke on this subject. The doctrine of the separation of powers was a core assumption underlying the drafting of our Constitution in 1787. Although the constitutional framers divided power among three principal branches of government, the checks and balances written into the Constitution assured that there would not be a tidy division of separated powers.

Political scientists from Woodrow Wilson to Edwin S. Corwin and Richard E. Neustadt have long been intrigued with how the separation of powers has worked.[1] They and numerous colleagues have applied a multitude of approaches to the problem—historical, legal, and behavioral. Most of them have concluded, as Neustadt did, that what we really have is not separation of powers, but rather "separate institutions *sharing* powers." [2]

Louis Fisher's book, *The Politics of Shared Power: Congress and the Executive,* fits directly into this tradition of careful, scholarly analysis. He brings to bear not only his own findings, but also thoughtful interpretations of countless court decisions, legislative enactments, and executive actions. The result is an imaginative and thorough critique of a central problem in American governance—how the executive and the legislature usually get along, sometimes agree to disagree, frequently clash, and occasionally stalemate one another.

Fisher provides many examples of congressional-executive interactions from George Washington to the Reagan administration. The main actors—presidents and bureaucrats, representatives and senators, Supreme Court and lower court judges—are brought into focus. For, of course, in the final analysis, there are no such entities as presidencies, Congresses, and courts except through the activities of the men and women who have held these positions over time.

The author is well qualified to write about deliberations and activities of the executive and legislative branches. After receiving his

Ph.D. degree in 1967 from the New School for Social Research, he taught courses in American government and constitutional law at several New York colleges. In 1970 Fisher joined the Government Division staff of the Congressional Research Service of the Library of Congress. He has written three books—*President and Congress: Power and Policy* (1972); *Presidential Spending Power* (1975); and *The Constitution Between Friends: Congress, the President, and the Law* (1978)—and numerous articles. These works provide some of the background for this broader, more integrative treatise.

In Chapter 1, Fisher lays the constitutional groundwork for his analysis of the workings of executive-legislative relationships. As he notes, by the late 1780s the doctrine of a separation of powers had all but given way to the operations of checks and balances in practice. Thus, from its conception, the American political system has operated on the basis of concurrent or shared powers. The president as legislator is the focal point of Chapter 2. Both formal powers, such as the right to recommend to Congress measures "as he shall judge necessary and expedient," as well as more informal sources of influence are analyzed. This chapter is rich in historical examples of executive lobbying, ranging from the nation's formative years through the post-World War II era and including the Reagan administration.

Chapter 3 examines congressional intervention in administrative matters. Fisher explores both the statutory and nonstatutory instruments of control that Congress exerts over the bureaucracy and the president. In Chapter 4 Fisher raises the thorny question of who the bureaucracy serves, Congress or the president. He explores the creation and reorganization of executive departments and the control of federal personnel.

Chapter 5 analyzes the role of the independent regulatory commissions in our government. Fisher examines the "independence" of the different commissions and how that independence has affected policy decisions.

In Chapter 6, the concluding chapter, Fisher takes a broader look at how the branches of government have shared the responsibility of representing the public's interest. The role of the courts is examined, as is the complex of congressional committee, interest group, and bureaucratic agency called the subgovernment.

As this book is being published, President Reagan and the members of the 97th Congress have been involved in a series of epic struggles, especially over the budget and tax measures. The struggle has been made even more complicated by divided party control of Congress. Louis Fisher's advice in his epilogue is on target—evaluations of executive and congressional actions in these troublesome times truly call for measuring our words. This book will aid students, practitioners, and citizens alike in coming to more informed and comprehensive understandings about the ways in which policies are made and implemented by the national government.

Robert L. Peabody

NOTES

1. Woodrow Wilson's *Congressional Government* (Boston: Houghton Mifflin Co., 1885); Edwin S. Corwin's *The President: Office and Powers,* 3d ed. (New York: New York University Press, 1957); and Richard E. Neustadt's *Presidential Power* (New York: John Wiley & Sons, 1960) are among central works in an extensive literature on presidential-legislative-judicial relationships.
2. Neustadt, *Presidential Power,* p. 33.

Preface

To study one branch of government in isolation from the others is usually an exercise in make-believe. Very few operations of Congress and the presidency are genuinely independent and autonomous. For the most part, an initiative by one branch will set in motion a series of compensatory actions by the other branch—sometimes of a cooperative nature, sometimes antagonistic. Like tuning forks when struck, the branches trigger complementary vibrations and reverberations.

Even a study on executive-legislative relations, if narrowly construed, is a contrivance. Congress and the presidency function within a political environment that consists of the judiciary, the bureaucracy, independent regulatory commissions, political parties, state and local governments, interest groups, and foreign nations. This book concentrates on the intersection where congressional and presidential interests converge. Despite the heavy traffic, head-on collisions are rare. Instead, individual drivers merge safely at high speeds. After passing through an elaborate cloverleaf, they exit to prepare for future exchanges. Standing in the midst of this intersection gives one the impression of anarchy and chaos, but distance and perspective bring a sense of order and purpose.

Although major personalities and pivotal events make their impacts, institutional patterns persist. The election of Jimmy Carter to the presidency, accompanied by Democratic majorities in each house of Congress, did not by itself assure a constructive and effective partnership between the executive and legislative branches. Party leadership and affiliation could not bridge the deep divisions existing then or the more enduring disagreements on policy goals and constitutional duties. The 1980 election of a Republican president, Ronald Reagan, presented a different set of power relationships. Though his party gained control of the Senate, he faced a Democratic House of Representatives. But regardless of who occupies the White House, members of Congress have their own constitutional obligations to discharge and their unique constituencies to represent.

A substantial part of the politics of executive-legislative relations is conducted through the courts. It is short-sighted to push this material to the side by calling it "judicial" or "legal." This activity is as political as anything else in the nation's capital. The courts review cases brought to them by members of Congress, the president, and agency heads. Judges referee disputes between the two political branches. When political activists decide that their interests will not be satisfied by Congress or the executive branch, they turn to the courts. Adjudication is politics by another name. Decisions by the judiciary determine individual rights, allocation of federal funds, and the prerogatives of the legislative and executive branches.

This book is shaped by a central question: how does the separation of power doctrine work in practice? This question gives rise to a number of issues. To what degree does the president participate as legislator? How much does Congress intervene in administrative matters? Are there political and constitutional problems for this sharing of power? Separate chapters on the bureaucracy and the independent regulatory commissions allow us to probe these questions more deeply and from different angles. A concluding chapter examines the representative function as carried out by Congress, the president, the bureaucracy, the courts, and subgovernments. An epilogue reviews some of the concepts and words in our vocabulary that interfere with an understanding of executive-legislative relations.

Publishing this book with Congressional Quarterly allowed me to appreciate first-hand the qualities that make an organization distinctive and distinguished. Jean L. Woy deserves a great deal of credit for suggesting this book. She worked with me on the early stages of conception, helping to pull individual segments into a coherent whole and tolerating delays on my part that went beyond the bounds of propriety. I was especially fortunate to have as professional reviewers Eric L. Davis, Robert L. Peabody, and James L. Sundquist. Their unsparing critiques spared me many embarrassments. I was helped at all times by two colleagues and friends, Roger H. Davidson and Walter J. Oleszek. The responsibility for converting a manuscript into a book fell to Sari Horwitz, who displayed a keen sense for organization and detail and led me through the mysteries of modern computerized book production.

Louis Fisher

Contents

1

Constitutional Underpinnings

Even perceptive students of government have described Congress and the presidency as detached and disconnected institutions. Writing in 1885, Woodrow Wilson claimed that it was impossible that the framers of the Constitution "could believe that executive and legislature could be brought into close relations of cooperation and mutual confidence without being tempted, nay, even bidden, to collude." How could either branch, he asked, maintain its independence "unless each were to have the guaranty of the Constitution that its own domain should be absolutely safe from invasion, its own prerogatives absolutely free from challenge?" [1]

Scholars today advocate an entirely different model, with the emphasis on sharing rather than separation. As noted by Richard Neustadt: "The constitutional convention of 1787 is supposed to have created a government of 'separated powers.' It did nothing of the sort. Rather, it created a government of separated institutions *sharing* powers." [2]

Close examination of executive-legislative disputes will illustrate the difficulty of capturing in a few words the essence of separated powers. Every concise formulation seems unsatisfactory in light of specific cases and circumstances. The Constitution, for both theoretical and practical reasons, anticipates a government of shared as well as separated powers.

SEPARATION DOCTRINE: THEORY AND PRACTICE

The record of the Continental Congress convinced the framers of the Constitution that they needed a separate branch of government to foster administrative efficiency. From 1774 to 1781, Congress performed all the functions of a national government: legislative, administrative, and adjudicative.

In an effort to allow more time for legislative duties, members of Congress experimented with various makeshift arrangements to handle administrative matters. First they relied on committees, then on boards staffed by men recruited from outside the legislature, and finally, in 1781, decided on single executives to administer four principal areas: foreign affairs, finance, war, and marine. Although these executives were agents of Congress and totally dependent upon the legislative body for their existence, a measure of independence and autonomy evolved.[3]

Between 1781 and 1787, the framers concluded that it was essential to vest administrative responsibilities and permanency in a separate executive branch. By the time of the Philadelphia Convention, however, no one was quite certain how much separation should exist between the legislative and executive branches. James Madison had not decided either the manner in which the executive should be constituted or "of the authorities with which it ought to be clothed."[4] The Virginia Plan, presented to the convention on May 29, 1787, authorized the legislature to select the executive. Many other "prerogatives" we now associate with the president were initially assigned to Congress. For example, the Virginia Plan called upon the legislature to choose members of a national judiciary. Two months later the delegates voted to have judges appointed solely by the Senate.[5] In a later draft of the Constitution, the Senate retained sole power to make treaties and appoint ambassadors.[6]

As the Convention progressed, these features of congressional government were replaced by the constitutional provisions familiar to us today. The Senate and the president share the appointment and treaty powers. The president is chosen by electors rather than by the legislature (unless a tie vote or three-candidate race throws the election into the House of Representatives), and the president possesses a qualified veto, in part as protection against legislative encroachments. The presidential veto may be overridden by a two-thirds majority of each house.

Other devices were considered to limit the legislative branch. Madison reminded the delegates that experience had proved "a tendency in our governments to throw all power into the Legislative vortex. The Executives of the States are in general little more than Cyphers; the legislatures omnipotent." James Wilson feared that the "natural operation of the Legislature will be to swallow up the Executive."

Gouverneur Morris and John Mercer also warned of legislative aggrandizement and usurpation.[7] Serious consideration was given to the creation of a revisionary council (joining the executive with the judiciary) to check legislative ambitions. Madison urged that the judiciary be introduced in "the business of Legislation—they will protect their Department, and uniting [with] the Executive render their Check or negative more respectable." [8]

Compared to the executive departments under the Articles of Confederation, the president possessed far greater independence and autonomy. Yet for government to function, all three branches had to cooperate as part of a common endeavor. The ironies and subtleties of our constitutional structure were captured by Justice Robert H. Jackson:

> While the Constitution diffused power the better to secure liberty, it also contemplates that practice will integrate the dispersed powers into a workable government. It enjoins upon its branches separatedness and interdependence, autonomy but reciprocity.[9]

By the late 1780s, the doctrine of a strict separation of powers had lost ground to the idea of checks and balances. Each branch shares in the powers of another branch: the Senate confirms presidential appointments and ratifies treaties, the House may impeach the president, and the president may veto bills but then can be overridden. A contemporary of the framers, publishing his views in 1788, ridiculed the separation doctrine as a "hackneyed principle" and a "trite maxim." [10] Madison, in *Federalist 37, 47,* and *48,* took great pains to emphasize the extent of sharing between the branches. Alexander Hamilton, in *Federalist 66,* said that the true meaning of the separation maxim was "entirely compatible with a partial intermixture" and that overlapping was not only "proper, but necessary to the mutual defence of the several members of the government, against each other."

Alexander White, a member of the First Congress, dismissed as fantasy the call for a separation of powers: "We are told, that we ought to keep the Legislative and Executive departments distinct; if we were forming a constitution, the observation would be worthy of due consideration, and we would agree to the principles; but the Constitution is formed, and the powers blended; the wished-for separation is therefore impracticable." [11] It is also worth recalling that the First Congress rejected a constitutional amendment that would have strictly allocated the powers of government among three separate branches.[12]

No one has successfully defined the boundaries between the legislative, executive, and judicial branches. In *Federalist 37,* Madison compared the problem to naturalists who had difficulty drawing an exact line between vegetable life and the animal world. Such difficulties, however, do not deny the existence of vegetables and animals. Nor is the distinction between earth, air, and water rendered meaningless by the existence of dust, mud, and clouds.[13]

Two principles, seemingly irreconcilable, must operate side by side to make the American system prosper: (1) the separation of powers and (2) the system of checks and balances. Far from being contradictory, they complement and support one another. An institution cannot check unless it has some measure of independence; it cannot retain that independence without the power to check.

EXCLUSIVE POWERS

The Supreme Court cautions against an indiscriminate use of the "sharing of power" thesis. As it noted in 1974, the judicial power vested in the federal courts by Article III of the Constitution "can no more be shared with the Executive Branch than the Chief Executive, for example, can share with the Judiciary the veto power, or the Congress share with the Judiciary the power to override a Presidential veto." [14]

The system of separated powers is secured by Article I, Section 6 of the Constitution, prohibiting members of Congress from holding appointive office. The delegates at the Philadelphia Convention wanted to avoid the corruption of the British system, which allowed members of Parliament to create offices for their own profit.[15] Other safeguards are placed within the Constitution to protect the independence of each branch. Congress is expressly proscribed from passing a bill of attainder, which would encroach upon the judiciary by inflicting punishment without a trial.[16] The Speech or Debate clause (Article I, Section 6) was added to protect legislators from executive or judicial harassment. For any speech or debate in either house, senators and representatives "shall not be questioned in any other place." [17] Congress may not reduce the compensation of the president or members of the federal judiciary. In practice, Congress has considered it an impermissible intrusion into executive matters to enact specific appropriations for the White House or even, in some cases, to insist on vouchers for presidential expenses.[18]

The budget process includes a number of discrete powers. The appropriations power belongs to Congress alone: "No Money shall be drawn from the Treasury, but in Consequence of Appropriations made by Law." To the House of Representatives is reserved the exclusive power to originate tax bills, although by custom it originates appropriation bills as well. Presidents have resisted efforts by Congress to dictate the submission of budget requests. In 1978 President Carter vetoed a bill that directed the secretaries of interior, agriculture, and defense to report to congressional authorizing committees whenever their budget requests for certain activities fell below the amount authorized. Carter called this provision "an unacceptable intrusion on the President's obligations and authority as Chief Executive." [19]

There are other exclusive powers for Congress. The House of Representatives has the sole power of impeachment; the Senate has the sole power to try all impeachments. Each house is the judge of the "Elections, Returns and Qualifications" of its own members, but Congress may not add to the qualifications specified in the Constitution.[20] Each house determines the rules of its proceedings and may punish and expel a member. In 1980 the House of Representatives expelled Pennsylvania Democrat Michael J. "Ozzie" Myers for his involvement in Abscam, an FBI undercover investigation of political corruption. He was the first member of the House to be dismissed in 119 years.

The president's "exclusive" powers fall principally under three headings: (1) the power to nominate; (2) the power to negotiate with foreign countries; and (3) the power to pardon. Exclusivity does not mean that these executive prerogatives operate without legislative participation. Depending on congressional interest and the intervention of outside groups, the exclusive nature of these powers expands and contracts but never disappears entirely. Legal doctrine and political reality limit all three powers.

Power to Nominate

Chief Justice John Marshall once called the nomination process the "sole act of the president" and "completely voluntary." [21] Congress may not establish a nominating procedure that puts before the president a single name. To design a method of selection that takes from the president the exercise of judgment and will, and limits him to one name and no other, is no different in constitutional principle from insisting that "he shall appoint John Doe to that office." [22] To preserve this constitutional discretion, the president is generally furnished at least three names for each vacancy.[23] There are situations, such as a senator's recommendation of someone for U.S. attorney, where the president's political options are limited to one name.

Congress has discovered a number of ways to circumscribe the president's authority to nominate. It may stipulate the qualifications of appointees, itemizing in great detail the qualities the president must consider before sending forth a name. For federal judges, U.S. attorneys, and marshals, it has been the custom for senators to "nominate" the individuals, allowing the president to give his "advice and consent." For appellate courts and some district courts, panels were formed under President Jimmy Carter to recommend nominees for federal judges. The element of presidential choice was preserved by having each panel recommend five candidates for each vacancy.[24]

President Ronald Reagan abolished the judicial nominating commissions established to select appellate judges. His administration also announced that the attorney general would invite Republican senators, with the assistance of advisory groups, to identify prospective candidates for federal district judges. For states with no Republican senators, the attorney general would solicit suggestions and recommendations from the Republican House members of that state.[25]

The president can decide whom to appoint but cannot decide whether an agency should exist and function.[26] Once an office has been authorized by Congress it must be filled. Otherwise the statutory purpose would be nullified by the president's failure to appoint officials to carry out the law. When an agency consists of several members at the top, and can operate without the full staff on board, there are precedents for not filling each office. The Interstate Commerce Commission is authorized eleven commissioners, but President Carter deliberately kept its size to seven by not filling all the vacancies.

Power to Negotiate

In terms of express constitutional powers, executive prerogatives in foreign affairs are quite limited. From the constitutional duty to receive "Ambassadors and public Ministers," the president serves as our primary channel of communication with other nations.[27] The Logan Act of 1799 attempted to protect this responsibility. It was directed against private citizens who "usurp the Executive authority of this Government, by commencing or carrying on any correspondence with the Governments of any foreign Prince or State...."[28]

Routinely violated, this statute has resulted in the indictment of only one individual, and he was found not guilty. The Logan Act is of doubtful constitutionality because it is vague in meaning and restrictive of First Amendment freedoms.[29] Its enforceability is reflected in this comment in 1979 by President Carter (the nation's chief law enforcement officer), after American blacks had traveled to the Mideast to talk to Arab and Israeli leaders:

> ... I don't have any authority, nor do I want to have any authority, to interrupt or to interfere with the right of American citizens to travel where they choose and to meet with whom they choose. I would not want that authority; I think it would be a violation of the basic constitutional rights that are precious to our Nation.[30]

A trip to Cuba in 1975 by Democratic Senators John Sparkman of Alabama and George McGovern of South Dakota raised the question of whether they had violated the Logan Act. The State Department concluded that nothing in the act "would appear to restrict members of the Congress from engaging in discussions with foreign officials in pursuance of their legislative duties under the Constitution." Both senators told the Cuban officials that they had no authority to negotiate on behalf of the United States.[31] When former President Richard Nixon's trip to China was challenged in 1976 as a possible violation of the Logan Act, the State Department answered that his visit was undertaken entirely as a private citizen and that the department was "unaware of any basis for believing that Mr. Nixon acted with the intent prohibited by the Logan Act." [32]

While more than 50 Americans were held hostage in Iran, beginning in November 1979, an assortment of American legislators, professors, clergymen, and parents of the hostages traveled to that country to try their hand at negotiation. Carter's patience ended the following summer when former Attorney General Ramsey Clark attended a conference in Iran despite a presidential ban. Carter announced his inclination to prosecute Clark and several others who had violated his directive.[33] This amounted to presidential pique, however, and the challenge to presidential power was soon forgotten.

From the constitutional power to "receive Ambassadors and other public Ministers," the president derives the exclusive power to recognize foreign governments. Courts consider themselves bound by the president's determination of which political group to recognize as the government of a foreign country.[34] Also flowing from the president's duty to receive ambassadors and to make treaties is the president's inherent authority, as recognized by the comptroller general, to provide Secret Service protection "of distinguished foreign visitors to this country or of official representatives of the United States while they are abroad." [35]

In 1979, when Congress attempted to keep open ten American consulates in foreign countries, President Carter argued that implicit in the Constitution is the right of the president to decide when and where an ambassador or consul should be appointed. Congress could not "mandate the establishment of consular relations at a time and place unacceptable to the President." To protect his prerogative, Carter signed the bill but treated the statutory language on consulates as a recommendation rather than a requirement.[36] The Senate countered the following year by invoking the power of the purse, prohibiting the use of funds to close the consulates, and earmarking $1.7 million to keep them open. By that time, however, Carter had directed that seven be closed, and the remaining three were shut down before Congress could complete action on the Senate bill.[37]

According to the standard annotated version of the Constitution, the process of drafting and negotiating a treaty is a "presidential monopoly."[38] Edward S. Corwin, in his classic study on the presidency, propounded the same theory. The president "alone has the power to negotiate treaties with foreign governments." [39] In that sentiment he followed the well-known position of Justice George Sutherland who claimed that the president alone negotiates: "Into the field of negotiation the Senate cannot intrude; and Congress itself is powerless to invade it." [40]

This strict reading of the negotiation process satisfies neither the constitutional text nor practical politics. The Constitution does not confer upon the president an exclusive role in negotiations. The president "shall have Power, by and with the Advice and Consent of the Senate, to make Treaties." This provision differs significantly from the constitutional procedure for appointments, for there the president "shall nominate, and by and with the Advice and Consent of the Senate, shall appoint Ambassadors." The responsibility for nomination is clearly set apart and reserved to the president, followed by Senate action. No such two-step procedure with a division of labor (negotiation by the president and ratification by the Senate) exists for treaties.

George Washington believed that the Constitution intended joint executive-legislative action on treaties. He advised the Senate that oral communications with the Senate regarding treaties "seem indispensably necessary; because in these a variety of matters are contained, all of which not only require consideration, but some of them may undergo much discussion; to do which by written communications would be tedious without being satisfactory." [41] It was his intention to send "propositions" to the Senate, allowing senators to make changes and offer recommendations to treaty drafts rather than simply voting up or down the finished product. [42]

His meeting with the Senate in August 1789, concerning an Indian treaty, often has been misinterpreted. Senator William Maclay of Pennsylvania described President Washington's frustration in trying to negotiate face-to-face with senators. [43] Although Washington never again resorted to personal consultation with the Senate on treaties, he continued to seek the advice of senators through *written* communications. The negotiation of treaties often has been shared with the Senate in order to secure legislative understanding and support. [44] After World War II, Democratic Senator Tom Connally of Texas and Republican Senator Arthur Vandenberg of Michigan participated in more than 200 meetings with Secretary of State James F. Byrnes in the negotiations that resulted in the peace treaties with Italy and the satellite states in 1947. [45]

Of course a president may, like Woodrow Wilson, exclude the Senate from the negotiation stage, but the results can be calamitous. The failure of the Senate to ratify the Treaty of Versailles is the most conspicuous casualty of a unilateral negotiation by the executive. [46] A healthier model of executive-legislative collaboration is the North Atlantic Treaty, developed by the State Department in close cooperation with the Senate Foreign Relations Committee. Secretary of State Dean Acheson, who participated in those negotiations as an executive official, later remarked that while the treaty process is formally divided into negotiation and ratification, "anybody with any sense would consult with certainly some of the members of the ratifying body before he got himself out on the very end of a limb from which he could be sawed off." [47]

Although the president and the Senate have the exclusive power to make treaties, the requirement of funds to implement the treaties has brought the House of Representatives increasingly into the picture. Throughout history the House has asserted its prerogatives whenever international agreements affected the purse. Acheson recognized this fact decades ago:

> The time has passed when the Senate monopolized the congressional function in this field [of foreign affairs], since it is the execution of policy, calling for legal authority, funds, and men, which is the ultimate test of success or failure. [48]

Many of the reservations attached to the Panama Canal Treaty of 1978, and many of the restrictions that appeared in implementing legislation adopted by the House in 1979, might have been avoided had President Carter reached out earlier to include key members of the House and Senate.

Power to Pardon

Article II reserves for the president the power to grant "Reprieves and Pardons for Offenses against the United States, except in Cases of Impeachment." This power may take a variety of forms: a full pardon, conditional pardon, clemency for a class of people (amnesty), amnesty on condition, commutation (substituting a lighter punishment for a heavier one), commutation on condition, and remission of fines and forfeitures.[49]

The power of pardon is one of the few "exclusive" powers available to the president. The responsibility fell to President Reagan alone, in 1981, to pardon former FBI officials Edward Miller and Mark Felt. As with other powers exercised by the government, however, a number of limitations and checks operate. The power of pardon is limited to offenses against the United States (not against the individual states and localities). The president cannot use the power to compensate individuals for what has been done or suffered. He cannot draw money from the treasury, except as expressly authorized by an act of Congress.[50]

Through its appropriations and taxing powers, Congress may remit fines, penalties, and forfeitures, thereby participating in "pardons." Congress, with the support of the Supreme Court and the Justice

Department, has vested that discretion in the secretary of the treasury and in other executive officials.[51] Congress may also legislate a general pardon or amnesty by repealing a law that had imposed criminal liability. It derives this power not by "sharing" the president's pardon power, but through its power to legislate and to repeal legislation.[52]

Certain statutory restrictions have been struck down by the Supreme Court as invalid interferences with the pardon power. During the Civil War, Congress required an oath of office for everyone in the federal service. In a further effort to discriminate between loyal and disloyal individuals in the Union, it extended the oath of office to attorneys who practiced in the federal courts. When President Andrew Johnson issued a pardon to Augustus H. Garland, a Confederate sympathizer and one of the nation's leading attorneys, Garland's inability to take the oath would have barred him from practicing in the federal courts. The Supreme Court, in upholding the pardon, stated that Congress could neither limit the effect of the pardon nor exclude from its exercise any class of offenders: "The benign prerogative of mercy reposed in him cannot be fettered by any legislative restrictions." [53] When a proviso in an appropriations act attempts to control the president's power to pardon, as well as prescribe to the judiciary the effect of a pardon, the statutory provision cannot stand.[54]

Many of these principles apply to two recent controversies over the pardon power: President Ford's pardon of Nixon, and President Carter's granting of amnesty to those who had violated the draft laws during the Vietnam war. On September 8, 1974, President Ford granted a full pardon "for all offenses against the United States which Richard Nixon has committed or may have committed or taken part in during the period from January 20, 1969, through August 9, 1974." Some members of Congress suspected that Nixon made a deal with Ford when nominating him to be vice president. If Nixon had conditioned the nomination on the promise of a pardon, or conditioned his own resignation on a pardon, the House might have charged Ford with accepting a bribe, which is itself an impeachable offense. To allay such concerns, Ford took the extraordinary step of appearing before the House Judiciary Committee to explain the basis for his action.[55]

To some legislators it seemed improper for Ford to grant a pardon before formal charges had been lodged against Nixon and without a formal admission of guilt from him. It is established, however, that a pardon may be granted prior to a conviction and even before indictment.[56] Still, it is generally regarded as unwise and inexpedient to invoke the power prior to trial and condemnation. The president, without the benefit of all the facts that can be produced through the normal trial procedure, may inadvertently grant a pardon for offenses quite unknown to him.[57]

A pardon carries an "imputation of guilt." Upon acceptance of a pardon, an individual in effect confesses guilt.[58] On both points—guilt and confession—Nixon equivocated. Philip W. Buchan, counsel to President Ford, interpreted Nixon's statement as one of "contrition," which is an expression of sorrow, not necessarily of guilt. Buchan believed that Nixon's words came "very close to saying that he did wrong, that he did not act forthrightly." [59]

In 1977, President Carter clashed with Congress over two appropriation acts that prohibited him from using funds to carry out his amnesty order. With certain exceptions, the order granted an unconditional pardon for Vietnam-era violators of the selective service laws. Some of the appropriation restrictions had no practical effect by the time that Carter signed the bills. His cancellation of indictments for certain violations of the selective service laws, and termination of investigations regarding those violations, did not depend on appropriations. But he objected, in particular, to a statutory prohibition concerning the exclusion of aliens because of possible violations of selective service laws. Carter considered this feature an unconstitutional interference with his power to pardon, a bill of attainder, and a denial of due process.[60]

CONCURRENT POWERS

The American political system operates primarily on the basis of concurrent powers. One branch can do very little without the support and countenance of the others. Justice Oliver Wendell Holmes, Jr. once noted:

> [H]owever we may disguise it by veiling words we do not and cannot carry out the distinction between legislative and executive action with mathematical precision and divide the branches into watertight compartments, were it ever so desirable to do so, which I am far from believing that it is, or that the Constitution requires.[61]

The framers tried to produce a document that would allow government to operate more effectively and with greater powers than were possible under the Articles of Confederation. They spent an entire decade prior to the Philadelphia Convention in an anxious and persistent search for a more workable form of government.[62] While the framers adopted a separation of powers, they "endeavored to prove that a rigid adherence to it in all cases would be subversive of the efficiency of the government, and result in the destruction of the public liberties." [63]

Justice Louis Brandeis argued that the doctrine of separated powers was adopted "not to promote efficiency but to preclude the exercise of arbitrary power." [64] However, the framers believed that a separation of powers would act in the interest of efficiency. To achieve that objective, public officials must act with moderation and common sense, ever respectful of the rights and privileges of other branches, constitutional limitations, and the larger purposes of government. The antithesis of that attitude took shape in the extremism and doctrinal wrangling of the Lyndon Johnson and Richard Nixon administrations.

Foreign and Domestic Sectors

Especially in the twentieth century, supporters of a strong presidency have argued for executive independence in external matters. They suggest that military and diplomatic questions are exclusively assigned to the chief executive. In a landmark decsion in 1936, Justice Sutherland claimed that foreign and domestic affairs were different "both in respect of their origin and their nature." [65] He elaborated on "this vast external realm" of international affairs, "with its important, complicated, delicate and manifold problems." According to his reasoning, legislation over this domain must accord to the president "a degree of discretion and freedom from statutory restriction which would not be admissible were domestic affairs alone involved." [66] In these remarks, which were extraneous to the specific issue before the Court, he borrowed from his private writings and also ventilated personal views of a "vigorous diplomacy which strongly, even belligerently, called always for an assertion of American rights." [67]

Sutherland based his assertion on his belief that the powers of external sovereignty "passed from the Crown not to the colonies severally, but to the colonies in their collective and corporate capacity as the United States of America." [68] This theory has been convincingly rejected by scholars as historically false. The states operated as sovereign entities, not as parts of a collective body. [69] Sutherland's thesis of an external-internal dichotomy has had a mixed reception. Aaron Wildavsky, in an influential study published in 1966, provided some support by describing "two presidencies": one for domestic and the other for international responsibilities. Covering the period from 1948 to 1964, Wildavsky wrote that presidents since World War II had "much greater success in controlling the nation's defense and foreign policies than in dominating its domestic policies." [70]

Eight years after the publication of Wildavsky's study, Donald Peppers discovered a different state of affairs. The years of Lyndon Johnson and Richard Nixon had narrowed the gap between presidential power in the domestic and foreign sectors. For Wildavsky, presidential power in foreign policy derived from the immediacy of the Cold War. Eight years later many of the Cold War tensions had subsided. The war in Vietnam and negotiations with Soviet Russia and Communist China transformed the climate. Also, congressional reassertion through such statutes as the War Powers Resolution of 1973 challenged some of the formal powers available to the president when Wildavsky wrote.[71] Court decisions and other legislative actions regarding executive agreements, freedom of information, the U.S. intelligence community, and electronic surveillance placed new limits on the president.

A new mood of legislative skepticism encouraged closer scrutiny of executive proposals in national security matters. Weapons systems, including the ABM (antiballistic missile) system and the B-1 bomber, were contested in Congress with unprecedented vigor. Moreover, "foreign policy" issues were having a demonstrably greater impact on the domestic economy. The American public learned that as the dollar declined abroad, prices rose at home. With stunning speed the Arab oil embargo of 1973-1974 doubled the price of gasoline and created long lines at the neighborhood service station. Grain sales to Russia brought the domestic and foreign arenas into close proximity. In 1980 the Carter administration imposed an embargo on grain sales to the Soviet Union in retaliation for the Soviet invasion of Afghanistan. The embargo, abandoned by President Reagan in 1981, immediately affected grain companies, grain elevators, and farmers, but the decision gradually had an impact on the entire domestic economy. Scholars (with some apologies) coined the word "intermestic" to describe events that are a blend of international and domestic.[72] Domestic constituencies are especially powerful in influencing foreign trade decisions such as the adoption of curbs on Japanese auto imports.

To support the "two presidencies" theory, Wildavsky relied heavily on a measure of presidential legislative success compiled by Congressional Quarterly until the mid-1970s. He examined 2,499 presidential proposals submitted to Congress from 1948 to 1964. In 1979, however, Lee Sigelman narrowed the focus to examine just key congressional votes on major issues, and a different picture emerged:

> ... in direct opposition to the two presidencies thesis, in votes on key issues since 1957 most presidents have not enjoyed a freer hand in the foreign and defense arenas than in domestic policy-making. Only Eisenhower and Nixon during his first term compiled appreciably better records of congressional support on foreign and defense than on domestic issues, while both Johnson and Ford did much better on domestic than on foreign and defense votes.[73]

When it suits their purpose, executive officials will sometimes argue that it is artificial to distinguish between external and internal affairs. For example, officials in the Nixon administration wanted full freedom to wiretap both foreign agents and domestic organizations. The government contended that foreign and domestic affairs are "inextricably intertwined and that any attempt to legally distinguish the impact of foreign affairs from the matters of internal subversive activities is an exercise in futility." [74]

Clash of Prerogatives

The exercise of prerogatives by Congress and the president often puts the two branches on a collision course, requiring an accommodation that is satisfactory to both. Two examples where this often occurs are (1) access to information and (2) the presidential veto.

In no area of federal activity is the need for compromise so essential as access to information. Although the courts have recognized that Congress has an implied power to investigate, and that the president has an implied power to withhold information, neither power is absolute. When legislators seek documents that an executive wants to withhold, something has to give.[75]

A recent illustration concerns the decision by Democratic Representative John Moss of California, operating through his subcommittee, to obtain from the American Telephone and Telegraph Company (AT&T) information on "national security" wiretaps by the administration. The Justice Department sued to prohibit the company from complying with the subpoena, arguing that compliance might lead to public disclosure of vital information and could adversely affect national security. A district court, in 1976, decided that if a final determination had to be made about the need for secrecy and the risk of disclosure, "it should be made by the constituent branch of government to which the primary role in these areas is entrusted. In the areas of national security and foreign policy, that role is given to the Executive." [76]

This attempt by the judiciary to assign discrete tasks to the executive and legislative branches was soon overturned. Five months later an appellate court remanded the decision to the district court, in part because the election of Jimmy Carter had raised the possibility that the two branches might be able to resolve their dispute without judicial compulsion. The appellate court, acting as referee, urged executive and legislative officials to settle their differences out of court. The appellate court believed that a compromise worked out between the branches was "most likely to meet their essential needs and the country's constitutional balance." [77]

The Justice Department and the subcommittee continued to disagree, however, forcing the appellate court to intervene and give additional guidance. Judge Harold Leventhal of the District of Columbia circuit rejected the idea that the dispute between the two branches represented a "political question." When a dispute consists of a clash of authority between the executive and legislative branches, "judicial abstention does not lead to orderly resolution of the dispute." Neither branch, he said, had "final authority in the area of concern." When the process of negotiation founders and stalemate beckons, the court may intervene to promote the "smooth functioning of government." [78]

Leventhal stressed to each party the necessity of resolving conflicting viewpoints and of seeking intermediate positions. He noted that the framers, in adopting a Constitution with general and overlapping provisions, anticipated that "a spirit of dynamic compromise would promote resolution of the dispute in the manner most likely to result in efficient and effective functioning of our governmental system." An adversary relationship, with neither party willing to be flexible, is alien to a system of coordinate branches. Leventhal advised the contestants to avoid polarization: "each branch should take cognizance of an implicit constitutional mandate to seek optimal accommodation through a realistic evaluation of the needs of the conflicting branches in the particular fact situation." [79] By putting pressure on both parties to clarify their major concerns, Leventhal continued to push in the direction of an acceptable compromise. The case was dismissed on December 21, 1978, after the Justice Department and the subcommittee amicably resolved their differences. [80]

The pocket veto controversy during President Nixon's term represents another clash of prerogatives: the president's power to veto and Congress's power to override. The Constitution provides that any bill not returned by the president within 10 days (Sundays excluded) shall become law "unless the Congress by their Adjournment prevent its Return, in which case it shall not be a law." The latter technique of negating a bill is known as the "pocket veto," in contrast to the regular veto returned to Congress.

Toward the end of 1970, Nixon returned the family practice of medicine bill to Congress as a pocket veto. The Senate was absent for four days during the Christmas holidays; the House was gone for five. To many congressional Democrats, Nixon had blatantly misused his pocket veto authority. In 1973 a district court held that the Christmas adjournment had not prevented Nixon from returning the bill to Congress as a regular bill, giving both houses a chance to override him. The following year an appellate court upheld that decision. The bill was eventually printed as a public law (P.L. 91-696) and backdated to December 25, 1970, which marked the end of the 10-day period provided in the Constitution for executive review of bills.

In deciding the case, the courts emphasized the twofold purpose of the veto power: (1) to give the president suitable opportunity to consider bills presented by Congress, and (2) to give Congress suitable opportunity to consider the objections in a veto message and to override them. [81] The process is subverted by allowing one opportunity to cancel another. The courts interpreted the pocket veto clause in a manner that would protect both legislative and executive interests. [82]

As a result of this litigation, the Justice Department announced an accommodation on April 13, 1976. It stated that President Ford would use the return veto rather than the pocket veto during congressional recesses and adjournments, whether in the middle of a session or between the first and second sessions. The pocket veto is now exercised only after the period following a final (*sine die*) adjournment at the end of the second session of a Congress. The two houses of Congress must specifically authorize an officer or other agent to receive return vetoes during recess periods.[83]

Reconciling Theory and Practice

The purpose of this book is to help the reader understand how the federal government operates within the context of the separation of powers theory. Action and theory have a symbiotic quality. Executive-legislative actions shape the theory; the theory constrains action. The constant interaction between the branches supplies definition and substance to the theory.

Chapters 2 and 3 examine the executive and legislative branches from two contrary and contrasting positions: president as legislator and Congress as administrator. These titles indulge in some hyperbole, but they allow us to examine the day-to-day functioning of the two political branches: the president engaged in the legislative process and members of Congress participating in the administration of programs. It took more than a century for us to accept—formally at least—the president's role in legislation. We are still resisting the right of Congress to intervene in administration.

After these two chapters, it is possible to probe more deeply into the structure of government, focusing first, in Chapter 4, on the bureaucracy in the executive departments and then, in Chapter 5, on the independent regulatory commissions. The executive departments are pulled in two directions, responding to Congress, which created them and provides authorizations and appropriations, and to the president, who appoints the principal officers to manage agency activities. Both Congress and the president, through longstanding practices, attempt to direct the operations of the executive departments. Indeed, it is inconceivable to think of the departments as wholly subservient to one branch.

The independent regulatory agencies, such as the Federal Trade Commission and the Interstate Commerce Commission, have been described variously as "arms of Congress," administrative bodies, and quasi-judicial agencies. No one is sure, at any given time, where these agencies are in the scheme of things. Some of them had their beginning within an executive department, only to gain independence at some later stage. They are an anomaly and defy orderly placement within the three branches of government. However mystifying they are in organizational terms, these agencies respond very concretely to the supervision of Congress and the president. In Chapter 5 the techniques of control are set forth, as well as recent recommendations designed to strengthen the president's hand.

The final chapter takes a look at efforts by Congress and the president, as well as by courts and the bureaucracy, to represent different interests in the nation. The epilogue identifies loaded words and concepts that prevent us from appreciating executive-legislative relations. When we say that Congress "emasculates" a bill, or that the president defends the "general interest," we cruise at too high a plane of abstraction, suggesting to others that we have said something of significance when in fact we close the door to further dialogue and inquiry. This study attempts to keep the door open.

NOTES

1. Woodrow Wilson, *Congressional Government* (Boston: Houghton Mifflin Co., 1885), p. 309.
2. Richard E. Neustadt, *Presidential Power* (New York: John Wiley & Sons, 1960), p. 33. Emphasis in original.
3. Louis Fisher, *President and Congress* (New York: Free Press, 1972), pp. 6-17.
4. Gaillard Hunt, ed., *The Writings of James Madison,* 9 vols. (New York: G. P. Putnam's Sons, 1900-1910), 2:339-340.
5. Max Farrand, ed., *The Records of the Federal Convention of 1787,* 4 vols. (New Haven: Yale University Press, 1937), 2:80-83.
6. Ibid., p. 183.
7. Ibid., 2:35 (Madison), 1:107 (Wilson), 2:52 (Morris), 2:298 (Mercer).
8. Ibid., 1:108. See also 1:105, 139; 2:77.
9. Youngstown Co. v. Sawyer, 343 U.S. 579, 635 (1952).
10. M. J. C. Vile, *Constitutionalism and the Separation of Powers* (New York: Oxford University Press, 1967), p. 153.
11. U.S., Congress, *Annals of Congress,* 1st Cong., May 19, 1789, p. 383.
12. Ibid., June 8, 1789, pp. 453-454, and August 18, 1789, pp. 789-790. For action by the Senate, see U.S., Senate, *Journals, 1789-1794,* 5 vols. (Washington, D.C.: Gales & Seaton, 1820), 1:64, 73-74.
13. Frederick Green, "Separation of Governmental Powers," *Yale Law Journal* 29 (1920):369, 371.
14. United States v. Nixon, 418 U.S. 683, 704 (1974).
15. Farrand, *Records of the Federal Convention,* 1:379-381, 383-390.
16. Ex parte Garland, 71 U.S. 333, 381 (1866); United States v. Lovett, 328 U.S. 303 (1946).
17. United States v. Johnson, 383 U.S. 169, 179 (1966).
18. Louis Fisher, "Confidential Spending and Governmental Accountability," *George Washington Law Review* 47 (1979):347, 373-382.
19. *Weekly Compilation of Presidential Documents* 14 (July 10, 1978):1250.
20. Powell v. McCormack, 395 U.S. 486 (1969).
21. Marbury v. Madison, 5 U.S. 137, 155 (1803).
22. 13 Op. Att'y Gen. 516 (1871).
23. For example, 5 U.S.C. 3317-3318 (1976).

24. Louis Fisher, *The Constitution Between Friends: Congress, the President, and the Law* (New York: St. Martin's Press, 1978), pp. 111-114.
25. *United States Law Week* 49 (March 24, 1981):2604.
26. Minnesota Chippewa Tribe v. Carlucci, 358 F.Supp. 973, 975-976 (D.D.C. 1973).
27. Fisher, *President and Congress,* pp. 62-66.
28. The resolution is cited in *Annals of Congress,* 5th Cong., 1799, p. 2489; 1 Stat. 613.
29. Detlev F. Vagts, "The Logan Act: Paper Tiger or Sleeping Giant?" *American Journal of International Law* 60 (1966):268.
30. *Weekly Compilation of Presidential Documents* 15 (October 10, 1979):1861.
31. *Digest of United States Practice in International Law, 1975* (Washington, D.C.: Government Printing Office), pp. 749-750.
32. *Digest of United States Practice in International Law, 1976,* pp. 75-76.
33. *Weekly Compilation of Presidential Documents* 16 (June 10, 1980):1087-1089.
34. Louis Henkin, *Foreign Affairs and the Constitution* (Mineola, N.Y.: The Foundation Press, 1972), p. 214; Guaranty Trust Co. v. United States, 304 U.S. 126, 137-138 (1938).
35. 53 Comp. Gen. 600, 602 (1974).
36. *Weekly Compilation of Presidential Documents* 15 (August 15, 1979):1434.
37. U.S., Congress, Senate, S. Rept. 738, 96th Cong., 2d sess., 1980, pp. 15-16, 33. See remarks by Senator Claiborne Pell, D-R.I., in U.S., Congress, Senate, *Congressional Record* (daily ed.), 96th Cong., 2d sess., May 7, 1980, 126:S4881-4882; August 6, 1980, 126:S10984-10985.
38. U.S., Congress, Senate, *The Constitution of the United States of America: Analysis and Interpretation,* S. Doc. No. 92-82, 1973, p. 481.
39. Edward S. Corwin, *The President: Office and Powers 1787-1957: History and Analysis of Practice and Opinion* (New York: New York University Press, 1957), pp. 211-212.
40. United States v. Curtiss-Wright, 299 U.S. 304, 319 (1936).
41. John C. Fitzpatrick, ed., *Writings of Washington,* 39 vols. (Washington, D.C.: Government Printing Office, 1931-1944), 30:373.
42. Ibid., p. 378.
43. William Maclay, *Sketches of Debate in the First Senate of the United States, 1789-91* (Harrisburg, Pa.: Lane S. Hart, 1880), pp. 122-126.
44. George H. Haynes, *The Senate of the United States: Its History and Practice,* 2 vols. (Boston: Houghton Mifflin Co., 1938), 2:576-602.
45. Francis O. Wilcox, *Congress, the Executive, and Foreign Policy* (New York: Harper & Row, 1971), p. 52.
46. Wilson's constitutional analysis of the treaty process has been decisively refuted by Forrest R. Black, "The United States Senate and the Treaty Power," *Rocky Mountain Law Review* 4 (1931):1, and by Richard E. Webb, "Treaty-Making and the President's Obligation to Seek the Advice and Consent of the Senate with Special Reference to the Vietnam Peace Negotiations," *Ohio State Law Review* 31 (1970):490.
47. U.S., Congress, Senate, Judiciary Committee, *Executive Privilege: The Withholding of Information by the Executive* (hearings), 92d Cong., 1st sess., 1971, pp. 262-264.
48. Dean Acheson, *A Citizen Looks at Congress* (New York: Harper & Bros., 1956), p. 83. See also Fisher, *The Constitution Between Friends,* pp. 197-204.

49. W. W. Humbert, *The Pardoning Power of the President* (Washington, D.C.: American Council on Public Affairs, 1941), p. 22. For the power of the president to commute a death sentence to life imprisonment, on the condition that the individual not be eligible for parole, see Schick v. Reed, 419 U.S. 256 (1974).
50. Knote v. United States, 95 U.S. 149, 153-154 (1877). On the primacy of the appropriations power when pitted against the pardon power, see Hart v. United States, 118 U.S. 62 (1886); 8 Op. Att'y Gen. 281, 282 (1857); 23 Op. Att'y Gen. 360, 363 (1901).
51. The Laura, 114 U.S. 411 (1885); 8 Op. Att'y Gen. 281, 282 (1857).
52. Humbert, *The Pardoning Power of the President*, pp. 43-45.
53. Ex parte Garland, 71 U.S. 333, 380 (1866). See 12 Stat. 502 (1862) and 13 Stat. 424 (1865).
54. United States v. Klein, 13 Wall. 128 (1872).
55. U.S., Congress, House, Judiciary Committee, *Pardon of Richard M. Nixon and Related Matters* (hearings), 93d Cong., 2d sess., 1974, pp. 87-158.
56. Ex parte Garland, 71 U.S. 333, 380; 1 Op. Att'y Gen. 341, 343 (1820); Murphy v. Ford, 390 F.Supp. 1372 (W.D. Mich. 1975).
57. 2 Op. Att'y Gen. 275 (1825); 6 Op. Att'y Gen. 20 (1853).
58. Burdick v. United States, 236 U.S. 79, 94 (1915).
59. *Weekly Compilation of Presidential Documents* 10 (September 8, 1974):1110.
60. Ibid., 13 (August 3, 1977):1164. See P.L. 95-26, 91 Stat. 114, sec. 306; P.L. 95-86, 91 Stat. 444, sec. 706.
61. Springer v. Philippine Islands, 277 U.S. 189, 211 (1928).
62. Fisher, *President and Congress*, pp. 1-27, 241-270.
63. Joseph Story, *Commentaries on the Constitution of the United States*, 2 vols. (Boston: Little, Brown & Co., 1905), 1:396.
64. Myers v. United States, 272 U.S. 52, 293 (1926).
65. United States v. Curtiss-Wright, 299 U.S. 304, 315 (1936).
66. Id. at 319, 320.
67. Joel Francis Paschal, *Mr. Justice Sutherland: A Man Against the State* (Princeton: Princeton University Press, 1951), p. 93. See also George Sutherland, *Constitutional Power and World Affairs* (New York: Columbia University Press, 1919).
68. United States v. Curtiss-Wright, 299 U.S. 304, 316 (1936).
69. Charles A. Lofgren, "United States v. Curtiss-Wright Export Corporation: An Historical Reassessment," *Yale Law Journal* 83 (1973):1; David M. Levitan, "The Foreign Relations Power: An Analysis of Mr. Justice Sutherland's Theory," *Yale Law Journal* 55 (1946):467. See also United States v. Butenko, 494 F.2d 593, 630-631 (3d Cir. 1974).
70. Aaron Wildavsky, "The Two Presidencies," *Perspectives on the Presidency*, ed. Aaron Wildavsky (Boston: Little, Brown & Co., 1975), pp. 448-461.
71. Donald A. Peppers, " 'The Two Presidencies': Eight Years Later," in *Perspectives on the Presidency*, pp. 462-471.
72. Bayless Manning, "The Congress, the Executive and Intermestic Affairs: Three Proposals," *Foreign Affairs* 55 (1977):306.
73. Lee Sigelman, "A Reassessment of the Two Presidencies Thesis," *Journal of Politics* 41 (1979):1195, 1203.
74. United States v. Hoffman, 334 F.Supp. 504, 506 (D.D.C. 1971). For a hybrid case, in which the activities of a domestic organization (the Jewish Defense League) affected foreign relations, leading the Justice Department to

wiretap the league's office without a warrant, see Zweibon v. Mitchell, 516 F.2d 594 (D.C. Cir. 1975).

75. Fisher, *The Constitution Between Friends,* chap. 6.
76. United States v. American Tel. & Tel. Co., 419 F.Supp. 454, 461 (D.D.C. 1976).
77. United States v. American Tel. & Tel. Co., 551 F.2d 384, 394 (D.C. Cir. 1976).
78. United States v. American Tel. & Tel. Co., 567 F.2d 121, 126 (D.C. Cir. 1977).
79. Id. at 127.
80. U.S., Congress, House, Select Committee on Congressional Operations, *Court Proceedings and Actions of Vital Interest to the Congress, Current to December 31, 1978,* 95th Cong., 2d sess., 1978, p. 50.
81. Kennedy v. Sampson, 364 F.Supp. 1075, 1084 (D.D.C. 1973).
82. Kennedy v. Sampson, 511 F.2d 430, 438 (D.C. Cir. 1974). See also Wright v. United States, 302 U.S. 583, 596 (1938).
83. *Congressional Record* (daily ed.), 94th Cong., 2d sess., April 26, 1976, 122:S5912.

2

President as Legislator

To a literalist, the Constitution limits the president to two forms of legislative activity: (1) the right to recommend to Congress such measures "as he shall judge necessary and expedient" and (2) the power to veto a bill. To this list can be added the president's power (shared with the Senate) to make treaties, which the Constitution defines as part of "the supreme Law of the Land." A fourth source of influence, which has been exercised on rare occasions in the past, permits him to convene both houses or either of them. In case they disagree on the time of adjournment, the president can adjourn them "to such Time as he shall think proper." [1]

The Supreme Court has held that in the "framework of our Constitution the President's power to see that the laws are faithfully executed refutes the idea that he is to be a lawmaker." According to this view the Constitution limits the president's functions in the lawmaking process to "the recommending of laws he thinks wise and the vetoing of laws he thinks bad." [2] And yet superimposed upon the president's express constitutional authorities are other legislative powers. These powers are either implied in the Constitution or developed by custom (often with the blessing of the courts). Some of these legislative powers Congress delegates to the president and the executive agencies. Others result from agency regulations, presidential proclamations, and the issuance of executive orders.

EXPRESS POWERS

Article II of the Constitution is remarkable for its laconic treatment of presidential power. Over 60 percent of the language is devoted to the term of office, election, qualifications, removal, compensation, and oath of office. The remainder of the article describes the president's power only in general terms; the veto power is set forth in Article I.

Recommending Legislation

The Constitution requires the president "from time to time" to give Congress "Information of the State of the Union, and recommend to their Consideration such Measures as he shall judge necessary and expedient...." The first presidents, George Washington and John Adams, appeared before Congress to deliver their annual messages, but in 1801 President Thomas Jefferson discontinued that practice, preferring to submit his message in writing. More than 100 years passed before President Woodrow Wilson, in 1913, resumed the custom of addressing Congress in person.[3]

The annual State of the Union message was typically a lackluster product, consisting mainly of departmental and agency reports on their activities. These messages were seldom used to recommend specific legislation. President William Henry Harrison, in his inaugural address of March 4, 1841, enunciated the classic Whig interpretation of the president's legislative role. He could not conceive that by a fair interpretation of the Constitution "any or either of its provisions would be found to constitute the President a part of the legislative power." The power to recommend, Harrison said, was "a privilege which he holds in common with every other citizen; and although there may be something more of confidence in the propriety of the measures recommended in the one case than in the other, in the obligations of ultimate decision there can be no difference."[4]

President Grover Cleveland broke ranks with this attitude by devoting his entire 1887 State of the Union message to the subject of tariff reform. The message had a profound impact on Congress and the press, created a split in Cleveland's Democratic party, and contributed to his defeat the following year.[5] Other presidents from time to time advocated legislation to satisfy party commitments. For example, President William Howard Taft believed the president could exercise

> a controlling influence in the securing of legislation by his personal intervention with members of his party who are in control in each House. I think he ought to have very great influence, because he is made responsible to the people for what the party does, and if the party is wise, it will bend to his leadership as long as it is tolerable, and

especially where it is in performance of promises that the party has made in its platform. . . .[6]

Since Taft's time, presidents regularly have used the State of the Union message to pursue legislative goals. The message, delivered in person to Congress, typically reviews the government's failures and successes (giving disproportionate attention to the latter), restates the administration's priorities, and appeals to Congress and the public at large for support. A separate written State of the Union message, released a few days after the oral message, covers in greater detail the administration bills not yet enacted and legislative recommendations to be submitted.

In addition to the constitutional requirement for the State of the Union message, statutes direct the president to submit legislative recommendations. The two major documents transmitted to Congress each year are the budget message, prescribed by the Budget and Accounting Act of 1921, and the economic report, submitted in compliance with the Employment Act of 1946. Hundreds of other presidential reports, messages, communications, and suggestions for legislation are sent to Capitol Hill on a regular basis as a result of statutory directives. Although members of Congress periodically criticize the president for trespassing into their legislative domain, major policy departures often await the president's initiative. Congress had the knowledge, institutional capability, and procedures to cut back on federal spending in the 1970s, but it took the leadership of President Reagan and his budget director, former Republican Representative David Stockman of Michigan, to set the process in motion. On April 28, 1981, President Reagan took the highly unusual step of appearing before a joint session of Congress to advocate a specific *amendment* to pending legislation (the Gramm-Latta amendment to the first budget resolution for fiscal 1982).

In modern times, members of Congress often expect the administration to present a bill as a starting point. One committee chairman reportedly advised an administration witness: "Don't expect us to start from scratch on what you people want. That's not the way we do things here—*you* draft the bills and *we* work them over." [7] Many bills, however, are conceived and drafted in Congress. (The specific steps the president takes to formulate legislation and mobilize support for its passage are covered later in this chapter.)

The Veto Power

The framers, after decisively rejecting a proposal for an absolute veto, gave the president a qualified veto, subject to an override by a two-thirds majority of each house of Congress. The Supreme Court later decided that two-thirds of a quorum present in each house, rather than of the total membership, would suffice.[8] This is still a demanding standard, generally requiring the support of more than 60 senators and 260 to 270 House members.

Some of the Antifederalists in 1788 were deeply offended by the veto power, claiming that it was an error to allow the executive power a negative "or in fact any kind of control over the proceedings of the legislature." [9] But Alexander Hamilton in *Federalist 73* argued that the power was an essential instrument for protecting the president against legislative encroachments. In addition to protecting the presidency, Hamilton singled out other justifications for the veto power. It would permit the president to prevent the enactment of "improper laws" that result from haste, inadvertence, or design. James Madison also described the veto as multipurpose, available not merely to restrain Congress from encroaching on other branches but also to prevent Congress "from passing laws unwise in their principle, or incorrect in their form" and from violating the rights of the people.[10]

The *threat* of a veto can be used as a lever to exact changes in a pending bill. In 1817, when President James Monroe announced that Congress lacked constitutional authority to appropriate money for internal improvements, a House committee reacted with indignation. It expressed shock that a president would try to interfere with the ability of Congress to express its will.[11] Such "interference," while common today, is not always effective. In 1980 President Carter told Congress that he would veto any bill that disapproved his gasoline conservation fee. Undaunted, Congress proceeded with the bill and then quickly and decisively overrode the veto. Though his veto was overridden, Carter could still gain political mileage, in an election year, by taking a stand for conservation and energy security and against inflation.[12] Members of Congress who manage a bill can also use the threat of a veto to their advantage. They can try to eliminate unwanted amendments by claiming that such modificiations run the risk of a veto.[13] Even entire bills are shelved in the face of presidential opposition. In 1975 both houses passed a consumer protection bill, but the legislation did not go to conference committee because President Ford threatened to veto it.[14]

The veto power today is fundamentally different from the original design. Both branches have forced changes in the system. Congress developed the practice of presenting to the president bills that had many elements, often unrelated, instead of allowing the president to consider a discrete measure. This practice became more coercive by attaching irrelevant amendments ("riders") to appropriation bills, assuming the president could not afford to veto a money bill in the closing days of a fiscal year. President Rutherford B. Hayes fought Congress on this issue and prevailed with a number of vetoes,[15] but presidents continue to receive complex bills filled with miscellaneous items.

Congress, despite House and Senate rules to the contrary, continues to add "legislation" to appropriation bills.[16] This practice reached epidemic proportions in the 1970s, delaying and sometimes preventing the passage of appropriation bills. The Hyde amendment (restricting the use of federal funds for abortion) is a prominent example of a rider to an appropriation bill.

Presidents have appropriated for themselves a form of "item veto." During the signing of a bill they sometimes refer to certain provisions as unconstitutional and therefore a nullity. When presidents believe that Congress has overstepped its boundaries, they have interpreted mandatory provisions as mere suggestions. Following this tradition, in 1979 President Carter decided to convert a statutory requirement into a "recommendation." He maintained that Congress had no authority to mandate the establishment of consular relations at a time and place unacceptable to the president; to do so would encroach upon executive responsibilities.[17] The constitutionality of this type of item veto has not been tested in the courts.[18]

Although this form of item veto has evolved by practice, the Constitution expressly recognizes a "pocket veto." Any bill not returned by the president within 10 days (Sundays excluded) shall become law "unless the Congress by their Adjournment prevent its Return, in which Case it shall not be a Law." First used by President Madison in 1812, the pocket veto required several decisions by the Supreme Court to determine what conduct by Congress would "prevent" the return of a bill for legislative consideration. As a result of a pocket veto by President Nixon in 1970, litigation by Democratic Senator Edward Kennedy of Massachusetts, and an announcement by the Ford administration in 1976, it is now established that pocket vetoes are impermissible (1) within a session of Congress or (2) during any adjournment of Congress between the first and second sessions, provided that the two houses make appropriate arrangements for the receipt of presidential messages. These precedents limit the pocket veto to the period following a final (*sine die*) adjournment at the end of the second session of a Congress.[19]

The veto is one of the more effective weapons in the president's arsenal. Of the 1,380 regular vetoes from Washington through Carter, Congress has managed to override only 94. More than half of these vetoes came during the administrations of Presidents Grover Cleveland and Franklin D. Roosevelt, with the vast majority aimed at private relief bills (see Table 2-1).[20] There have also been 1,011 pocket vetoes, with Cleveland and Roosevelt again accounting for more than half. The record shows that Congress typically drops a number of suspect and often indefensible bills on the president, with a few days remaining before adjournment, confident that the use of the regular or pocket veto

Table 2-1   Presidential Vetoes, 1789-1981

Years	President	Regular Vetoes	Vetoes Over-ridden	Pocket Vetoes	Total Vetoes
1789-1797	George Washington	2	0	0	2
1797-1801	John Adams	0	0	0	0
1801-1809	Thomas Jefferson	0	0	0	0
1809-1817	James Madison	5	0	2	7
1817-1825	James Monroe	1	0	0	1
1825-1829	John Q. Adams	0	0	0	0
1829-1837	Andrew Jackson	5	0	7	12
1837-1841	Martin Van Buren	0	0	1	1
1841-1841	W. H. Harrison	0	0	0	0
1841-1845	John Tyler	6	1	4	10
1845-1849	James K. Polk	2	0	1	3
1849-1850	Zachary Taylor	0	0	0	0
1850-1853	Millard Fillmore	0	0	0	0
1853-1857	Franklin Pierce	9	5	0	9
1857-1861	James Buchanan	4	0	3	7
1861-1865	Abraham Lincoln	2	0	5	7
1865-1869	Andrew Johnson	21	15	8	29
1869-1877	Ulysses S. Grant	45	4	48	93
1877-1881	Rutherford B. Hayes	12	1	1	13
1881-1881	James A. Garfield	0	0	0	0
1881-1885	Chester A. Arthur	4	1	8	12
1885-1889	Grover Cleveland	304	2	110	414
1889-1893	Benjamin Harrison	19	1	25	44
1893-1897	Grover Cleveland	42	5	128	170
1897-1901	William McKinley	6	0	36	42
1901-1909	Theodore Roosevelt	42	1	40	82
1909-1913	William H. Taft	30	1	9	39
1913-1921	Woodrow Wilson	33	6	11	44
1921-1923	Warren G. Harding	5	0	1	6
1923-1929	Calvin Coolidge	20	4	30	50
1929-1933	Herbert Hoover	21	3	16	37
1933-1945	Franklin D. Roosevelt	372	9	263	635
1945-1953	Harry S Truman	180	12	70	250
1953-1961	Dwight D. Eisenhower	73	2	108	181
1961-1963	John F. Kennedy	12	0	9	21
1963-1969	Lyndon B. Johnson	16	0	14	30
1969-1974	Richard M. Nixon[1]	26	7	17	43
1974-1977	Gerald R. Ford	48	12	18	66
1977-1981	Jimmy Carter	13	2	18	31
	Total	1,380	94	1,011	2,391

[1] Two "pocket vetoes," overruled in the courts, are counted here as regular vetoes.

SOURCE: *Presidential Vetoes, 1789-1976*, compiled by the Senate Library (Washington, D.C.: Government Printing Office, 1978), p. ix; Carter figures are taken from *Weekly Compilation of Presidential Documents.*

will prevent these measures (usually private bills for the relief of an individual from a member's district) from becoming law. After the veto, legislators can tell the affected constituents or interest groups that they had done their best, placing responsibility for the failure of enactment on the president.

Treaties and Executive Agreements

The Constitution, statutes, and treaties are collectively called "the supreme Law of the Land." [21] Treaties have legislative as well as executive qualities. In *Federalist 75*, Hamilton remarked that the power of making treaties "will be found to partake more of the legislative than of the executive character, though it does not seem strictly to fall within the definition of either of them." Opponents of the Constitution considered it improper for the president to be part of this lawmaking process. To the contention that laws should be made "only by men invested with legislative authority," thereby excluding the president from the treaty process, John Jay answered in *Federalist 64* that decisions by the courts and the executive were as binding on the people as laws passed by Congress. Indeed, treaties may supersede prior conflicting statutes.[22] The Constitution was also criticized for permitting action by the Senate and the president to "have all the force of the law paramount without the aid or interference of the House of Representatives. . . ." [23]

When the Senate refuses to support a treaty by the necessary two-thirds majority, the president may present an international compact to both houses in the form of a joint resolution, which requires only a simple majority in each house. Annexation of Texas in 1845 and of Hawaii in 1898 were accomplished by this method. Years after the Senate had rejected the St. Lawrence Seaway plan, President Dwight D. Eisenhower submitted it to Congress in the form of a regular bill and won legislative approval.

If treaties are laws, must they be terminated by both Congress and the president? On December 15, 1978, President Carter announced that the United States would recognize the People's Republic of China as the sole legitimate government of China. As a consequence, the defense treaty with Taiwan was scheduled to terminate on January 1, 1980. Republican Senator Barry Goldwater of Arizona and several other members of Congress filed suit to contest this action, claiming that terminating a treaty, "like making one, is a legislative, not an executive act. . . ." Since treaties are law, Goldwater argued that both branches had to participate in their termination: "It is taken for granted that terminating a statute requires the same procedures as enacting one." [24] After an initial setback in the district court, the Carter administration eventually prevailed on this particular treaty termination, especially since Congress failed to take all of the legislative steps that were available to challenge Carter. The decisions left unclear how the courts might decide future treaty-termination cases.[25] Senator Goldwater, calling for joint executive-legislative participation, introduced legislation in 1981 to establish procedures for terminating military or defense treaties.[26]

Presidents have also entered into "executive agreements" with foreign nations, initially on the basis of statutory authority. Although such agreements lacked what the Supreme Court called the "dignity" of a treaty, they have been considered valid international compacts.[27] More disturbing to Congress are international agreements entered into without statutory authority. Often these executive initiatives are taken a year or two before Congress has an opportunity to pass a statute or the Senate has a chance to ratify a treaty.[28]

Executive agreements based neither on statutory nor treaty authority have been upheld by the Supreme Court when the president operates on an implied constitutional power, such as the power to recognize foreign governments.[29] The State Department concedes, however, that an executive agreement cannot be "inconsistent with legislation enacted by Congress in the exercise of its constitutional authority."[30] In cases where executive agreements contravene an existing statute in a field delegated to Congress by the Constitution, or where they violate rights secured by the Constitution, the agreements have been struck down by the courts.[31]

Largely as a result of hearings by a Senate subcommittee in 1969 and 1970, Congress passed legislation in 1972 to require the secretary of state to transmit to Congress within 60 days the text of "any international agreement, other than a treaty," to which the United States is a party. Congress later discovered that a large number of agreements were being reported after the 60-day period and in some cases were not being reported at all. The basic problem was late reports from agencies to the Department of State. To remedy this defect, the legislation was rewritten in 1977 to require all departments and agencies to transmit to the Department of State the text of any international agreement not later than 20 days after its signing.[32]

IMPLIED AND EVOLVED POWERS

Some constitutional scholars believe that an act of the federal government is illegal unless based upon a power enumerated in the Constitution. They take comfort in the statement of Henry Lee at the Virginia ratification convention: "When a question arises with respect to the legality of any power, exercised or assumed," the question will be "Is it enumerated in the Constitution? ... It is otherwise arbitrary and unconstitutional." [33] Not only is this doctrine impractical and unrealistic, but these scholars must themselves make room for implied powers: the power of Congress to investigate, the president's power to remove executive officials, and the power of the Supreme Court to review legislative actions.[34] Executive authority in the legislative domain has been enlarged by several powers not enumerated in the Constitution: authority that Congress delegates and the issuance of regulations, proclamations, and executive orders.

Delegated Authority

Strict interpretations of the Constitution would prohibit Congress from delegating its power to another branch. This notion finds expression in the ancient maxim, *delegata potestas non potest delegari* (delegated power cannot be delegated). According to this doctrine, the power delegated by the people to Congress may not be transferred elsewhere.[35]

Practice has not kept pace with theory, however. From an early date the Supreme Court allowed Congress to supply general guidelines for national policy, leaving to other branches the responsibility for "filling in the details." [36] Although time after time the Court has paid homage to the nondelegation doctrine, claiming that it would be "a breach of the National fundamental law" were Congress to transfer its legislative power to the president, the Court typically upholds the delegation in question.[37] Delegation is permissible in the presence of clear and unambiguous language. Delegation by Congress, said the Court in 1940, "has long been recognized as necessary in order that the exertion of legislative power does not become a futility. ... The burdens of minutiae would be apt to clog the administration of the law and deprive the agency of that flexibility and dispatch which are its salient virtues." [38]

Only on two occasions, both occurring in 1935, did the Supreme Court strike down a delegation of legislative authority to the president.[39] The Court objected to vague language and inadequate legislative standards. How little bearing those cases have on delegation today is underscored by the Economic Stabilization Act of 1970, which authorized the president to "issue such orders and regulations as he may deem appropriate to stabilize prices, rents, wages, and salaries at levels not less than those prevailing on May 25, 1970." Nowhere in the statute does one find the procedural safeguards that usually accompany broad delegations of power: giving notice to interested parties before issuing a presidential order, providing a hearing for affected groups, and establishing the machinery for judicial review. A federal court upheld the delegation by noting that some of these congressional guidelines were imbedded in committee reports and other portions of the legislative history.[40] Allowing Congress to pass laws by placing crucial details outside the bill, however, is not always satisfactory, as Congress periodically discovers. Agencies are bound by law, but not necessarily by nonstatutory controls (see pp. 81-83).

The nondelegation doctrine has not lost its force entirely. Justices of the Supreme Court, usually in dissent, still raise it as a standard for reviewing statutes passed by Congress.[41] A decision in 1980 was significant because four members of the *majority* (in particular Justice William H. Rehnquist) challenged the scope of power granted to an agency by Congress. The other three members, Chief Justice Warren Burger and Justices John Paul Stevens and Potter Stewart, appeared to insist that Congress at least clarify its policy by using less ambiguous language.[42] In 1981 the Court once again refused to accept vague statutory language as a mandate for compulsory action. While the question of an unconstitutional delegation of legislative power was not the central issue, the Court did insist that Congress speak with a clear voice in directing agency activities.[43]

Regulations, Proclamations, and Executive Orders

To carry out authority delegated by Congress, executive officials often issue rules and regulations that "must be received as the acts of the executive, and as such, be binding upon all within the sphere of his legal and constitutional authority." [44] In theory, regulations are not a substitute for general policymaking. That power is reserved to Congress and may be enacted only in the form of public law.[45] While administrative regulations are entitled to respect, "the authority to prescribe rules and regulations is not the power to make laws, for no such power can be delegated by the Congress." [46] According to the courts, a regulation that is out of harmony with a statute "is a mere nullity." [47]

So much for general theory. Vague grants of delegated power by Congress give administrators substantial discretion to make policy. During the Senate vote in 1981 to confirm James Watt as secretary of the interior, Democratic Senator Dale Bumpers of Arkansas recalled that Watt had told his committee: "I believe in complying with the law." Bumpers continued: "Do you know what the law is so far as the management of the public lands is concerned? Most of the time it is whatever the Secretary of the Interior says it is." [48]

Even when statutory language is relatively clear and specific, one provision may conflict with another in the same bill. Faced with inconsistent and perhaps contradictory congressional demands, the president and agency officials try to "harmonize" competing provisions. In 1979 a federal court ruled that the Environmental Protection Agency acted properly by adopting a regulatory scheme that bridged conflicting provisions in the Clean Air Act. Instead of Congress resolving the policy conflict, the Environmental Protection Agency manufactured an administrative solution.[49]

In response to an antiregulation mood in the 1970s, Presidents Ford, Carter, and Reagan tried to create a system to monitor government regulations that impose heavy costs on businesses and consumers. The Council on Wage and Price Stability (COWPS) within the White House was one effort, followed by the creation of executive units such as the Regulatory Analysis Review Group (RARG). The most ambitious attempt so far in centralizing control over agency regulations is Executive Order 12291 issued by President Reagan on February 17, 1981. He designated the Office of Management and Budget (OMB) as the central agency to review regulations and subject them to cost-benefit analysis. The purpose was to "reduce the burdens of existing and future regulations, increase agency accountability for regulatory actions, provide for presidential oversight of the regulatory process, minimize duplication and conflict of regulations, and insure well-reasoned regulations." [50]

Presidential proclamations are a second instrument of administrative legislation. Often they are routine in nature, without legislative effect. During 1980 President Carter used proclamations to make statements for Mother's Day, Father's Day, Jewish Heritage Week, and Salute to Learning Day.[51] Also during that period, however, he issued proclamations that had substantive impact, including import quotas on cotton and on television parts.[52] Several other substantive proclamations issued by Carter in 1980, imposing a fee on imported oil, were declared illegal by a federal court.[53] The judicial decision came against a backdrop of congressional moves to strip Carter of his power to impose import fees.[54]

In a controversial action in 1971, President Nixon issued a proclamation imposing a 10 percent surcharge on articles imported into the United States. After extensive litigation a federal court decided that although the president lacks an independent power to regulate commerce or set tariffs, and any valid proclamation had to be based on authority delegated by Congress, in this case Nixon had acted consistent with statutory authority.[55] But when a statute prescribes a particular procedure and the president follows a different course, his proclamation can be declared illegal and void.[56]

A third form of administrative legislation is the executive order. President Franklin D. Roosevelt issued a number of executive orders in 1941 to seize industrial plants, shipbuilding companies, a cable company, a munitions plant, and approximately 4,000 coal companies. Two years passed before Congress supplied statutory authority for his actions.[57] During World War II, President Roosevelt created several agencies by executive order, without the slightest shred of statutory support. Democratic Senator Richard Russell of Georgia, opposing this practice, said he "never believed that the President of the United States was vested with one scintilla of authority to create by an Executive order an action agency of Government without the approval of the Congress of the United States." Russell successfully secured the adoption of an amendment, still in effect today, that prohibited the use of any appropriation to pay the expenses of an agency established by executive order "if the Congress has not appropriated any money specifically for such agency or instrumentality or specifically authorized the expenditure of funds by it." [58] Congress adopted similar restrictions at the end of President Lyndon Johnson's administration to prohibit the use of appropriated funds for interdepartmental boards, commissions, councils, committees, or similar groups that did not have prior and specific congressional approval. This provision is repeated each year in appropriation bills.[59]

The use of executive orders to eliminate employment discrimination in private industry began with President Franklin D. Roosevelt and continued with Presidents Truman, Eisenhower, Kennedy, and Johnson. These initiatives were further carried forward by President Nixon, who issued an executive order that required federal contractors to set specific goals for hiring members of minority groups (the "Philadelphia Plan"). The comptroller general concluded that the plan conflicted with the Civil Rights Act of 1964. Here the federal courts upheld the administration's action.[60] Another executive order by Nixon that was contested attempted to rejuvenate the Subversive Activities Control Board. Congress intervened in this case to prohibit the administration from using appropriated funds to carry out the order.[61] When executive orders exceed presidential authority, the judiciary has struck them down.[62] However, as a federal court noted in 1981, the issuance of an executive order is not expected to be preceded by formal notice, hearing, or other procedures as are agency regulations mandated by the Administrative Procedure Act.[63]

An executive order by President Carter in 1978 used the government's procurement power to fight inflation. Contracts were to be funneled to firms whose wage and price decisions followed the administration's guidelines. A district court held that President Carter had exceeded his constitutional authority by trying to establish a mandatory system of wage and price controls. An appellate court reversed that decision by arguing that the guidelines were "voluntary" rather than mandatory.[64]

EXECUTIVE ORGANIZATION AND LEADERSHIP

The process of government requires constant interaction between executive and legislative leaders. Congress and the president can seldom afford to spin in separate orbits. Among the fundamental duties of the executive branch, since 1789, is the need to maintain a continuing dialogue with Congress regarding legislation, appointments, and other matters that demand close consultation and cooperation.

Early Networks and Linkages

Contacts between Congress and George Washington's administration were smoothed by common bonds of familiarity, friendship, and public service that had been forged in the years of the Continental Congress. Many of the delegates to the Constitutional Convention in Philadelphia were later to serve in the First Congress and in Washington's administration. In the midst of partisan strains between Federalists and Antifederalists, public officials tried to place the new government on secure footing while at the same time protecting the prerogatives of the branch they served.

James Madison, while serving in the First Congress, provided valued counsel to Washington on many legislative matters. Washington sought his advice concerning a possible veto of a bill for compensation to members of Congress.[65] Even though Madison was a member of the House of Representatives, with no constitutional responsibility for reviewing nominations submitted by the president, Washington wanted Madison's opinion on specific nominations. He also turned to him to ask whether executive communications to the Senate should be transmitted by written or oral means. Washington's correspondence contains other efforts to solicit the advice of senators on nominations.[66]

Through various communications to the Senate, Washington suggested that senators function as an advisory council on appointment and treaty matters. In the handling of treaties, Washington told the Senate, "oral communications seem indispensably necessary." The issues not only required careful consideration, "but some of them may undergo much discussion; to do which by written communications would be tedious without being satisfactory." [67] Although he was severely disappointed by his effort to discuss an Indian treaty with senators, face to face, Washington continued to seek the Senate's advice by written communications.[68]

Presidential bill-drafting is sometimes considered a twentieth-century phenomenon, but the practice was with us at the start. Washington wrote down his ideas for a bill on the national militia and sent them to Henry Knox, his secretary of war, for legislative action. In

1790 Washington conferred with two senators in an effort to reverse an action the House had taken on appropriations for the foreign service. Two years later he sent Secretary of State Jefferson to speak privately to members of a House committee investigating the heavy losses by Major General Arthur St. Clair in an Indian raid.[69]

As another way to link the executive branch with Congress, legislators were invited to dine with the president. Washington, sensitive to the precedents being established, entertained members of Congress with great reserve. Senator William Maclay of Pennsylvania, not one of Washington's greatest admirers, remembered these occasions as stiff and formal. After returning from one he wrote: "[I]t was the most solemn dinner ever I sat at." The next year, following another evening with Washington, he recorded in his diary: "The President is a cold, formal man; but I must declare that he treated me with great attention." [70]

Legislative-executive contacts during the Washington administration were tentative and sporadic. Each branch tested the limits of the constitutional system, ever on the watch for transgressions and encroachments. This sensitivity is illustrated by the opposition of Congress in 1789 to a proposal which would have authorized the secretary of the treasury to report to Congress on financial recommendations. Some members feared that this might open the door to excessive executive influence, especially in the hands of so formidable a secretary as Alexander Hamilton. The particular language under consideration would have directed the secretary to "digest and report" plans for the improvement and management of the revenue. Representative John Page of Virginia warned that the bill would establish a precedent "which might be extended, until we admitted all the ministers of the Government on the floor, to explain and support the plans they have digested and reported; thus laying a foundation for an aristocracy or a detestable monarchy." [71]

As enacted into law, the language was changed to "digest and prepare." And yet the statute also required the secretary of the treasury to "make report, and give information to either branch of the legislature, in person or in writing (as he may be required), respecting all matters referred to him by the Senate or House of Representatives, or which shall appertain to his office." Some scholars credit Hamilton with drafting the bill that created the Treasury Department.[72]

This statutory language seemed to suggest that the secretary of the treasury would help bridge the gap between the executive and legislative branches. The secretary, although the head of an executive department, would also serve as an agent of Congress. Executive assistance to Congress seems underscored by the fact that the Ways and Means

Committee, established by the House on July 24, 1789, was disbanded several weeks after creation of the Treasury Department.[73]

Hamilton assumed an activist role in Washington's cabinet. According to the journals of Senator William Maclay, Hamilton believed that his official duties required close contact with legislative leaders. When his plan for a funding system was in jeopardy, Hamilton "was here early to wait on the Speaker, and I believe spent most of his time in running from place to place among the members." When the Senate considered the excise bill, Hamilton "sat close with the committee." Hamilton attended to each detail of the legislative process. After a Senate committee agreed that the power of excise inspectors should extend only to importations and distillations, Maclay discovered that Hamilton "will have even to modify this to his mind. Nothing is done without him." The loyalty of some Federalist legislators to the administration prompted Maclay to remark: "It was, however, only for Elsworth, King, or some of Hamilton's people to rise, and the thing was generally done." [74]

Eventually Congress rebelled against Hamilton. In 1792, when he asked to come before Congress to answer questions concerning the public debt, legislators vehemently objected to this mixing of the two branches. Some took the position that departmental heads should never originate legislation or even voice an opinion that might affect congressional decisions. Legislative investigations in 1793 and 1794, although fruitless in unearthing damaging information about Hamilton, so poisoned the relationship between the branches that he resigned from office. In March 1794, during Hamilton's last year as secretary, the House revived its Ways and Means Committee.[75]

The Jeffersonians

Much of the suspicion and tension between the executive and legislative branches eased during Thomas Jefferson's first term as president. The use of the congressional caucus to nominate presidential candidates provided chief executives a ready circle of supporters (and some political debts) on Capitol Hill. By the time Jefferson was ensconced in office, the party apparatus had so joined the branches that he could draft bills and give them to friendly members of Congress for action. On one occasion he told Albert Gallatin, his secretary of the treasury, of a proposed draft on embargo enforcement: "If you will prepare something on these or any other ideas you like better ... Mr. Newton [of Virginia] ... will push them through the House." The periodicals of the day referred to Representative William B. Giles, D-Va., as the leader of the "ministerial phalanx." Giles served as Jefferson's link to Congress for a few years and was succeeded by John

Randolph, another Virginian. When the post of House majority leader again fell vacant, Jefferson urged·Wilson Cary Nicholas, also of Virginia, to make himself available as administration leader in the House.[76]

Critics of the administration objected to these organizational ties, complaining that Jefferson's methods were those of an autocrat. Senator Timothy Pickering, a Federalist from Massachusetts, said that Jefferson was deceptive in his public deference to the legislative branch: "[H]e secretly dictates every measure which is seriously proposed and supported." [77] But Jefferson could not operate by mere command, even among his close followers. He had to work within the political limits imposed by the times:

> It was in this calm and seductive manner, careful to avoid all appearance of being a master, that he had drawn around him his great party, and held it together, year after year, until he had marched with it to victory. And it was this spirit which was to give him such marked success in directing the work of his administration. Such methods only could succeed in handling followers like Giles, Randolph, and Macon, men often responding readily to suggestion and capable of loyalty but perfectly independent and ready to resent too free a use of the party lash.[78]

The record shows that Jefferson employed the same liaison techniques that had been pioneered by Hamilton. So long as the executive departments assisted Congress "subtly and with proper deference," the drafting of a few bills by the executive "for guidance only" was acceptable to most legislators.[79] Jefferson and Gallatin took responsibility for initiating the main outlines of party measures. They followed legislative deliberations carefully, intervening whenever necessary to preserve the basic goals of the administration. Gallatin, who had previously served on the House Ways and Means Committee, remained in close touch with his former colleagues, attending committee meetings in the same manner as Hamilton.[80] By maintaining his residence on Capitol Hill, Gallatin was able to continue his friendships with legislators. As noted by Henry Adams, the principal supporters of the administration in Congress were

> always on terms of intimacy in Mr. Gallatin's house, and much of the confidential communication between Mr. Jefferson and his party in the Legislature passed through this channel. . . . But the communication was almost entirely oral, and hardly a trace of it has been preserved either in the writings of Mr. Gallatin or in those of his contemporaries.[81]

Jefferson had cultivated many personal relationships from the time he served in the Continental Congress. From 1797 to 1801 his ties with Congress were deepened by his experience as vice president. Much of his time was devoted to the constitutional duty of president of the Senate.

He took time out to write a manual on Senate rules. While in that service he lived at one of the largest boardinghouses on Capitol Hill, sharing company, food, and political insights with congressmen.[82]

As president, Jefferson laid heavy emphasis on the wining and dining of legislators at the executive mansion. In contrast to the practices established by Washington, he held small dinners

> almost nightly when Congress was in session, with legislators predominating among the guests. The dinners were the talk of Washington. In the judgment of observant diplomats from abroad, for whom food and wine were standard accessories of political persuasion, they were the secret of Jefferson's influence.[83]

Jefferson's persuasive innovations did not survive his administration. After the collapse of the rival Federalist party (a rallying point for Jefferson's followers), his own Democratic party developed signs of division and factionalism. President James Madison and his immediate successors in the White House lacked the personal qualities and political skills that Jefferson had used to maintain party unity and executive-legislative cooperation.

Other structural and organizational changes complicated presidential influence on Capitol Hill. The executive departments, as they grew in number, responsibility, and complexity, drifted beyond the president's immediate control. And in those early decades of the nineteenth century, Congress evolved its present system of standing committees, dispersing power away from congressional leaders to "little legislatures." As a result of such changes, presidents succeeding Jefferson had to face decentralized and independent blocs of power, within both the executive branch and Congress.

Reform Efforts, 1864-1921

In the decades following the Civil War, various proposals were put forth to stimulate closer contacts between the executive and legislative branches. In 1864 Democrat George Pendleton of Ohio introduced a bill to provide that departmental heads "may occupy seats on the floor of the House of Representatives." In later years this reform was associated with greater executive influence, but Pendleton thought his proposal would make more information about departmental activities available to Congress. Cabinet officers would have the right to participate in debate and explain the business of their departments. The clerk of the House would keep a "notice book" that contained questions requiring a response from cabinet officials. The objective was to make the executive more accountable, converting a secret and unauthorized mode of operation into one that was "open, declared and authorized." [84]

Opponents of Pendleton's bill predicted that departmental heads would either be put through the "torture of a cross-examination" or, alternatively, exhibit such awesome mastery of the legislative process that disreputable bills would be enacted into law. In addition, if departmental heads refused to appear, what sanctions (short of impeachment) could Congress use to enforce compliance? Opponents doubted that the Pendleton procedure would put an end to executive "intrigue" in lawmaking. They warned that passage of the bill would be "a step toward the absorption of the power of Congress by the Executive." After extensive debate, the bill was put aside without further action.[85]

Pendleton returned to Congress in 1879, this time as an Ohio senator, and promptly reintroduced his bill to allow cabinet officials to speak on the floor of each house. Two years later a Senate select committee reported the bill favorably, recommending that departmental heads attend the Senate and the House on specific days "to give information asked by resolution, or in reply to questions which may be propounded to them under the rules of the Senate and House. . . ." The bill never came up for a vote because Pendleton devoted his energy to enacting civil service legislation in 1883.[86]

During Theodore Roosevelt's administration, Congress explicitly acknowledged the president's role as legislative leader. In 1906 Congress passed a bill authorizing up to $25,000 a year in traveling expenses for the president.[87] In prior years the railroads had given the president free transportation, a privilege about to be eliminated by the Hepburn Act. Democratic Representative Charles Cochran of Missouri argued that these expenses should now be covered by Congress, because in the

> operation of our constitutional system the President has become the chief leader of public thought and exponent of public opinion — quite as much a source of valuable suggestion for the enactment of laws as a mere executive charged with enforcing the laws, and since the circulation of the President throughout the country aids practically and decisively in promoting salutary legislation, by giving effective direction to public opinion, should not his expenses incurred in rendering such important public service be borne out of the public Treasury?[88]

To Democratic Representative J. Swagar Sherley of Kentucky, Roosevelt's travels "not only did good by his speeches, but I think his traveling did him a tremendous amount of good." Trips to different sections of the country helped educate the president on the "actual conditions that confront us, and make him a better President for the whole people of the United States."[89]

Pendleton's proposal continued to resurface, but its purpose was changed to give executive officials a dominant voice in the legislative process. One study in 1913, in addition to recommending seats in both houses for cabinet members, advocated two other ways to augment presidential power: (1) by restricting executive messages to "a few definite recommendations embodying the policies in favor of which the party has pronounced in its platform or those for which the President is willing to assume the responsibility," and (2) by allowing the president to initiate bills and giving precedence to administration bills over other measures.[90]

A similar theory of government was implicit in much of the drive for budget reform. Democratic Representative John J. Fitzgerald of New York announced in 1915 his support for restrictions on Congress's power of the purse. As chairman of the House Appropriations Committee, he believed that Congress should be prohibited from appropriating any money "unless it has been requested by the head of the department, unless by a two-thirds vote, or unless it was to pay a claim against the government or for its own expenses." Congress was urged to relinquish its power to increase appropriations requested by the departments unless specifically asked to do so by the executive. David Houston, as secretary of the treasury under President Woodrow Wilson, asked Congress in 1920 to refrain from adding to the president's budget unless requested by the secretary of the treasury or approved by a two-thirds vote of Congress.[91]

By the time Congress passed the Budget and Accounting Act of 1921, it had rejected all of these proposals. The budget to be submitted by the president was "executive" only in the sense that the president was responsible for the estimates. Congress retained full power to increase or decrease those estimates. As explained by the House Select Committee on the Budget, the proposed law "does not change in the slightest degree the duty of Congress to make the minutest examination of the budget .... The bill does not in the slightest degree give the Executive any greater power than he now has over the consideration of appropriations by Congress." [92]

Pendleton's proposal continued to attract interest. Under the "question period" advocated by Democratic Senator Estes Kefauver of Tennessee from 1943 to 1953, the heads of executive departments and agencies would appear periodically before Congress, for up to two hours, to answer written or oral questions. In 1978 Democratic Representative Lee Hamilton of Indiana and his staff assistant recommended that senior executive officials appear frequently before Congress in a "question hour" as part of a cooperative process in foreign affairs and national defense.[93]

Despite the logic and apparent good sense behind these proposals, they consistently have failed to generate the necessary support. Part of the reason is that the advantages, by this time, are largely theoretical. The political process adjusted long ago to permit departmental heads a formal role in presenting their ideas to Congress. President Wilson relied on legislative leaders in Congress to link the branches, but he also depended on Postmaster General Albert Burleson to carry out the duties of congressional liaison. A former member of Congress from Texas, Burleson received credit for much of the success of Wilson's legislative program.[94]

Institutionalizing Power, 1921-1981

By creating the Budget Bureau in 1921, Congress added an institution that inadvertently enhanced the president's role as legislative leader. As will be explained, this influence grew predominantly as a result of executive initiatives and statutory interpretation, at times with the support of important power centers in Congress.

The first budget director, Charles G. Dawes, established procedures to control the flow of bills traveling from the executive branch to Congress. The Budget Bureau derived this responsibility from Section 206 of the Budget and Accounting Act, which prohibited agencies from submitting their financial proposals to Congress unless first requested by either house. The bureau reasoned that Congress expected it to review all departmental reports to Congress on proposed or pending legislation. Although Section 206 related only to estimates or requests for appropriations, Dawes concluded that "it is necessary for a full compliance with its spirit that all requests or recommendations for legislation, the effect of which would be to create a charge upon the public Treasury or commit the Government to obligations which would later require appropriations to meet them, should be first submitted to the President before being presented to Congress." Several years passed before this policy was systematically enforced.[95]

Dawes's directive appeared to be a power grab by the Budget Bureau, but the initiative came from Congress. The House Appropriations Committee had expressed concern about the lack of supervision over agency requests. Chairman Martin Madden, R-Ill., learned that an agency had asked a legislative committee for authority to divert appropriated funds from the purposes originally specified. Madden told Dawes that "matters of this character should come through the Bureau of the Budget. . . . I have called them to your attention in order that you may take . . . steps . . . to include [such] requests . . . in the control which the Bureau has over direct estimates."[96]

This process of "central clearance" evolved over the years until it embraced three main functions. The Budget Bureau reviewed agency proposals sent to Congress to determine that they were "in accord with the program of the president." It coordinated departmental advice on legislation originating in Congress and advised the president to sign or veto enrolled bills presented to him by Congress. By 1939, when the Budget Bureau was transferred from the Treasury Department to the Executive Office of the President, it had become responsible for clearing proposed executive orders and proclamations and for reviewing the testimony of executive officials who appeared before congressional committees.[97]

Until recent years, central clearance was carried out by a staff of Budget Bureau professionals in the legislative reference division. Other participants included the budget examiners assigned to various departments and agencies, with assistance from the general counsel's office in the White House.

The Budget Bureau was expected to supply objective, analytical advice on the merits of bills, leaving political and partisan judgments to the White House. The influence of the legislative reference division declined during the Kennedy and Johnson administrations, due to competition from White House staff. Central clearance was increasingly relegated to handling the "thousands of legislative items not commanding presidential attention, with the White House handling the major items and articulating the president's priorities."[98] In 1970 the Budget Bureau was replaced by the Office of Management and Budget (OMB). Much of the leverage within the OMB shifted from career civil servants to political appointees; objectivity and professionalism lost ground to a politicized operation.[99]

Initiating Legislation

The search for the source of legislation inevitably takes the traveler on a convoluted and twisted journey, full of surprises. Peel away one "source," and you will discover another. The process continues to repeat itself with little hope of reaching bottom. As Woodrow Wilson remarked, "Legislation unquestionably generates legislation. Every statute may be said to have a long lineage of statutes behind it. . . ."[100]

Democratic Senator James E. Murray of Montana is generally credited with supplying the "spark of will" that transformed an idea into the Employment Act of 1946. This legislative achievement, however, owes a major intellectual debt to two British economists, John Maynard Keynes and Sir William Beveridge; to such private associations as the National Planning Association; and to legislative staff members who worked in concert with executive agencies, interest groups, and private individuals. An annotated bibliography of the major books and articles on full employment, written between 1943 and 1945, came to "fifty-six tightly packed pages."[101]

Robert A. Dahl expressed a widely held view of legislative activity in foreign policy: "Perhaps the single most important fact about

Congress and its role in foreign policy . . . is that it rarely provides the initiative."[102] Yet other studies credit individual representatives and senators with a significant voice in shaping foreign policy. Francis O. Wilcox, writing from the perspective of chief of staff for the Senate Foreign Relations Committee from 1947 to 1955 and assistant secretary of state for international organization affairs from 1955 to 1961, concluded that "some of the most imaginative and constructive foreign policies since World War II have originated in Congress." As leading examples he cited the exchange-of-persons program, the use of surplus agricultural commodities in the foreign aid program, the International Development Association, the Peace Corps, and the U.S. Arms Control and Disarmament Agency. "Not infrequently," he noted, "an idea is born on Capitol Hill and then, when it is brought to fruition, the President receives political credit for it." [103]

More recently, as a result of the build-up in professional staff within Congress, structural changes within the institution, and greater visibility of foreign policy issues among the public, Congress is now able and willing to assert itself on a continuous basis. Legislative actions over the past decade—such as terminating the war in Vietnam, restricting presidential policy in Cyprus and Angola, enacting the War Powers Resolution in 1973 over Nixon's veto, restricting the Central Intelligence Agency, and scrutinizing arms sales—have been initiated by Congress with the assistance of outside groups and individuals. Presidents Ford and Carter appealed to Congress to remove many of these restrictions on their freedom to act in foreign affairs, but Congress generally resisted these appeals.[104]

Legislation is often rooted in causes that do not come to light. A member of a legislator's staff, after playing a pivotal role in initiating and shaping a bill, may decide to conceal that contribution out of deference to a member or because of a self-imposed anonymity. A private organization that conceives the idea embodied in legislation, and perhaps even drafts the bill, might prefer to hide its influence in order to improve the bill's chance for passage. Further complicating the picture, an administration may allow a member of Congress to take the lead in advocating a proposal, not because the legislator conceived the idea but to avoid anticipated criticism that the executive branch is extending its power and promoting expensive programs.[105]

Bills that "originate" in the executive branch are subsequently modified and refined by the suggestions of private groups, committee hearings and markups, and the adoption of floor amendments. Decentralization of Congress in recent years, associated with largely autonomous and well-staffed subcommittees, has produced more floor amendments and challenges to reported bills. As a result, the White House faces the prospect of substantial revisions and often radical alterations in administration bills. In the rare case when an administration bill sails through Congress with little change, this may reflect not so much the president's influence but rather a decision by the White House to have a draft bill cleared first by the major powers on Capitol Hill.[106]

Scholars devote considerable time and energy in debating which branch of government—legislative or executive—deserves credit for originating most legislation. Writing in 1953, George B. Galloway concluded that very little legislation found its source in Congress. For the most part, he said, legislators are "merely conduits for the executive departments, private organizations, and individual constituents." Samuel P. Huntington, in a 1965 study, suggested that 80 percent of the bills enacted into law originate in the executive branch.[107]

These studies by Galloway and Huntington give far too much credit to the executive branch. Lawrence Chamberlain, after studying 90 major enactments from 1890 to 1940, concluded that no less than 77 developed from bills that had been introduced in earlier years without sponsorship from the administration. A more recent study by Ronald Moe and Steven Teel, published in 1970, agreed with Chamberlain that Congress plays a substantial role in initiating and developing legislation. Chamberlain frames the issue accurately: the *ideas* for legislation seldom originate either in Congress or the executive branch. "Most legislation is in reality the product of forces external to any governmental agency." [108]

EXECUTIVE LOBBYING

Prior to World War II, presidents relied on personal assistants within the White House or the executive departments to handle contacts with Congress. The Budget Bureau, created in 1921, was the starting point for an *institutionalized* liaison operation with Congress.

The Executive Office of the President (EOP), established in 1939, contained not only the Budget Bureau but also other units to improve executive-legislative relations. The EOP White House Office was composed, in part, of secretaries to the president charged with the following mission: "To facilitate and maintain quick and easy communication with the Congress, the individual members of the Congress, the heads of executive departments and agencies, the press, the radio, and the general public." The administrative assistants to the president were expected to bridge the gap between the branches.[109]

Some of the key aides of President Franklin D. Roosevelt did not even work for the White House. Benjamin Cohen, while serving in a number of government positions outside the White House, helped draft the Securities Act of 1933, the Securities and Exchange Act of 1934, the Utility Holding Company Act of 1935, and the Fair Labor Standards

Act of 1937. Thomas Corcoran, assigned primarily to the Reconstruction Finance Corporation, assisted with those measures as well as the Federal Housing Act of 1933. A White House official said of Corcoran: "[A]s frequent emissary from the White House some felt that he played the Congress as well as he played the accordion, to the delight of FDR." [110]

Agency Initiatives

Although departments had promoted legislation throughout the history of the country, agencies in the 1930s began to realize the value of centralizing control for bill-drafting in the counsel's office and assigning to someone in that office a definite responsibility for the task. Most departments had detailed someone in their organization to watch legislation, but usually on a part-time and sporadic basis. In 1934 the Treasury Department created a legislative division within the office of the general counsel. This division was responsible for drafting treasury bills, monitoring their progress after they were introduced in Congress, and working with legislative staff in preparing amendments desired by congressional committees. [111]

In 1909 the State Department created the post of counselor, which President Wilson used as special adviser on congressional relations. The job became full-time and of high rank in 1940 when Secretary Cordell Hull appointed Breckinridge Long as assistant secretary in charge of legislative relations. [112]

By 1941, some political scientists were wondering whether executive lobbying had fundamentally altered the governmental process:

> No one would deny that this familiar, slow, democratic process has been materially modified. It is scarcely too strong to say that today the government leads and the people follow; and by government is meant, as all would agree, the executive, or the administrative bureaucracy. This is not to say the executive leadership is new or uncommon in American politics. The strong presidents have all been spirited leaders in legislation. Yet never before in peacetime has there been the degree of legislative direction from administrative quarters that the last few years has brought. [113]

Beginning in 1942, two months after the attack on Pearl Harbor, the War Department reorganized its general staff. Under the leadership of Brigadier General Wilton B. Persons, the reorganization included the army's first elaborate congressional unit, the legislative and liaison division. The Army Organization Act of 1950 established a department legal counselor—a senior civilian reporting directly to the secretary of the army and responsible for monitoring the activities of the office of legislative liaison. In other departments, legislative liaison also developed out of the departments' general counsels or solicitors. [114]

Organizing the White House, 1941-1969

During the emergency atmosphere of World War II, the task of coordinating the president's program was shared by the White House, the Budget Bureau, and the Office of War Mobilization and Reconversion. After Roosevelt's death in 1945, Truman tried to pull the entire function back into the Budget Bureau. To coordinate the State of the Union message, the budget message, and the economic report, Truman asked the Budget Bureau to obtain from the agencies a preliminary listing of their ideas for legislation. The Budget Bureau was expected to work closely with congressional committees to determine whether the central clearance process could be "tied more closely to the committees' desire for the scheduling of items to come before them." [115]

A small congressional liaison unit was established within the Truman White House. Two assistants were appointed in 1949, one assigned to the Senate and the other to the House. Neither had been a long-time associate or close personal friend of President Truman. Neither had any experience in partisan politics or as congressional staff.[116] Significant liaison responsibilities were carried out by Truman or his associates in the White House, particularly Clark Clifford and Charles S. Murphy. Senior members of the Truman White House characterized the formal liaison unit as:

> understaffed and relatively ineffectual. The legislative assistants attended the President's staff meetings but rarely spoke up. In the Congress they had litle discretion to commit the President or to speak authoritatively for him so as to influence votes, strategy or tactics ... the legislative assistants were primarily messengers rather than responsible political agents.[117]

By 1953, the first year of the Eisenhower administration, a staff of senior assistants in the White House had been assigned the responsibility of legislative liaison. Starting with three, the unit's staff was increased to eight by 1961.[118] Eisenhower's initial chief liaison officer was Brigadier General Wilton B. Persons, a close personal friend and longtime military associate. Persons had served as a liaison officer for the military under two Democratic administrations. Another member of the liaison team, Bryce Harlow, had known Eisenhower during World War II when Harlow carried out legislative liaison for General George Marshall and Secretary of War Henry Stimson. Later serving as general counsel for the House Armed Services Committee, Harlow's contact with Eisenhower continued.[119] Eventually Harlow replaced Persons as head of the White House liaison unit.

The operation of the liaison staff was limited by Eisenhower's strong belief in the separation of powers doctrine and his respect for congressional prerogatives in legislative matters. But Eisenhower took seriously the promises in his party's platform and the commitments made during the campaign. In 1954 alone he made 232 specific requests for legislation to Congress.[120]

The Kennedy administration, pledged to activist leadership, had an extensive legislative program. Kennedy's razor-thin presidential victory convinced him that a sophisticated, aggressive liaison operation with Congress was indispensable to White House objectives. The chief of the liaison unit, Larry O'Brien, anticipated complaints about encroachments on congressional authority, and even charges of violating the separation of powers doctrine, but the choice seemed clear: "Either we fought for our program or we would have no program." [121]

The liaison unit in the Kennedy White House numbered about six full-time professionals. Compared with the Eisenhower staff, they were younger, possessed less experience in dealing with Congress, and had served in highly partisan positions before joining the administration. Several were criticized for displaying "a lack of respect for their elders in the Congress and with using crude tactics more appropriate to the rough-and-tumble of party conventions than to the political process in a coequal branch of the national government." [122]

O'Brien initially performed two jobs: congressional relations and the allocation of top-level political appointments. To protect the liaison operation, he soon decided not to be viewed as Kennedy's patronage chief, "lest the ill will from the people I had to say 'no' to would hurt Kennedy on the Hill." He worked out an arrangement that made John Bailey, chairman of the Democratic National Committee, the bearer of bad news, retaining for the White House the more pleasant duty of announcing who got a job. O'Brien also allowed supporters in Congress to make the first announcement of federal grants and projects awarded to their districts.[123]

O'Brien's liaison unit did not try to monopolize congressional relations. Appropriations remained the responsibility of the Budget Bureau. Foreign affairs were left to the president's adviser on foreign affairs, the secretary of state, and the assistant secretary for congressional relations in the State Department (although on some issues, such as foreign aid, the White House liaison team intervened).[124]

When President Johnson, a former Senate majority leader, entered office he stressed the importance of the congressional liaison operation. He told cabinet members and agency heads:

> There's no one more important in your department or agency than the man responsible for congressional relations. You have the responsibility to see to it that you have the best possible man available. You see to it that he's adequately staffed, and you see to it that you maintain your relationship with the Congress every day of the week.[125]

In O'Brien's estimate, Johnson's approach to congressional liaison represented a "hard-sell, arm-twisting style of operation which contrasted with Kennedy's more restrained approach." [126]

Nixon to Reagan, 1969-1981

Nixon, like Johnson, came to the presidency with considerable congressional experience: member of the House of Representatives, senator, and vice president. And yet more than any president before or since, he displayed a contemptuous attitude toward the legislative branch and never seemed comfortable dealing with its members.

To manage his congressional relations staff, President Nixon first turned to Bryce Harlow, veteran White House lobbyist of the Eisenhower years, and to William E. Timmons, who had served as an aide to Republican members of Congress. On December 9, 1970, Harlow resigned his post as counselor to the president. Despite his long experience as a liaison officer, Harlow's two years with the Nixon administration had been marred by reports of poor communication and consultation. His record from the Eisenhower years, however, would have been difficult to match. During that period Harlow enjoyed close relationships with Speaker Sam Rayburn and Senate Majority Leader Lyndon Johnson. He later recalled that Eisenhower, Rayburn, and Johnson "were the dearest of friends. I'd put them together about every six weeks in the dead of night over there on the second floor of the White House Mansion with branch water and bourbon whiskey and they'd just have a ball." [127] This level of intimacy did not exist in the Nixon administration.

Harlow's job was complicated by attitudes within the Nixon White House. Some senior staffers, including John D. Ehrlichman and H. R. Haldeman, had a limited understanding of Congress or the constitutional system of separated powers and little inclination to learn. Another source of difficulty lay in the heightened expectations of Republican legislators. Many of them remembered Harlow from the Eisenhower days, "when they were so respectful of the General, they asked for little. Part of their trouble is that they expected a greater deal of Richard Nixon, who was one of them for so long, who has always been reliably political and completely responsive to their problems." [128]

Harlow was replaced by Clark MacGregor, who had just completed ten years in the House of Representatives. Republican members of Congress praised MacGregor's appointment. On his lapel he wore a button that proclaimed: "I care about Congress." But shortly after MacGregor took office, Nixon issued a sharp attack on the 91st Congress. He said that Congress, because of its record over the previous two years, "will be remembered and remarked upon in history not so much for what it did, but for what it failed to do." The nation, he said, had watched a legislative body "that had seemingly lost the capacity to decide and the will to act." [129]

MacGregor, objecting to this speech, extracted from Nixon a promise that future messages to Capitol Hill would first be routed through him. MacGregor believed that the tense atmosphere of confrontation tactics employed by the Nixon White House should be replaced by a more conciliatory approach. The philosophy he expressed to Nixon, upon accepting the job, was that "bloody defeats in Congress are not helpful to him or the country. My view is that the best politics for Richard Nixon is success for the legislative program." [130]

But the Nixon administration was bent on confrontation politics. MacGregor departed to make way for Timmons's hard-hitting style. On July 6, 1972, setting the tone for Nixon's reelection effort, Timmons denounced Congress as "miserable," "irresponsible," "appalling," and "cynical." In the words of one political scientist, Democrats were suspicious of Timmons's "almost exclusive ties with Republican organizations and representatives prior to his joining the Nixon White House; they saw his office as more overtly partisan than Harlow's." [131]

The bitterness of the 1972 campaign produced several changes in the Nixon White House. Informal consultations with Congress were now offered by top presidential advisers, including Haldeman, Ehrlichman, Henry Kissinger, and Peter Flanigan. Timmons gained control over contacts with outside interest groups, a job formerly held by Charles Colson. Nixon agreed to meet weekly with the "Big Four" Republican leaders in Congress: the minority leaders and whips of both houses. He also agreed to meet more frequently with Senate Majority Leader Mike Mansfield and House Speaker Carl Albert.[132]

The resignations of Ehrlichman and Haldeman on April 30, 1973, offered another opportunity to mend relations with Congress. Nixon appointed Harlow and Melvin Laird (a former member of Congress and Nixon's first secretary of defense) to the post of White House counselor, where they were supposed to function as Nixon's "ambassadors" to Capitol Hill. Within a year, as pressure mounted for Nixon's resignation, they departed from the adminstration.[133]

Max Friedersdorf, Timmons's deputy for House liaison, was appointed to head the liaison unit in the Ford White House. Gerald Ford had spent 25 years in the House of Representatives, many of them as minority leader for the Republicans. He was therefore accustomed to the give-and-take of politics. Congressional relations appeared to be off to a good start on August 12, 1974, when President Ford addressed Congress three days after he took office. In contrast to the truculent, pugnacious tone of the Nixon administration, Ford looked forward to a period of trust and harmony: "As President, within the limits of basic

principles, my motto toward the Congress is communication, concilia-
tion, compromise, and cooperation."

White House actions were not always consistent with this posture.
On May 27, 1975, in a nationwide radio and television address, Ford
castigated legislators for acting slowly on his energy proposals: "The
Congress cannot drift, dawdle and debate forever with America's
future." Some of the White House lobbyists were accused of heavy-
handedness (see p. 58), and Ford issued almost twice as many regular
vetoes in his two-and-a-half years as Nixon did in his five-and-a-half. Of
Ford's 48 vetoes, Congress overrode 12. On the whole, however, executive-legislative relationships improved considerably during the Ford
years. Timmons, after leaving his post as White House liaison chief,
compared the styles of Nixon and Ford:

> If you put in a suggestion for Ford to call up someone, a conferee or a
> ranking member, he'll do it. Nixon was not comfortable doing that. He
> did some of it, of course, but it wasn't often, and when he did he really
> wouldn't like it. It was awkward for him. It was not his nature. Ford is
> comfortable doing it and he's pretty persuasive in personal negotia-
> tions.[134]

Jimmy Carter selected Frank Moore to head his congressional
relations team. A native of Georgia, Moore had served as liaison with
the Georgia legislature during Carter's term as governor. Later he
served as Carter's executive secretary. At no time had Moore ever
worked in Washington or on Capitol Hill. Even before Carter took
office, congressional Democrats began criticizing Moore's performance.
Unreturned phone calls and missed meetings were part of the objections, but the complaints soon broadened to include inadequate consultation on presidential appointments and the energy program.[135]

Some of the problems stemmed from the inexperience of Carter's
liaison staff, but other factors contributed to the breakdown in executive-legislative relations. Congressional sensitivity had been heightened
by the acerbity of the Nixon years, there were fears that Carter viewed
Congress as little more than a national version of the Georgia legislature, and House Speaker Tip O'Neill and Senate Majority Leader
Robert Byrd were much more assertive as party leaders than their
predecessors, Carl Albert and Mike Mansfield. Moreover, changes in the
delegate selection process at the Democratic National Convention
allowed someone like Carter to win nomination with less than the usual
support from Congress. Carter came in as an "outsider" and would
remain one.

Previous administrations had organized their liaison teams around
geographical areas, assigning White House staff to legislators from the
Northeast, South, and West. The purpose was to prevent liaison staffers
from developing special interests in substantive areas and becoming

identified with congressional committees, interest groups, and administrative agencies devoted to particular programs.[136] The Carter White House, by dividing its liaison team into "issue clusters" instead of geographical areas, tried to change the nature of executive lobbying. Under the geographical system, White House aides could attempt to manipulate federal program grants and contracts in return for favorable votes by legislators. Vote-trading was not as easy with the "issue cluster" system. As a former Carter aide explained: "A White House liaison officer is no longer in a position to discuss a sewage treatment plant in the context of a foreign aid vote because the liaison aide who handles foreign policy does not also handle environmental issues...."[137] The House liaison team in the Carter White House eventually returned to a geographical division of labor.

Although studies initially described Carter as reluctant to use project grants to influence votes on Capitol Hill,[138] by 1979, with the presidential campaign in full swing, Republican members of Congress denounced the White House for using public funds and grants to influence governors and mayors before key primaries. The amount of discretionary funds available to the White House was estimated at $29 billion.[139]

President Reagan's liaison team operated smoothly from the start. Friedersdorf, who had served Nixon and Ford in congressional relations, was selected to head the Reagan liaison unit. His principal assistants, Powell A. Moore (handling the Senate) and Kenneth M. Duberstein (responsible for the House), both had substantial experience on Capitol Hill. As if to underscore the importance of congressional relations to the Reagan administration, Friedersdorf's staff worked out of the White House rather than the rooms in the Old Executive Office Building that had been occupied by Frank Moore's staff.

Other units in the Executive Office of the President, including staff from the OMB and the Office of Policy Development (OPD), assist with congressional relations. OPD, consisting of about 40 staffers in the Reagan administration, is the successor agency to Nixon's Domestic Council and Carter's Domestic Policy Staff. It helps formulate and coordinate a legislative policy for the president, oversees the drafting of administration bills, and resolves conflicts between agency proposals.[140] Once a program is introduced in Congress as a bill, the White House liaison team assumes responsibility for passage, working together with departmental liaison staff. Stuart Eizenstat, head of Carter's Domestic Policy Staff, had worked the Hill on a regular basis and acquired a reputation as one of the most effective members of Carter's staff.

The vice president, acting in his constitutional capacity as presiding officer of the Senate, seems ideally located to serve as liaison to Congress. Early interpretations of the office, however, considered the vice president as essentially a legislative officer who could not be assigned executive duties without violating the separation of powers doctrine. James Sherman, vice president under Taft, decided he would not intercede with legislative leaders: "I am to be Vice-President and acting as a messenger boy is not part of the duties of a Vice-President." But political considerations explain Sherman's decision better than constitutional theory. As a former representative, he had been a confidant of House Speaker Joseph Cannon and did not want to be used by Taft in the pending battle against Cannon. Even as late as the 1940s and 1950s, Harry S Truman and Dwight D. Eisenhower believed that the vice president was not formally part of the executive branch, although Truman recognized that the vice president could be an influential force behind the scenes. Indeed, it would have been strange for Truman not to take advantage of Vice President Alben Barkley's legislative experience: fourteen years in the House of Representatives and more than two decades in the Senate.[141]

Lyndon Johnson, despite his vast experience on Capitol Hill, was given little responsibility for legislative liaison during his three years as vice president in the Kennedy administration. With the assistance of Mike Mansfield, his successor as Senate majority leader, Johnson was elected to preside over Senate Democratic caucuses. Seventeen senators voted against him (with forty-six in favor). His opponents argued that the arrangement violated the spirit of the separation of powers, but they were principally concerned that Johnson would actually run the Senate instead of the self-effacing Mansfield. Their fears were reinforced when Mansfield announced that he would retain Bobby Baker, Johnson's former personal aide, as secretary of the Senate. According to one account:

> Johnson grieved deeply and emotionally over those seventeen votes. No other single event in those formative days of the New Frontier cut deeper, and none more influenced his conduct as Vice-President after January 20. Indeed, he retired from the Senate — physically as well as legally.[142]

When Johnson became president, he delegated substantially more Hill duties to Vice President Hubert Humphrey, who had spent many years in the Senate.[143] Vice President Walter Mondale, another former senator, became an effective link to Congress for the Carter administration. Mondale had offices both in the Capitol and the Dirksen Senate Office Building, where he conducted congressional relations. Drawing on old friendships in Congress, he supported White House proposals such as the Panama Canal treaties and Carter's energy program.[144] Reagan's vice president, George Bush, has an opportunity to lobby Congress effectively because of his earlier experience as a member of the House of Representatives.

Federal agencies are in a continuous process of acquiring and losing the values and attitudes needed for effective lobbying. As a top official in the Department of State noted in 1980:

> Five years ago our LMO's (congressional relations staff) went up to the Hill to "sell." Today they consider the legislators as partners and, therefore, communicate in both directions, bringing Executive Branch views to Congress and returning to the State Department with Congressional insights.[145]

Reciprocity requires mutual respect. It is not uncommon, however, for lobbyists from the executive branch to conduct their operations with a thinly disguised contempt for members of Congress. Bryce Harlow recalls that some members of the Kennedy liaison unit held a low opinion of legislators, considering them "cheap ward politicians and ward heelers," while Carter and his White House aides thought Congress was "a bunch of toads." [146] Subjected to this treatment, members of Congress will respond in kind, scuttling many of the administration's legislative aspirations.

RESTRICTIONS ON EXECUTIVE LOBBYING

Executive branch lobbying is subject to legal and political constraints. These constraints date as far back as 1913, when Congress passed an appropriation bill with this language: "No money appropriated by this or any other Act shall be used for the compensation of any publicity expert unless specifically appropriated for that purpose." [147] Republican Representative Frederick Gillett of Massachusetts sponsored this provision after learning that the Civil Service Commission had advertised for a "publicity expert" in the Department of Agriculture. Democrat John Fitzgerald of New York, chairman of the House Appropriations Committee, agreed with Gillett that there was "no place in the Government service for an employee whose sole duty was to extol and to advertise the activities of any particular service of the Government." [148]

In response to this statutory language, agencies simply concocted new titles for employees. Instead of "publicity expert," agencies created positions for director of information, chief educational officer, supervisor of information research, director of publications, and other imaginative names that circumvented the law.[149] The 1913 legislation remains part of the permanent body of federal law (5 U.S.C. 3107), but it has been diluted by other statutes that specifically authorize and fund publicity efforts. In contrast to the attitude of Representatives Gillett and Fitzgerald, today it is commonplace for Congress to supply funds to agencies and departments for public information officers.[150]

A more significant law passed in 1919. Debate in the House of Representatives reveals that members were offended by bureau chiefs and departmental heads "writing letters throughout the country, sending telegrams throughout the country, for this organization, for this man, for that company to write his Congressman, to wire his Congressman, in behalf of this or that legislation." Statutory language was devised to "absolutely put a stop to that sort of thing." [151] As currently codified (18 U.S.C. 1913), the provision reads:

> No part of the money appropriated by an enactment of Congress shall, in the absence of express authorization by Congress, be used directly or indirectly to pay for any personal service, advertisement, telegram, telephone, letter, printed or written matter, or other device, intended or designed to influence in any manner a Member of Congress, to favor or oppose, by vote or otherwise, any legislation or appropriation by Congress, whether before or after the introduction of any bill or resolution proposing such legislation or appropriation; but this shall not prevent officers or employees of the United States or of its departments or agencies from communicating to Members of Congress on the request of any Member or to Congress, through the proper official channels, requests for legislation or appropriations which they deem necessary for the efficient conduct of the public business.

In addition to Section 1913 (also known as the "Lobbying With Appropriated Moneys Act"), Congress enacts other restrictions on departmental lobbying and public relations.[152] Several studies have used the term "legal fiction" to describe these statutory restrictions,[153] but laws have been somewhat effective in limiting the ability of departments to mobilize grass-roots support for or against pending legislation.

Enforcing Statutory Restrictions

Part of the difficulty in controlling executive lobbying by statute is disagreement on what constitutes "publicity," "propaganda," and "liaison." But beyond this issue of definitions is a more fundamental problem. Members of Congress simultaneously resent and invite executive lobbying. Those who advocate restrictions on departmental lobbying also understand that the legislative process depends on a free flow of information from the executive branch. Even critics of administrative lobbying steer clear of a blanket condemnation. As one legislator remarked: "Certainly, any administration should be expected to use all legal means at its disposal to encourage acceptance of its programs." [154] During an investigation of executive lobbying in 1950, Democratic Representative Frank Buchanan of Pennsylvania explained·

> ... it is necessary in a democracy, for our citizens, individually or collectively, to seek to influence legislation. It is equally necessary for

the executive branch of Government to be able to make its views known to Congress on all matters in which it has responsibilities, duties, and opinions. The executive agencies have a definite requirement to express views to Congress, to make suggestions, to request needed legislation, to draft proposed bills or amendments, and so on.[155]

Congress has even passed legislation to *encourage* agency personnel to inform members of Congress about their operations. In a provision that dates back to 1912 (and is reiterated in the Civil Service Reform Act of 1978), Congress declared that the right of federal employees, "individually or collectively, to petition Congress or a Member of Congress, or to furnish information to either House of Congress, or to a committee or Member thereof, may not be interfered with or denied." [156] An appropriation bill for fiscal 1980 contained a standard prohibition on agency publicity and propaganda efforts designed to support or defeat legislation pending before Congress. Immediately following this interdiction, however, is an invitation to lower-level employees of the Postal Service to inform Congress about the operations of their agency. These communications may be at the initiative of the employee or in response to a request or inquiry by a member or committee. Administrators in the Postal Service who interfere with this flow of information to Congress can be penalized.[157]

Members of Congress do not question the right of presidents to advocate legislative measures, either through the constitutional prerogative to present to Congress information on the state of the union or other recommendations judged to be necessary or expedient. The president is at liberty to present personal views through press conferences, news broadcasts, and television appearances. The president's opportunity to appeal to the public and to build support for legislative recommendations has been enhanced by access to the media. Vice President Mondale remarked in 1980: "If you asked me, if I had to give up one—the opportunity to get on the evening news, or the veto power, I think I'd throw the veto power away." [158]

Section 1913 does not prevent executive officials from responding, through appropriate channels, to a legislator's request. Rather, the purpose is to prevent administrators from using their offices to drum up support or opposition to pending legislation. Members of Congress do not want to be on the receiving end of constituent pressures artificially manufactured by agency phone calls, telegrams, departmental threats and coercion, and other stimuli originating from within an administration. The General Accounting Office (GAO), as well as the former Budget Bureau, has objected to agency publications that are proselytizing in tone and propagandistic in substance. Agency lobbying is thus subject to legislative as well as executive constraints.

Controversial Actions

A former official of the Budget Bureau, Roger W. Jones, recalled one instance "in which there was a clear-cut case which, by any standards, would have been improper proselytizing, under a hidden appropriation, [and] the situation was brought into the open." The Budget Bureau, through its authority to clear agency publications, disapproved a proposed pamphlet prepared by a regional office of the Bureau of Reclamation (now the Water and Power Resources Service) on the grounds that the pamphlet constituted propaganda. In a few cases the GAO has been able to collect from executive officials telegram and telephone expenses incurred for the specific purpose of influencing a pending bill. Lobbying by telephone presents a special problem for GAO. Without a recorder or eavesdropper, it is difficult to judge the purpose and motivation behind a call.[159] In addition, it is often difficult to discriminate between violations of Section 1913 and the exercise of statutory authority to disseminate information.[160]

In 1948 the House Subcommittee on Publicity and Propaganda reported what it considered a number of illegal and improper agency practices. It expressed particular concern about "an unprecedented flood of news releases from the executive agencies ... much of it ... sheer propaganda designed to influence public thinking and to bring pressure upon Congress." The subcommittee found especially objectionable the administration's efforts to promote national health insurance. Following President Truman's message to Congress on November 19, 1945, urging enactment of legislation, a number of federal agencies established "health workshops" around the country to discuss the issue. When Subcommittee Chairman Republican Forest Harness of Indiana asked one of the agency officials whether all sides of the question were being explored, the official responded that the purpose of the workshops was to present supporting material to carry out the president's order: "We would naturally give emphasis to that, because that is why we are in Government. Otherwise, we should get out of Government." Only two health workshops were held, both before the subcommittee's investigation. Federal agencies cancelled their plans to hold other workshops.[161]

The subcommittee also investigated lobbying efforts by the War Department with regard to universal military training and a campaign by the Department of Agriculture to organize a farmers' protest against a congressional cut in funds. It concluded that the "greatest and most effective lobby in the Nation today is that conducted by Federal administrative agencies." Despite this critique, the subcommittee hesitated to make specific recommendations for reform, recognizing that

there is a fine line between legitimate information service, and activity on the part of agencies and individuals which is designed to condition the public mind, and [the subcommittee] cautions that it will take legislation drawn with meticulous care to prevent improper action without infringing on legitimate services or the rights of the individual public official.[162]

During the fall of 1961, the Kennedy administration sponsored a series of White House regional conferences around the country. President Kennedy declared that it was

vitally important that the Government remain close to the people, and therefore we have arranged to have representatives of the various agencies and departments of Government travel through some of the major cities of the United States, to talk to informed and interested citizens on the problems that our people are facing and on those governmental actions which might assist our country to move forward.[163]

Republican Representative Ancher Nelsen of Minnesota charged that the conferences were efforts at the grass roots to foster the objectives of the White House. He claimed that private citizens who had participated in the discussions with agency officials were first cleared to guarantee the "soundness" of their views. Postcards were handed out to permit the audience to tell the president about their support. The GAO decided that a finding of illegality was unwarranted, even though executive officials had urged the audience to support the administration's legislative proposals. Also, since Section 1913 carried criminal penalties, enforcement "would be for determination in the first instance by the Department of Justice." Representative Nelsen noted that one of the agencies participating in the conferences was the Justice Department, forcing it to pass judgment on its own conduct.[164]

In 1962, during House debate on a public debt ceiling, Republican Gerald Ford of Michigan complained that the Defense Department had tried to convince military contractors that a failure to raise the debt limit would result in defense cutbacks. Republican John Byrnes of Wisconsin protested that the Kennedy administration's tactic "smacks of blackmail." Roy Walter Riehlman, a Republican representative from New York for 16 years, said that never before had someone from industry approached him to warn that his unwillingness to increase the debt limit would lead to a loss of federal contracts for his district. "Through the enormous power the President wields," charged Riehlman, "he now has representatives of industry doing his dirty work for him." [165]

Also during the Kennedy administration, Republican Representative Odin Langen of Minnesota protested that an official from the Agricultural Stabilization and Conservation Service had sent a directive to federally licensed radio and television stations, implying that the licenses might not be renewed unless the stations gave free time to present the government's position on agricultural issues. Citizens who served on Department of Agriculture committees reported that the meetings were being used primarily to propagandize administration programs. At the urging of the Senate Appropriations Committee, Congress enacted specific language to prohibit the use of appropriated funds to influence the vote of farmers in any referendum and to influence agricultural legislation, except as permitted by Section 1913. The legislation also prohibited funds for salaries or other expenses of members of county and community committees for engaging in any activities other than advisory and supervisory duties and delegated program functions prescribed in administrative regulations.[166]

Several key members of Congress were outraged in 1973 when the Nixon White House prepared a 145-page kit of materials to be used against Congress in the "Battle of the Budget." The kit consisted of guidelines for speeches, "one liners," and "horror stories" about wasteful federal programs—all to be used as part of a coordinated attack on the "spendthrift" Democratic-controlled Congress. Some of the suggested epithets, distributed to top agency officials and public relations aides, included "the buck-passing Congress," "the credit-card Congress," and the "maverick Congress (ignoring the will of the people)." Following are examples of quips to be used in lampooning Congress:

> This may look like a Santa Claus Congress—but it's got a bagful of bad news for the taxpayers.

> Just because the Congress passes the buck doesn't mean the President has to spend it.

> When Congress can't add, Senator Scott (the Republican leader) has said the President must subtract. Otherwise the budget will keep on multiplying and the taxpayer's dollars will keep on dividing.

> When one man helps himself to another man's bank account, that's called embezzlement. But when a big-spending congressman helps himself to the taxpayer's income with higher prices and taxes, then it's called "compassion." [167]

Democratic Senators Edmund Muskie of Maine and Hubert Humphrey of Minnesota asked the GAO to determine whether the White House operation violated Section 1913. Comptroller General Elmer Staats concluded that the kit violated language in an appropriation act, which restricted funds for publicity or propaganda purposes designed to support or defeat pending legislation, but deferred to the Justice Department on the question of Section 1913: "Since 18 U.S.C. 1913 contains fine and imprisonment provisions which may be enforced only through judicial criminal proceedings, it is not within our jurisdiction to determine the statute's applicability in any given circumstances." While the GAO was reviewing the matter, a Ralph Nader litigation unit (Public Citizen, Inc.) went to court claiming that the White House had violated Section 1913. Shortly thereafter a White House official, in an affidavit, stated that all copies of the kit had been returned for destruction. The suit was subsequently dismissed on the ground that it was moot.[168]

The Justice Department did not prosecute the White House aides responsible for the budget kit. Assistant Attorney General Henry Peterson added his interpretation to Section 1913 by claiming that the "apparent intention" of Congress was to bar "gross solicitations of public support, i.e., conduct that would propagandize and generate public backing, financed with appropriated funds. Such gross solicitation does not appear to have occurred in this case." (The GAO had determined that most of the kits had been printed and paid for by the Republican National Committee.) Peterson further narrowed the reach of Section 1913 by dismissing *de minimis* (small) violations of the law.[169]

Lobbying by the Ford administration came under fire when several Republican members of Congress announced that White House staffers had threatened to withhold federal favors unless the legislators voted with the administration. In 1975, Maine Republican Representatives William Cohen and David Emery said that a White House lobbyist had told them that Ford's appointment of a former Republican governor from Maine to a federal post hinged on their willingness to support Ford's veto of a tax bill. Both legislators voted to override the veto—two of only nineteen Republicans in the House to do so.[170]

A year later, Republican Representative Larry Pressler of South Dakota publicly rebuked a White House lobbyist. Pressler said that the lobbyist told him he would be in "political trouble" if he voted against the Ford administration on the natural gas vote. Attacking Pressler in his home district's leading newspaper, the lobbyist called him "paranoid and defensive" and described his reaction to White House pressure as "typical of a freshman Congressman." After the lobbyist apologized, Pressler told President Ford that such tactics were counterproductive and intolerable.[171]

During Carter's administration, criticism of executive lobbying was aimed primarily at departmental and agency officials. The Interior Department appropriation act in 1977 prohibited the use of funds for any activity or the publication or distribution of literature that "in any way tends to promote public support or opposition to any legislative proposal on which congressional action is not complete," in accordance with Section 1913. The same language was enacted the next year.[172]

Despite this statutory restriction, the Senate Appropriations Committee learned that "intensive public communication efforts" were being conducted by the secretary of the interior and several agencies in support of the administration's proposal to designate millions of acres of federal land in Alaska as national parks. The communications went "far beyond" the typical press release. They included wide distribution of editorial columns signed by the secretary, special mailings to environmental groups urging them to "make your views known," regional releases by the Fish and Wildlife Service, "elaborate supporting brochures" by the Bureau of Land Management, and other efforts. The literature "clearly favored" the administration's version of the Alaska lands legislation. All of it, the committee noted, was produced, printed, and mailed at federal expense. The committee refused to approve "elaborate propaganda campaigns at the expense of the taxpayer." [173] Carter eventually signed the bill into law (P.L. 96-487) in 1980.

Several complaints were made about the Carter administration's use of public funds to campaign for the SALT II arms control treaty.[174] Also high on the list of agencies criticized for lobbying activities were the Indian Health Services, Commission on Civil Rights, Office of Juvenile Justice, Maritime Administration, and Office of Surface Mining.[175] Especially irritating to some members of Congress was the use of federal funds by the Legal Services Corporation and ACTION to lobby Congress and state and local lawmakers.[176] Three suits were filed in federal court to challenge the attempt by the Carter administration to promote SALT II, trucking deregulation, and civil service reform.[177] The SALT case—brought to court by six senators, four representatives, and the American Conservative Union—was dismissed because they failed to establish specific injury under the standing doctrine.[178]

Sanctions against executive lobbying are largely ineffective because the Justice Department believes that Congress intended Section 1913 to bar "gross solicitations" of public support, and the GAO lacks jurisdiction to determine violations of the criminal code. Furthermore, statutory restrictions generally do not reach administrative lobbying in matters of state referenda, state elections, or ratification of amendments to the Constitution.[179] Congressional ambivalence has undercut any principled or consistent objection to executive lobbying, especially when conducted by presidential staff. The White House post of public liaison chief, held by Elizabeth Hanford Dole in the Reagan administration, deliberately orchestrates the lobbying efforts of private constituent groups, urging them to pressure Congress to pass the president's program.[180] From the few judicial decisions, it is apparent that the courts are inclined to defer to the judgment of Congress and the president on the definition of appropriate lobbying activity by executive officials.[181]

CONCLUSIONS

Even in the days of patronage and the spoils system, the administration of sanctions and favors by the president was time-consuming and quite likely to irritate and alienate important members of Congress. Civil service reforms and the rise of the welfare state, which automatically dispenses benefits through entitlement programs, have removed much of the leverage previously available to the White House. In addition, since members of Congress are increasingly independent of the White House in their reelection campaigns, they may vote as they please with little worry of presidential retaliation.

The president is left essentially with modest powers of persuasion, bargaining, negotiation, favors, services, flattery, appeals to national interest, and personal loyalty. Success in enlisting the support of a legislator comes at a cost, at least in time and energy; often the price is a specific benefit that the legislator wants, and expects, in return. All these tactics may fail when legislators decide that a presidential request is injurious to their constituents or contrary to their own principles and conscience.[182]

An ambitious program to "care and feed" legislators carries a high risk. If a president extends favors to fence-sitters to secure their votes, other legislators may resent the fact that they have routinely supported the administration without receiving comparable assistance. Such thoughts might encourage signs of "disloyalty" until the White House takes notice and demonstrates its appreciation. "Vote-trading" is carried out by all parties in the legislative process. Legislators, heads of administrative agencies, and lobbyists "continually do unto others in the hope that others will do at least as well by them." The president, as a manager of patronage, is "simply one trader in a market system."[183]

A president's election rarely provides a "mandate" for his program. Legislators successful in the same election usually enter office with mandates of their own, quite different from the values and objectives of the president-elect. Seldom will these legislators depend on the president's "coattail effect." Consequently, they owe him little. Two-thirds of the senators gained their seats by winning elections two to four years earlier. In the words of one perceptive journalist:

> Ironically, Congress and the President get along so badly partly because they are so similar. Mr. Carter ran for President as a man with no ties and no obligations. So did many of the newer members of Congress. Like him, they are independent outsiders, free agents with no entangling alliances. Now that he's President, and needs and wants their loyalty, it simply is not there.[184]

Reagan's election in 1980 interrupted this pattern. The goals he stressed—budget reductions, less federal regulation, and a stronger defense—were shared by many of the legislators who also won election. But even in the spring of 1981, still in Reagan's "honeymoon" period, it was evident that both houses of Congress had fundamentally different notions of what ought to be done about social security reform and tax cuts. Further gaps between the branches can be expected in the process of converting broad generalities of budget cuts, regulatory reform, and national defense into specific program decisions.

Leadership from the White House will always be possible, whether Congress is centralized or decentralized. It is often argued that the decentralization of Congress in the 1970s, which took power from committee chairmen and dispersed it to House and Senate subcommittees, thwarted the legislative goals of Presidents Ford and Carter. They could not contact a handful of influential chairmen to push forward the White House program.

This is a convenient excuse, but it ignores the fact that earlier presidents complained that the *centralization* of power in Congress made it impossible to get bills past uncooperative committee chairmen. Legislative decentralization can be an opportunity, not an obstacle, because it opens up lines of communication. Presidents can turn to legislators and subcommittee chairmen to bring to the floor a bill that might have been buried in the past by a committee chairman.

Part of presidential leadership consists in fashioning a broad coalition of support, capable of adjusting to new circumstances and conditions. It is irresponsible to complain that conditions are not like they used to be (or not like we *thought* they used to be). A good leader makes the best of a situation that is never ideal. President Franklin D. Roosevelt once told an aide: "I am the captain of this ship, but the seas control the captain." He recognized that the strength of forces, impulses, and opinions at any given time would determine what he had to do.[185] A skillful leader can find some margin for action in any situation.

NOTES

1. There are political benefits as well as liabilities in convening Congress for special session. See Wilfred E. Binkley, "The President as Chief Legislator," *The Annals* 307 (1956):92, 99-100; Joseph E. Kallenbach, *The American Chief Executive* (New York: Harper & Row, 1966), pp. 324-333.
2. Youngstown Co. v. Sawyer, 343 U.S. 579, 587 (1952).
3. *Hinds' Precedents of the House of Representatives* (Washington, D.C.: Government Printing Office, 1907), 5:6629; *Cannon's Precedents of the House of Representatives* (Washington, D.C.: Government Printing Office, 1935), 8:3333; Kallenbach, *The American Chief Executive*, pp. 333-336.
4. James D. Richardson, ed., *A Compilation of Messages and Papers of the Presidents*, 20 vols. (New York: Bureau of National Literature, 1897-1925), 4:1864.
5. H. Wayne Morgan, *From Hayes to McKinley* (Syracuse, N.Y.: Syracuse University Press, 1969), pp. 274-319.
6. Donald F. Anderson, *William Howard Taft: A Conservative's Conception of the Presidency* (Ithaca, N.Y.: Cornell University Press, 1973), p. 299.
7. Richard E. Neustadt, "Presidency and Legislation: Planning the Presi-

dent's Program," *American Political Science Review* 49 (1955):980, 1015.

8. Missouri Pac. Ry. Co. v. Kansas, 248 U.S. 277 (1919). A president may sign a bill after Congress recesses; see La Abra Silver Mining Co. v. United States, 175 U.S. 423 (1899). He may also sign a bill after a final adjournment of Congress; see Edwards v. United States, 286 U.S. 482 (1932).

9. Anonymous "William Penn" writing in the Philadelphia *Independent Gazetteer*, January 3, 1788, cited in *The Antifederalist Papers*, ed. Morton Borden (East Lansing: Michigan State University Press, 1965), p. 210.

10. Max Farrand, ed., *The Records of the Federal Convention of 1787*, 4 vols. (New Haven: Yale University Press, 1937), 1:139. See also 2:74, 586-587; 4:81.

11. U.S., Congress, *Annals of Congress*, 15th Cong., 1st sess., 1817, pp. 18, 451-452.

12. *Weekly Compilation of Presidential Documents* 16 (May 30, 1980):1012; June 4, 1980, pp. 1027-1028; June 5, 1980, pp. 1037, 1041-1043. After Congress overrode the veto, the bill became P.L. 96-264.

13. U.S., Congress, *Congressional Record* (daily ed.), 96th Cong., 2d sess., June 19, 1980, 126:H5402-5407.

14. U.S., Congress, Senate, Committee on Governmental Affairs, *Study on Federal Regulation*, Vol. 3, S. Doc. 95-71, 95th Cong., 1st sess., July 1977, p. 65.

15. Richardson, *Messages and Papers of the Presidents*, 9:4475, 4488, 4494 (April 29, May 29, and June 23, 1879); T. Harry Williams, ed., *Hayes: The Diary of a President* (New York: David McKay, 1964), pp. 193-234.

16. Louis Fisher, "The Authorization-Appropriation Process in Congress: Formal Rules and Informal Practices," *Catholic University Law Review* 29 (1979):51.

17. *Weekly Compilation of Presidential Documents* 15 (August 15, 1979):1434.

18. Louis Fisher, *The Constitution Between Friends: Congress, the President, and the Law* (New York: St. Martin's Press, 1978), pp. 90-96.

19. Kennedy v. Sampson, 511 F.2d 430 (D.C. Cir. 1974); *Congressional Record* (daily ed.), 94th Cong., 2d sess., April 26, 1976, 122:S5912; Fisher, *The Constitution Between Friends*, pp. 96-99.

20. For an analysis of the factors behind vetoes and congressional overrides of vetoes, see Jong R. Lee, "Presidential Vetoes from Washington to Nixon," *Journal of Politics* 37 (1975):522.

21. *U.S. Constitution*, Article VI, Section 2. The Supremacy Clause applies with particular force to treaties that are self-executing; see Foster v. Neilson, 27 U.S. 253, 314 (1829).

22. United States v. Schooner Peggy, 5 U.S. 103 (1801); memorandum by Monroe Leigh, legal adviser to the State Department, on October 8, 1975, reprinted in *Congressional Record* (daily ed.), 93d Cong., 2d sess., November 14, 1975, 121:S20104.

23. Statement by George Clinton on December 16, 1787, cited in *The Antifederalists*, ed. Cecelia M. Kenyon (New York: Bobbs-Merrill, 1966), p. 317.

24. *Congressional Record* (daily ed.), 96th Cong., 1st sess., April 26, 1979, 125:S4839.

25. Ibid., June 6, 1979, pp. S7062-7064; Goldwater v. Carter, 481 F.Supp. 949 (D.D.C. 1979); Goldwater v. Carter, 617 F.2d 697 (D.C. Cir. 1979);

Goldwater v. Carter, 444 U.S. 996 (1979).

26. *Congressional Record* (daily ed.), 97th Cong., 1st sess., February 17, 1981, 127:S1344.
27. Altman & Co. v. United States, 224 U.S. 583, 601 (1912). For an early example of statutory authority for executive agreements, see 1 Stat. 239 (1792).
28. Louis Fisher, *President and Congress* (New York: Free Press, 1972), pp. 44-45.
29. United States v. Belmont, 301 U.S. 324 (1937); United States v. Pink, 315 U.S. 203 (1942). For a more recent decision upholding the president's authority to enter into international executive agreements, based solely on his constitutional authority, see Dole v. Carter, 444 F.Supp. 1065 (D. Kans. 1977). An appellate court, declining to enter into a controversy relating to distinctions between treaties and executive agreements, held that the action did not present a justiciable controversy; see Dole v. Carter, 569 F.2d 1109 (10th Cir. 1977).
30. *Foreign Affairs Manual* 11 (1974):721.2(b)(3).
31. United States v. Guy W. Capps, Inc., 204 F.2d 655, 660 (4th Cir. 1953); Seery v. United States, 127 F.Supp. 601, 606 (Ct. Cl. 1955); and Reid v. Covert, 354 U.S. 1, 16 (1957).
32. 86 Stat. 619 (1972), 1 U.S.C. 112b (1976); P.L. 95-45, 91 Stat. 224, sec. 5 (1977). For more detail on treaties and executive agreements, see Fisher, *The Constitution Between Friends,* pp. 192-213.
33. Cited in Raoul Berger, *Government by Judiciary* (Cambridge: Harvard University Press, 1977), pp. 117, 407. See also Raoul Berger, *Executive Privilege* (Cambridge: Harvard University Press, 1974), pp. 57-58.
34. See Louis Fisher, "Raoul Berger on Public Law," *Political Science Reviewer* 8 (1978):173.
35. Patrick W. Duff and Horace E. Whiteside, "Delegata Potestas Non Potest Delegari: A Maxim of American Constitutional Law," *Cornell Law Quarterly* 14 (1929):168; and Horst P. Ehmke, " 'Delegata Potestas Non Potest Delegari,' A Maxim of American Constitutional Law," *Cornell Law Quarterly* 47 (1961):50.
36. Wayman v. Southard, 10 Wheat. 1, 46 (1825).
37. Hampton & Co. v. United States, 276 U.S. 394, 406 (1928). See also Field v. Clark, 143 U.S. 649, 692 (1891).
38. Sunshine Coal Co. v. Adkins, 310 U.S. 381, 398 (1940). See also the discussion in Fisher, *President and Congress,* pp. 55-57.
39. Panama Refining Co. v. Ryan, 293 U.S. 388 (1935); Schechter Corp. v. United States, 295 U.S. 495 (1935).
40. 84 Stat. 799 (1970); Amalgamated Meat Cutters & Butcher Work. v. Connelly, 337 F.Supp. 737, 750 (D.D.C. 1971).
41. California Bankers Assn. v. Shultz, 416 U.S. 21, 90-93 (1974), Justices Douglas and Brennan dissenting; Arizona v. California, 373 U.S. 546, 624-627 (1963), Justice Harlan dissenting; Zemel v. Rusk, 381 U.S. 1, 21-22 (1965), Justice Douglas dissenting.
42. Industrial Union v. American Petroleum (July 2, 1980), sometimes referred to as the "Benzene Case."
43. Pennhurst State School v. Halderman (April 20, 1981). The majority opinion was written by Justice Rehnquist, joined by Chief Justice Burger and Justices Stewart, Powell, and Stevens.
44. United States v. Eliason, 41 U.S. 291, 301 (1842).

45. 6 Op. Att'y Gen. 10 (1853).
46. Lincoln Electric Co. v. Commissioner of Int. Rev., 190 F.2d 326, 330 (6th Cir. 1951). See James Hart, *The Ordinance Making Powers of the President of the United States,* a 1925 classic reprinted by Da Capo Press in 1970.
47. Manhattan Co. v. Commissioner, 297 U.S. 129, 134 (1936). See also Ernst & Ernst v. Hochfelder, 425 U.S. 185, 213-214 (1976).
48. *Congressional Record* (daily ed.), 97th Cong., 1st sess., January 22, 1981, 127:S500.
49. Citizens to Save Spencer Cty. v. EPA, 600 F.2d 844 (D.D.C. 1979).
50. *Weekly Compilation of Presidential Documents* 17 (February 17, 1981):124; "OMB Turf Wars Show Lobbying Targets," *Legal Times of Washington,* May 11, 1981, pp. 1, 9.
51. *Weekly Compilation of Presidential Documents* 16 (1980):583, 768, 841, 901.
52. Ibid., pp. 575, 922.
53. Proclamation 4744, *Federal Register* 45 (1980):22864, as amended by Proclamations 4748 and 4751; Independent Gasoline Marketers Council, Inc. v. Duncan, 492 F.Supp. 614 (D.D.C. 1980).
54. U.S., Congress, House, Ways and Means Committee, *Oil Import Fees: The Administration of the Program and its Impact* (hearings), 96th Cong., 2d sess., 1980.
55. United States v. Yoshida Intern., Inc., 526 F.2d 560 (Ct. Cust. & Pat. App. 1975); Fisher, *The Constitution Between Friends,* pp. 126-127.
56. Schmidt Pritchard & Co. v. United States, 167 F.Supp. 272 (Cust. Ct. 1958); Carl Zeiss, Inc. v. United States, 76 F.2d 412 (Ct. Cust. & Pat. App. 1935).
57. See John L. Blackmun, Jr., *Presidential Seizure in Labor Disputes* (Cambridge: Harvard University Press, 1967).
58. *Congressional Record,* 78th Cong., 2d sess., 1944, 90:6022; 58 Stat. 387, sec. 213 (1944); 31 U.S.C. 696 (1976). See also 31 U.S.C. 691 (1976) and 31 U.S.C. 673 (1976).
59. U.S., Congress, Senate, S. Rept. 1275, 90th Cong., 2d sess., 1968, pp. 2-3; U.S., Congress, House, H. Rept. 1348, 90th Cong., 2d sess., 1968, p. 8; 82 Stat. 444-445, sec. 302 (1968). For recent language in an appropriation bill, see P.L. 96-74, 93 Stat. 575, sec. 608 (1979).
60. 49 Comp. Gen. 59 (1969); 42 Op. Att'y Gen. 405 (1969); Contractors Assn. of Eastern Pa. v. Secretary of Labor, 442 F.2d 159, 171 (3d Cir. 1971), certiorari denied, 404 U.S. 854 (1971).
61. Fisher, *The Constitution Between Friends,* pp. 131-132. See also Joel L. Fleishman and Arthur A. Aufses, "Law and Orders: The Problem of Presidential Legislation," *Law and Contemporary Problems* 40 (1976):1.
62. Cole v. Young, 351 U.S. 536 (1956); Youngstown Co. v. Sawyer, 343 U.S. 579 (1952); Panama Refining Co. v. Ryan, 293 U.S. 388, 433 (1935); United States v. Symonds, 120 U.S. 46 (1887); Little v. Barreme, 2 Cr. 170 (1804).
63. Metzenbaum v. Edwards (D.D.C. March 4, 1981), *United States Law Week* 49 (1981):2601.
64. Executive Order 12092, *Federal Register* 43 (1978):51375; American Fed. of Labor v. Kahn, 472 F.Supp. 88 (D.D.C. 1979); American Federation of Labor, Etc. v. Kahn, 618 F.2d 784 (D.C. Cir. 1979), certiorari denied, 443 U.S. 915 (1979).
65. John C. Fitzpatrick, ed., *Writings of Washington,* 39 vols. (Washington,

D.C.: Government Printing Office, 1931-1944), 30:394.

66. Ibid., pp. 369-370, 375, 393-394. See also Washington's letter to Senator Pierce Butler, August 10, 1789, p. 379.
67. Washington's letter to Senator Pierce Butler, p. 373.
68. Richardson, *Messages and Papers of the Presidents*, 1:64-65, 68-69, 71-72, 81ff, 110, 115 (February 9, 1790, to March 8, 1792).
69. For information on the Knox incident, see James Hart, *The American Presidency in Action* (New York: Macmillan, 1948), p. 77. For 1790 and 1792 actions, see Leonard D. White, *The Federalists* (New York: Macmillan, 1948), p. 57.
70. William Maclay, *Sketches of Debate in the First Senate of the United States* (Frederick Ungar, 1965), pp. 135, 172. See also pp. 201, 251.
71. *Annals of Congress*, 1st Cong., June 25, 1789, pp. 592-593.
72. 1 Stat. 65 (1789); White, *The Federalists*, p. 118n.
73. *Annals of Congress*, 1st Cong., July 24, 1789, pp. 670-671; and September 17, 1789, p. 895. See also Patrick H. Furlong, "The Origins of the House Committee on Ways and Means," *William and Mary Quarterly* 25 (1956):587.
74. Maclay, *Sketches of Debate in the First Senate* (1965 ed.), pp. 185, 373, 374, 376, 399. For Hamilton's other activities to influence Congress, see pp. 377, 397-398.
75. *Annals of Congress*, 2d Cong., 1st-2d sess., November 20, 1792, pp. 703-708. On the 1793 and 1794 investigations, see ibid., February 28 to March 1, 1793, pp. 899-963; ibid., 3d Cong., 1st-2d sess., February 19, 1794, p. 458; ibid., February 24, 1794, pp. 463-466, and December 2, 1794, p. 954. See also Broadus Mitchell, *Alexander Hamilton*, 2 vols. (New York: Macmillan, 1957-1962), 2:245-286. For some strategic errors that caused Hamilton political problems, see James Willard Hurst, "Alexander Hamilton, Law Maker," *Columbia Law Review* 78 (1978):483. On reviving the Ways and Means Committee, see *Annals of Congress*, 2d Cong., 1st sess., March 26, 1794, pp. 532-533.
76. On Jefferson to Gallatin, see Henry Adams, ed., *The Writings of Albert Gallatin*, 3 vols. (New York: Antiquarian Press, 1960), 1:380. On Representative Giles, see Ralph Volney Harlow, *The History of Legislative Methods in the Period before 1825* (New Haven: Yale University Press, 1917), p. 168, citing the *Washington Federalist* of February 17, 1802. On Jefferson to Nicholas, see *The Writings of Thomas Jefferson* (Memorial Edition, 1904), 11:162.
77. Harlow, *The History of Legislative Methods*, p. 175.
78. Dice Robins Anderson, *William Branch Giles* (Menasha, Wis.: George Banta, 1914), p. 82.
79. Robert M. Johnstone, Jr., *Jefferson and the Presidency* (Ithaca, N.Y.: Cornell University Press, 1978), p. 140.
80. Charles Francis Adams, ed., *Memoirs of John Quincy Adams*, 12 vols. (Philadelphia: J. B. Lippincott, 1874-1877), 1:447.
81. Henry Adams, *The Life of Albert Gallatin* (New York: Peter Smith, 1943), pp. 302-303. See also Johnstone, *Jefferson and the Presidency*, pp. 140-143.
82. James Sterling Young, *The Washington Community: 1800-1828* (New York: Columbia University Press, 1966), pp. 16, 162.
83. Ibid., p. 168.
84. Stephen Horn, *The Cabinet and Congress* (New York: Columbia Univer-

sity Press, 1960), pp. 55-59.

85. Ibid., pp. 63-71.

86. Ibid., pp. 78-92. See also Gamaliel Bradford, "Congress and the Cabinet," *Annals of the American Academy of Political and Social Science* 2 (November 1891):289-290.

87. 34 Stat. 454 (1906).

88. *Congressional Record*, 59th Cong., 1st sess., 1906, 40:8810-8811.

89. Ibid., p. 8812.

90. James W. Garner, "Executive Participation in Legislation as a Means of Increasing Legislative Efficiency" (Proceedings of the annual meeting of the American Political Science Association, Washington, D.C., December 30, 1913-January 1, 1914), 10:183-184.

91. On Fitzgerald, see "Budget Systems," *Municipal Research* 62 (June 1915):312, 327, 340. See also William Franklin Willoughby, *The Problem of a National Budget* (New York: D. Appleton, 1918), pp. 146-149; Fisher, *The Constitution Between Friends*, pp. 176-177; and David Houston, *Eight Years with Wilson's Cabinet*, 2 vols. (Garden City, N.Y.: Doubleday, Page, 1926), 2:88.

92. U.S., Congress, House, H. Rept. 14, 67th Cong., 1st sess., 1921, pp. 6-7.

93. Estes Kefauver, "Executive-Congressional Liaison," *The Annals* 289 (1953):108; Horn, *The Cabinet and Congress*, pp. 136-175; Lee H. Hamilton and Michael H. Van Dusen, "Making the Separation of Powers Work," *Foreign Affairs* 57 (1978):17, 37-38.

94. Richard F. Fenno, Jr., *The President's Cabinet* (Cambridge: Harvard University Press, 1959), pp. 200-202.

95. Bureau of the Budget, Circular No. 49 (December 19, 1921); Stephen J. Wayne, *The Legislative Presidency* (New York: Harper & Row, 1978), pp. 96-97, note 1.

96. Richard E. Neustadt, "Presidency and Legislation: The Growth of Central Clearance," *American Political Science Review* 48 (1954):641, 643.

97. On executive orders and proclamations, see Executive Order 8247, *Federal Register* 4 (1939):3864, sec. II.2(f); Horace W. Wilkie, "Legal Basis for Increased Activities of the Federal Budget Bureau," *George Washington Law Review* 11 (1943):265, 273. See also Carl R. Sapp, "Executive Assistance in the Legislative Process," *Public Administration Review* 6 (1946):10. On reviewing testimony, see John H. Reese, "The Role of the Bureau of the Budget in the Legislative Process," *Journal of Public Law* 15 (1966):63, 77-78; and Neustadt, "Presidency and Legislation," pp. 649-650. The current policy for central clearance is embodied in OMB Circular No. A-19, revised September 20, 1979. For personal opinion by officials, see OMB Circular No. A-10, November 12, 1976.

98. Allen Schick, "The Budget Bureau That Was: Thoughts on the Rise, Decline, and Future of a Presidential Agency," *Law and Contemporary Problems* 35 (1970):519, 527. See also Robert S. Gilmour, "Central Legislative Clearance: A Revised Perspective," *Public Administration Review* 31 (1971):150.

99. Wayne, *The Legislative Presidency*, pp. 70-100. For other recent studies on central clearance, see James W. Davis and Randall B. Ripley, "The Bureau of the Budget and Executive Branch Agencies: Notes on their Interaction," *Journal of Politics* 29 (1967):749; and Larry Berman, *The Office of Management and Budget and the Presidency, 1921-1979* (Princeton: Princeton University Press, 1979), pp. 116-125.

100. Woodrow Wilson, *Congressional Government* (Boston: Houghton Mifflin Co., 1885), p. 297.
101. Stephen Kemp Bailey, *Congress Makes a Law* (New York: Columbia University Press, 1950), pp. 9, 41.
102. Robert A. Dahl, *Congress and Foreign Policy* (New York: Harcourt Brace Jovanovich, 1950), p. 58.
103. Francis O. Wilcox, *Congress, the Executive, and Foreign Policy* (New York: Harper & Row, 1971), p. 14.
104. See James A. Robinson, *Congress and Foreign Policy-Making* (Homewood, Ill.: Dorsey Press, 1967); and David Baldwin, "Congressional Initiative in Foreign Policy," *Journal of Politics* 28 (1966):754. Studies crediting Congress with significant voice include: James A. Robinson, *The Monroney Resolution: Congressional Initiative in Foreign Policy Making* (New York: Henry Holt, 1959); Thomas M. Franck and Edward Weisband, *Foreign Policy by Congress* (New York: Oxford University Press, 1979); and Cecil V. Crabb, Jr., and Pat M. Holt, *Invitation to Struggle: Congress, the President and Foreign Policy* (Washington, D.C.: Congressional Quarterly Press, 1980).
105. Robinson, *Congress and Foreign Policy-Making*, pp. 44-46.
106. For thoughtful analyses by John R. Johannes, see his *Policy Innovation in Congress* (Morristown, N.J.: General Learning Corporation, 1972); "Where Does the Buck Stop—Congress, President, and the Responsibility for Legislative Initiation," *Western Politics Quarterly* 25 (1972):396; "Congress and the Initiation of Legislation," *Public Policy* 20 (1972):281; and "The President Proposes and the Congress Disposes, But Not Always: Legislative Initiation on Capitol Hill," *Review of Politics* 36 (1974):356. See also David E. Price, *Who Makes the Laws?: Creativity and Power in Senate Committees* (Cambridge: Schenkman, 1972); and Gary Orfield, *Congressional Power: Congress and Social Change* (New York: Harcourt Brace Jovanovich, 1975).
107. George B. Galloway, *The Legislative Process in Congress* (New York: Thomas Y. Crowell, 1953), p. 38; Samuel P. Huntington, "Congressional Responses to the Twentieth Century," *The Congress and America's Future*, ed. David B. Truman (Englewood Cliffs, N.J.: Prentice-Hall, 1965), p. 23.
108. Lawrence H. Chamberlain, *The President, Congress and Legislation* (New York: Columbia University Press, 1946), pp. 23, 454; Ronald C. Moe and Steven C. Teel, "Congress as Policy-Maker: A Necessary Reappraisal," *Political Science Quarterly* 85 (1970):443. See also Nelson W. Polsby, "Policy Analysis and Congress," *Public Policy* 18 (1969):61.
109. *Public Papers and Addresses of Franklin D. Roosevelt*, 13:491, 497; 53 Stat. 565 (1939).
110. Jonathan Daniels, *White House Witness* (Garden City, N.Y.: Doubleday, 1975), p. 40. For a political profile on Corcoran, see Patrick Anderson, *The President's Men* (Garden City, N.Y.: Doubleday, 1968), pp. 40-53.
111. Edwin E. Witte, "The Preparation of Proposed Legislative Measures by Administrative Departments," The President's Committee on Administrative Management, *The Exercise of Rule-Making Power and the Preparation of Proposed Legislative Measures By Administrative Departments* (Washington, D.C.: Government Printing Office, 1937), pp. 52, 57, 57n. See also O. Douglas Weeks, "Initiation of Legislation by Administrative Agencies," *Brooklyn Law Review* 9 (1940):117; and Edwin E. Witte,

"Administrative Agencies and Statute Lawmaking," *Public Administration Review* 2 (1942):116.

112. The Commission on Organization of the Executive Branch of the Government (Hoover Commission), *Task Force Report on Foreign Affairs* [Appendix H], January 1949, pp. 131-132. For Dean Acheson's experience as assistant secretary for congressional relations at the State Department, see his memoir, *Present at the Creation* (New York: Norton, 1969), pp. 87-238. See also Ben H. Brown, Jr., "Congress and the Department of State," *The Annals* 289 (1953):100; and Robinson, *Congress and Foreign Policy-Making*, pp. 95-144.

113. Harold W. Stoke, "Executive Leadership and the Growth of Propaganda," *American Political Science Review* 35 (1941):490, 491.

114. On Brig. Gen. Persons, see Bryce Harlow, "Text of Address at Nashville Symposium, October 21, 1973," *Center House Bulletin of the Center for the Study of the Presidency* 4 (Winter 1974), cited by Maura E. Heaphy in "Executive Legislative Liaison," *Presidential Studies Quarterly* 5 (1975):42. On the legal counselor in 1950, see Earl D. Johnson, "Legislative-Executive Relationships in the Formulation of Public Policy as Viewed by the Executive," in *Legislative-Executive Relationships in the Government of the United States*, ed. O. B. Conway (Washington, D.C.: The Graduate School of the U.S. Department of Agriculture, 1954), p. 30. See also Abraham Holtzman, *Legislative Liaison* (Chicago: Rand McNally, 1970), p. 11; and Thomas P. Murphy, "Congressional Liaison: The NASA Case," *Western Politics Quarterly* 25 (1972):192.

115. U.S., Congress, House, Select Committee on Lobbying Activities, *Legislative Activities of Executive Agencies (Part 10)* (hearings), 81st Cong., 2d sess., 1950, pp. 9-10.

116. Holtzman, *Legislative Liaison*, pp. 231-233, 236, 259.

117. Ibid., p. 233.

118. Maura E. Heaphy, "Executive Legislative Liaison," *Presidential Studies Quarterly* 5 (1975):42, 43.

119. Holtzman, *Legislative Liaison*, pp. 232-237.

120. Dwight D. Eisenhower, *Mandate for Change* (Garden City, N.Y.: Doubleday, 1963), p. 298; see also chaps. 8, 12.

121. Lawrence F. O'Brien, *No Final Victories* (Garden City, N.Y.: Doubleday, 1974), pp. 109-110.

122. Holtzman, *Legislative Liaison*, p. 239. For additional criticism of Kennedy liaison staffers, characterized as young and arrogant, see Meg Greenfield, "Why Are You Calling Me, Son?" *The Reporter*, August 16, 1962, pp. 29-31.

123. O'Brien, *No Final Victories*, pp. 107-108, 119, 183. See also *Time* (September 1, 1961):10-11.

124. G. Russell Pipe, "Congressional Liaison: The Executive Branch Consolidates its Relations With Congress," *Public Administration Review* 26 (1966):14, 21.

125. Interview with Lawrence F. O'Brien, "From White House to Capitol ... How Things Get Done," *U.S. News & World Report* (September 20, 1965):73.

126. O'Brien, *No Final Victories*, p. 176.

127. John Osborne "Gabbing with Harlow," *The New Republic* (May 13, 1978):13. For Harlow's record in the Nixon administration, see *Washington Post*, February 8, 1969, p. A2; and *Washington Star*, February 11,

1969, p. A7.

128. Mary McGrory, "GOP Dream Still Unfulfilled," *Washington Star*, February 11, 1969, p. A7.

129. *Public Papers of the Presidents*, 1971, pp. 23-25.

130. *New York Times*, July 3, 1972, p. 15; *The Washington Lobby* (Washington, D.C.: Congressional Quarterly, 1971), p. 142.

131. Wayne, *The Legislative Presidency*, p. 157. On Timmons's blast at Congress, see *New York Times*, July 7, 1972, p. 10.

132. *Washington Post*, January 1, 1973, p. A1; *National Journal*, January 13, 1973, pp. 35-43.

133. *New York Times*, June 30, 1973, p. 16; *Christian Science Monitor*, February 26, 1974, p. 1; *Washington Star*, April 13, 1974, p. A2.

134. *Washington Post*, January 2, 1975, p. A28.

135. "Hill Democrats Unhappy with Carter's Emissary," *Washington Post*, November 5, 1976, p. A1; "Hill Leaders Ask Carter to Improve Consultation," *Washington Post*, January 28, 1977, p. A4. See also *Christian Science Monitor*, January 27, 1977, p. 3; and *New York Times*, January 27, 1977, p. 1.

136. Eric L. Davis, "Building Presidential Coalitions in Congress: Legislative Liaison in the Johnson White House" (Doctoral dissertation, Stanford University, 1977), p. 38.

137. F. T. Merrill, Jr., "How Carter Stopped Playing Politics and Started Having Trouble with Congress," *Washington Monthly* (July-August 1977):30.

138. Eric L. Davis, "Legislative Liaison in the Carter Administration," *Political Science Quarterly* 94 (1979):287, 294-295.

139. *Congressional Record* (daily ed.), 96th Cong., 1st sess., October 22, 1979, 125:S14854-14855; "White House Grants: Carter's $29 Billion Campaign Fund?" in *U.S. News & World Report*, reprinted in *Congressional Record* (daily ed.), 96th Cong., 2d sess., June 17, 1980, 126:E2993-2994.

140. "White House Domestic Policy Staff Plays an Important Role in Formulating Legislation," Congressional Quarterly *Weekly Report*, October 6, 1979, p. 2199; "Reagan Sings of Cabinet Government, and Anderson Leads the Chorus," *National Journal*, May 9, 1981, pp. 824-827. See also John H. Kessel, *The Domestic Presidency: Decision-Making in the White House* (North Scituate, Mass.: Duxbury Press, 1975).

141. On Vice President Sherman, see Irving G. Williams, *The Rise of the Vice Presidency* (Washington, D.C.: Public Affairs Press, 1956), p. 93; Harry S Truman, *Year of Decisions* (Garden City, N.Y.: Doubleday, 1955), p. 197; Dwight D. Eisenhower, *Waging Peace* (Garden City, N.Y.: Doubleday, 1965), p. 6.

142. Rowland Evans and Robert Novak, *Lyndon B. Johnson: The Exercise of Power* (New York: The New American Library, 1968), p. 326.

143. Joel Kramer Goldstein, *The American Vice Presidency, 1953-1978*, (Doctoral dissertation, Nuffield College, University of Oxford, Trinity Term, 1978), pp. 175-183.

144. "Vice President Mondale—Carter's Partner With Portfolio," *National Journal*, March 11, 1978, p. 381.

145. Charles W. Whalen, Jr., "A Decade of Reform in the U.S. House of Representatives, 1969-1979: Its Impact Upon American Foreign Policy" (Paper presented at a colloquium sponsored by the Woodrow Wilson International Center for Scholars, November 20, 1980).

146. *Congressional Record* (daily ed.), 96th Cong., 1st sess., December 5, 1979, 125:S17879.
147. 38 Stat. 212.
148. *Congressional Record,* 63rd Cong., 1st sess., 1913, 50:4409.
149. James L. McCamy, *Government Publicity: Its Practices in Federal Administration* (Chicago: University of Chicago Press, 1939), p. 7.
150. *Washington Star,* August 31, 1975, p. A2. See also "Agencies Resist Nixon Directive to Cut Back Spending on Public Relations," *National Journal,* July 24, 1971, pp. 1551-1556.
151. For statement of Representative Good, see *Congressional Record,* 66th Cong., 1st sess., 1919, 58:403.
152. Two early restrictions appeared in 1949 in the Agriculture and Interior Department appropriation acts (63 Stat. 342, 765). Another restriction appeared in 1962 (76 Stat. 739). More recent examples, for fiscal 1978, cover agriculture (91 Stat. 824); defense (91 Stat. 904-905, sec. 828); foreign assistance (91 Stat. 1239, sec. 501); interior (91 Stat. 307, sec. 304); labor and health, education, and welfare (90 Stat. 1437, sec. 407, as continued by P.L. 95-205); state, justice, and commerce (91 Stat. 443, sec. 701); and treasury, postal service (91 Stat. 355, sec. 607a).
153. J. Leiper Freeman, *The Political Process: Executive Bureau-Legislative Committee Relations* (New York: Random House, 1966), p. 39; Richard L. Engstrom and Thomas G. Walker, "Statutory Restraints on Administrative Lobbying—'Legal Fiction,'" *Journal of Public Law* 19 (1970):89.
154. Ancher Nelsen, "Lobbying by the Administration," *We Propose: A Modern Congress,* ed. Mary McInnis (New York: McGraw-Hill, 1966), p. 145.
155. *Legislative Activities of Executive Agencies (Part 10),* p. 2.
156. 92 Stat. 1217, sec. 7211 (1978). This provision originally appeared at 37 Stat. 555, sec. 6 (1912).
157. P.L. 96-74, 93 Stat. 575, sec. 607 (1979).
158. *Washington Post,* October 10, 1980, p. A3. See also Elmer E. Cornwell, Jr., *Presidential Leadership of Public Opinion* (Bloomington: Indiana University Press, 1965).
159. *Legislative Activities of Executive Agencies (Part 10),* pp. 24-25, 31-33.
160. For example, 7 U.S.C. 2201 (1976); 29 U.S.C. 1 (1976); and 49 U.S.C. 1352 (1976).
161. U.S., Congress, House, H. Rept. 2474, 80th Cong., 2d sess., 1948, pp. 2-4.
162. Ibid., pp. 7, 9.
163. *Public Papers of the Presidents,* 1961, p. 700.
164. Nelsen, "Lobbying by the Administration," p. 149.
165. *Congressional Record,* 87th Congress, 2d sess., 1962, 108:10410. See also 108:10408.
166. *Congressional Record,* 88th Congress, 1st sess., 1963, 109:11213-11214, 24767-24768; 77 Stat. 827 (1963). See also U.S., Congress, H. Rept. 355, 88th Cong., 1st sess., 1963, pp. 28-29; S. Rept. 497, 88th Cong., 1st sess., 1963, p. 23; and H. Rept. 1088, 88th Cong., 1st sess., 1963, p. 10.
167. Mike Causey, "Administration Supplies One Liners," *Washington Post,* April 6, 1973, p. D17.
168. On Staats, see *Congressional Record,* 93d Cong., 1st sess., 1973, 119:14484. See also pp. 11872, 13060; and Public Citizen, Inc. v. Clawson, Civil Action No. 759-73 (D.D.C. July 30, 1973).
169. Letter to Senator Hubert H. Humphrey, July 19, 1973. See Mike Causey, "No Action Planned Over Speech Kits," *Washington Post,* July 30, 1973,

p. D11.

170. *New York Times,* December 19, 1975, p. 23.
171. *Congressional Record* (daily ed.), 94th Cong., 2d sess. February 10, 1976, 122:570-572. See also "Turning Screws: Winning Votes in Congress," Congressional Quarterly *Weekly Report,* April 24, 1976, pp. 947-954.
172. 91 Stat. 307, sec. 304 (1977); 92 Stat. 1302, sec. 304 (1978).
173. U.S., Congress, Senate, S. Rept. 1063, 95th Cong., 2d sess., 1978, pp. 47-48. See also H. Rept. 1672, 95th Cong., 2d sess., 1978, p. 19; and U.S., Congress, Senate, Committee on Appropriations, *Department of the Interior and Related Agencies Appropriations for Fiscal Year 1979 (Part 3)* (hearings), 95th Cong., 2d sess., 1979, pp. 1023-1106.
174. *Congressional Record* (daily ed.), 96th Cong., 1st sess., October 25, 1979, 125:E5301-5302; ibid., May 10, 1979, 125:S5651-5653; and Kenneth L. Adelman, "Rafshooning the Armageddon: The Selling of SALT," *Policy Review* 9 (Summer 1979):85-102. In the case of American Conservative Union v. Carter, Civil Action No. 79-2495 (D.D.C. December 14, 1979), a federal court concluded that the plaintiffs lacked standing to bring suit against the administration's effort to promote SALT II.
175. On Indian Health Services, see U.S., Congress, Senate, S. Rept. 363, 96th Cong., 1st sess., 1979, p. 94. On the Commission on Civil Rights, see S. Rept. 706, 96th Cong., 2d sess., 1980, pp. 9-11; and *Congressional Record* (daily ed.), 96th Cong., 2d sess., May 20, 1980, 126:S5609-5613; May 22, 1980, pp. S5721-5723; June 3, 1980, pp. H4447-4448. On the Office of Juvenile Justice, see U.S., Congress, House, H. Rept. 946, 96th Cong., 2d sess., 1980, pp. 78-80. On the Maritime Administration, see *Washington Post,* January 28, 1979, p. A5. On the Office of Surface Mining, see *Congressional Record* (daily ed.), 96th Cong. 2d sess., March 27, 1980, 126:S3104-3115.
176. On the Legal Services Corporation, see 93 Stat. 422 (1979); *Congressional Record* (daily ed.), 96th Cong., 2d sess., May 15, 1980, 126:H3738-3739; May 29, 1980, pp. E2653-2655; and June 13, 1980, pp. S6870-6876, 6886-6896. See also U.S., Congress, House, Committee on Appropriations, *Department of State, Justice, and Commerce, the Judiciary, and Related Agencies Appropriations for 1981 (Part 9)* (hearings), 96th Cong., 2d sess., 1980, pp. 142, 153-154; *Congressional Record* (daily ed.), 97th Cong., 1st sess., February 6, 1981, 127:S1209-1212. On ACTION, see U.S., Congress, House, H. Rept. 164, 96th Cong., 1st sess., 1979, pp. 6, 29-30, 49-51, 69-96; and *Congressional Record* (daily ed.), 96th Cong., 1st sess., June 20, 1979, 125:S8125-8127.
177. *Legal Times of Washington,* October 29, 1979, p. 1.
178. American Conservative Union v. Carter, Civil Action No. 79-2495 (D.D.C. December 14, 1979).
179. On referenda, see U.S., Congress, General Accounting Office, *Evaluation of the Publication and Distribution of "Shedding Light on Facts About Nuclear Energy,"* September 30, 1976, p. 32. On constitutional amendments, see Hall v. Siegel, No. 77-1028 (S.D. Ill. June 8, 1977), memorandum opinion. See also Mulqueeny v. Nat. Com'n on the Observance, Etc., 549 F.2d 1115 (7th Cir. 1977).
180. See statements by Representatives Schroeder and Harris, *Congressional Record* (daily ed.), 95th Cong., 2d sess., April 13, 1978, 124:H2865-2867, and statements by Representatives Wiggins and Danielson on April 20, 1978, pp. H3077-3078. See also "Public Liaison Chief Dole Reaches to

Outside Groups to Sell Reagan's Programs," Congressional Quarterly *Weekly Report*, June 6, 1981, pp. 975-978.

181. American Conservative Union v. Carter, Civil Action No. 79-2495 (D.D.C. December 14, 1979); Hall v. Siegel, No. 77-1028 (S.D. Ill. June 8, 1977), memorandum opinion at 5; Am. Public Gas Ass'n v. Fed. Energy Administration, 408 F.Supp. 640 (D.D.C. 1976); National Ass'n for Community Development v. Hodgson, 356 F.Supp. 1399 (D.D.C. 1973).

182. George C. Edwards III, *Presidential Influence in Congress* (San Francisco: W. H. Freeman and Co., 1980), pp. 116-202.

183. Stanley Kelley, Jr., "Patronage and Presidential Legislative Leadership," in *The Presidency*, ed. Aaron Wildavsky (Boston: Little, Brown & Co., 1969), p. 270. See also comments by Tom Korologos, Ford's lobbyist to the Senate, in *Washington Post*, August 18, 1974, p. A9; John A. Ferejohn, *Pork Barrel Politics* (Stanford: Stanford University Press, 1974), pp. 146-147; and Wayne, *The Legislative Presidency*, p. 160.

184. Steven V. Roberts, "Congress in No Mood to Help Out Carter," *New York Times*, May 27, 1979, p. 4.

185. *The White House: Organization and Operations* (New York: Center for the Study of the Presidency, 1971), p. 94. Recollection of Thomas Corcoran, former FDR adviser.

3

Congress as Administrator

It has become customary to reprimand legislators for interfering with administrative matters. Woodrow Wilson chided Congress in 1885 for entering "more and more into the details of administration, until it has virtually taken into its own hands all the substantial powers of government." Despite almost 25 years of congressional service, President Ford warned Congress that its attempt to become a "virtual co-administrator" in operational decisions would seriously distract from its proper legislative role.[1]

High on the list of accused congressional "meddling" are these practices: excessive detail in statutes, passage of private bills, the use of "riders" in appropriation bills to direct and confine administrative actions, statutory restrictions on personnel policy, legislative vetoes, redundant and intrusive investigations, casework demands that consume agency time, and the creation of independent commissions to perform regulatory tasks that could be carried out by existing executive departments. These congressional initiatives are criticized for undermining the unity of the presidency, violating hierarchical principles of public administration, disrupting the orderly functioning of agencies, and threatening the stability of the constitutional system. Congress is advised to confine itself to legislative duties and leave administration to the president and the executive branch.

Yet members of Congress will continue to participate in administration because they have learned time and again that "details" are the crucial building blocks of policy. No better formula for legislative impotence has ever been devised than to allocate "broad policy questions" to Congress and assign "administrative details" to the executive. A law professor once recalled that when he married it was agreed that he would decide all the important questions and his wife all the unimportant questions. "And you know," he reflected, "that after forty years of marriage we haven't had an important question yet." [2]

CONSTITUTIONAL BASIS

Administration is not a monopoly of the executive. Congress has a legitimate role and responsibility in supervising the efforts of federal agencies. Little was said at the Philadelphia Convention concerning the president's power as administrator. Certainly the framers were keenly aware of the failings of the Continental Congress, especially its lack of administrative accountability and efficiency.[3] Moreover, Madison discovered in the state legislatures an appetite for usurpation: "The Executives of the States are in general little more than Cyphers; the legislatures omnipotent." James Wilson, Gouverneur Morris, and John Mercer were among the delegates at the Convention who warned against legislative aggrandizement. The delegates rejected the idea of a plural executive, preferring to anchor that responsibility in a single individual. Said John Rutledge: "A single man would feel the greatest responsibility and administer the public affairs best." [4]

It can be argued that congressional participation in administrative matters creates a divided executive, something the framers explicitly rejected. Nevertheless, at the Convention, Roger Sherman considered the executive "nothing more than an institution for carrying the will of the Legislature into effect," and although Hamilton, Jefferson, and others had criticized the Continental Congress for meddling in administrative details, the framers were never able to distinguish clearly between legislative and executive duties.[5]

Agencies have a direct responsibility to Congress which created them. In 1854 Attorney General Caleb Cushing admitted that departmental heads are created by law and "most of their duties are prescribed by law." Congress "may at all times call on them for information or explanation in matters of official duty; and it may, if it see fit, interpose by legislation concerning them, when required by the interests of the Government." The extent to which Congress could direct officials prompted Cushing to warn that Congress might by statute so divide the executive power as to subvert the government "and to change it into a parliamentary despotism, like that of Venice or Great

Britain, with a nominal executive chief utterly powerless—whether under the name of Doge, or King, or President. . . ." [6]

Not only is the administrative process today open to congressional intervention, but parties from the private sector are invited to participate in agency operations. The Administrative Procedure Act of 1946 requires public notice and comment in rulemaking and provides for group representation in adjudicatory proceedings. The statutory requirement for boards, committees, and task forces allows interested parties from the private sector to advise federal agencies on the implementation of laws. Programs from the Johnson administration called for participation by citizens in antipoverty and urban programs. The Freedom of Information Act, the Sunshine Act of 1976, and funding of public participation in agency proceedings have given citizens and interest groups greater access to the administrative process. [7]

The judiciary is another important participant in the administrative process, reviewing agency decisions to see that they conform to legislative intent, satisfy standards of procedural fairness, and meet the test of constitutionality. Courts are routinely criticized for intervening so deeply in the administrative process that they usurp the policymaking functions of Congress and the agencies. [8]

With participation of this breadth in the administrative process, it seems anomalous to ask Congress to stay out. When members of Congress believe that an agency has departed from its statutory purpose, they are entitled, if not obligated, to express their views through individual statements on the floor, questions at committee hearings, or direct contact with agency officials. The legislative function does not cease with a bill that creates an agency. Only by monitoring the operation of a law can members uncover statutory defects and correct agency misinterpretations.

In a study basically sympathetic to congressional supervision of agencies, Frank Neuman and Harry Keaton concluded: "One point seems obvious. Congress goes too far if it spends so much time supervising that not enough time is left for legislating." [9] This attitude presumes that supervision and legislation are distinct duties, whereas it is impossible to legislate intelligently and effectively without close supervision. Only through regular feedback from administrators can laws be perfected. How much time to allocate for supervision is a decision left solely to Congress.

INSTRUMENTS OF LEGISLATIVE CONTROL

A number of express or implied constitutional powers allow Congress to direct administrative matters. Congress has the power to create an office, define its powers and duration, and determine the compensation for officials. Additional legislative guidance comes from the process of confirming presidential appointees, advisory participation in the administrative process, the investigatory and appropriations powers, private bills, casework, and nonstatutory controls. One of the prime devices for congressional control—the "legislative veto"—is discussed later in this chapter in a separate section.

Personnel Policy

The U.S. Code contains extraordinarily detailed instructions from Congress to cover personnel policy for agencies: examination, selection, and placement of employees; training, performance ratings, and incentive awards; classification of positions, pay rates, and travel expenses; hours of work, leave, and holidays; rights of employees; preferential points in hiring veterans; medical plans and life insurance; and restrictions on political activities by federal employees.[10]

In creating departments, Congress may require that the appointment of certain executive officials be subject to the advice and consent of the Senate. It may stipulate the qualifications of appointees, itemizing in great detail the characteristics a president must consider before submitting a name for Senate action. Congress has the power to delegate the appointment of officers to departmental heads; it may also specify grounds for removal and impose procedural safeguards before administrators suspend or dismiss employees.

During confirmation hearings, senators have an opportunity to explore a nominee's depth of knowledge and policy commitments. Promises may be extracted at that time with regard to keeping the committees informed of proposed actions and even requiring prior approval from the committees on specific issues. In 1972 President Nixon invoked executive privilege to prevent White House aide Peter Flanigan from testifying before the Senate Judiciary Committee. In an adroit countermove, Democratic Senator Sam Ervin of North Carolina asked the committee to delay the consideration of Richard Kleindienst's nomination as attorney general until Nixon let Flanigan testify. The tactic worked. Flanigan was permitted to appear before the committee under special ground rules.[11]

Participating as Advisers

The Constitution specifically prohibits persons from simultaneously holding federal office and serving as members of Congress. This Incompatibility Clause is one of the supporting structures of the separation of powers doctrine. Nevertheless, some statutes allow members of Congress to take part in the implementation of laws. The Trade

Expansion Act of 1962 directed the president, before each negotiation, to select four members from the congressional tax committees to be accredited as members of the U.S. delegation. Under the Trade Act of 1974, ten members of Congress are accredited by the president as official advisers to U.S. delegations at international conferences, meetings, and negotiation sessions relating to trade agreements. In assigning Secret Service protection for major presidential or vice presidential candidates, the secretary of the treasury consults with an advisory committee consisting of the Speaker of the House, the House minority leader, the Senate majority leader, the Senate minority leader, and a fifth member selected by those four officers.[12]

Congress appoints members of various commissions to oversee the implementation of federal policy. In 1976 Congress established a Commission on Security and Cooperation in Europe to monitor compliance with the Helsinki Agreement regarding human rights. Congress appoints twelve of its members to the commission. The president appoints three, drawing from the Departments of State, Defense, and Commerce. The Speaker of the House designates the chairman from one of the House members.[13] As if to underscore the mixed executive-legislative nature of this commission, it is funded not from the legislative branch appropriation bill but from the state-justice appropriation bill.

Investigations

Congress uses the investigative power to scrutinize the administration of programs. The power of Congress to conduct investigations, the Supreme Court noted in 1957, "comprehends probes into departments of the Federal Government to expose corruption, inefficiency or waste." Even Joseph Harris, the author of a 1965 study critical of congressional involvement in administration, recognized that it is not enough for Congress to enact policies and programs into law. Members of Congress "must check to see how those policies are being executed, whether they are accomplishing the desired results, and, if not, what corrective action the legislature may appropriately prescribe."[14]

The House of Representatives sharpens its investigative power through the use of "resolutions of inquiry." A member may introduce a resolution authorizing a committee to request information from the heads of executive departments. All resolutions of inquiry must be reported to the House within one week after presentation. Resolutions of inquiry are answered by departmental officials, either directly or through the president.[15] If the executive branch resists the call for certain papers, Congress can invoke its contempt power to enlist the cooperation of agency officials. Contempt proceedings produced material from Secretary of Commerce Rogers Morton, during the Ford administration, and from Secretary of Energy Charles W. Duncan, Jr., during the Carter administration.[16]

Restrictions on the investigative power generally protect private citizens rather than agency officials. Citizens are entitled to First Amendment rights of free speech and association, the Fourth Amendment right to be free of unreasonable searches and seizures, the Fifth Amendment right that protects witnesses against self-incrimination, and certain Sixth Amendment rights of due process. Committee hearings must be properly authorized; the judiciary insists that committee questions be pertinent and directed toward a legislative purpose.

These limitations on the investigative power do not apply to committee inquiries into agency activities. Agencies are expected to cooperate with legislative efforts to determine the expenditure of taxpayer funds. Presidents may raise the barrier of executive privilege, claiming a constitutional right to withhold information from Congress, but such defenses are rarely employed.[17]

The courts have added a few restrictions on congressional investigations into agency affairs. Committees may not intervene in a pending adjudicatory proceeding by focusing on the process used by agency officials to reach a decision; here the congressional interference is not in an agency's "*legislative* function, but rather, in its *judicial* function."[18] The legislative (rulemaking) function of an agency is more open to congressional inquiries than adjudicatory proceedings, but a member may not force an executive official to take into account considerations that Congress had not intended.[19]

For the most part, however, the courts assume that agency officials possess the necessary "backbone" to withstand searching inquiries by congressional committees.[20] Even when pressure during a congressional hearing is the direct impetus for a change in agency policy, the courts treat such influence as "part of the give and take of democratic government."[21]

Appropriations

The power of the purse allows Congress to closely monitor and control the administration of programs. At the end of each appropriation bill lies a "General Provisions" section that contains dozens of limitations, riders, and restrictions on agency operations. Within each appropriation account are additional restrictions that take the form of "provisos," as illustrated by the following account for the Legal Services Corporation:

> For payment to the Legal Services Corporation to carry out the purposes of the Legal Services Corporation Act of 1974, as amended,

$300,000,000: *Provided,* That no part of this appropriation shall be used for publicity or propaganda purposes designed to support or defeat legislation pending before Congress or any State Legislature: *Provided further,* That none of the funds appropriated in this title may be used to carry out any activities for or on behalf of any individual who is known to be an alien in the United States in violation of the Immigration and Nationality Act or any other law, convention, or treaty of the United States relating to the immigration, exclusion, deportation, or expulsion of aliens: *Provided further,* That none of the funds contained in this paragraph shall be used to increase funds allocated to programs serving those areas of the country already funded at the minimum access level or to activities directly administered by the Corporation unless minimum access to civil legal assistance is available or provided in all parts of the country.[22]

Audits by the General Accounting Office (GAO) permit Congress to hold executive officers accountable for the use of public funds. The GAO has the power to "disallow" an expenditure, thereby making the disbursing officer liable for the funds involved in an illegal transaction. For example, in 1974 GAO used this power to stop the expenditure of funds for Secret Service protection to Spiro Agnew after he had resigned as vice president.[23]

The power of the purse cannot be protected merely through the authorization and appropriation process. The abuse of discretionary authority by executive officials has forced Congress to place specific controls and limitations on the expenditure of funds. Members of Congress find it necessary to exercise statutory and nonstatutory controls over administrative operations such as transfer of funds, reprogramming of funds, year-end buying, deficiency spending, impoundment, carryover balances, and contractor expenses.[24]

Very few constitutional limits operate on the appropriations power. While the flow of federal money is not "the final arbiter of constitutionally protected rights," [25] only rarely has the judiciary placed restrictions on the power of the purse. For example, Congress may not diminish the compensation of members of the federal judiciary, since this is specifically proscribed by the Constitution.[26] In addition, the Supreme Court, in *United States* v. *Lovett* (1946), declared invalid a section of an appropriation act that prohibited the payment of federal salaries to three named "subversives." The language in the statute was struck down because it represented a bill of attainder which Article II, Section 3 of the Constitution forbids.[27]

Private Bills

Members of Congress introduce private bills to overcome injustices and inadequacies in the administrative process. They rely heavily on the Court of Claims to evaluate private claims.[28] The flood of private bills after the Civil War to assist constituents who had been turned down by the Pension Bureau was particularly flagrant. President Grover Cleveland declared open season on these measures, often employing sarcastic language in his veto messages to communicate his contempt for legislative efforts to circumvent the established administrative procedure. During the 49th Congress (1885-1887) there were over twice as many private laws as public laws: 1,031 to 434. The ratio climbed to 3-to-1 by the 56th Congress (1899-1901)—1,498 private laws and 443 public laws. Private bills introduced in the 59th Congress (1905-1907) topped 6,000.[29]

In an effort to reduce the private bill workload, the Legislative Reorganization Act of 1946 prohibited the consideration of any private bill or resolution (including omnibus claims or pension bills) or an amendment to any bill or resolution authorizing or directing: (1) the payment of money for property damages, for personal injuries or death for suits that could be instituted under the Federal Tort Claims Act (Title IV of the 1946 act), or for a pension (other than to carry out a provision of law or treaty stipulation); (2) the construction of a bridge across a navigable stream (Title V of the act); or (3) the correction of a military or naval record.[30]

Due to a surge in legislative activity regarding immigration from 1949 through 1955, private laws averaged more than 1,000 a Congress, but during 1971 to 1979 they were reduced sharply, averaging about 150 a Congress. Private bills need not be *enacted* to affect the administrative process. Whenever a senator or representative introduces an immigration bill and the judiciary committees request a report from the Immigration and Naturalization Service, a deportation is delayed until action is taken on the bill. Although private bills are subject to abuse, they allow Congress to correct mistakes in past legislation or current administration.

Casework

Members of Congress often are alerted to administrative problems by attending to "casework"—assisting a constituent's contact with the bureaucracy. Much of the literature on Congress refers disparagingly to casework because it supposedly diverts members from more significant matters, making them "errand boys" instead of legislators. But casework, aside from its importance for reelection, helps educate legislators on the actual workings of a law. It forces them to descend from the lofty and often abstract universe of statutes to the mundane world of administration. By responding to constituent requests, legislators obtain information that allows them to perfect laws and improve agency procedures. One member of Congress advised his colleagues:

You should not underestimate the value of constituent work on the legislative process. Don't you get a lot of your ideas about needed changes in the laws from the problems of your constituents? In processing a problem before the VA or a draft problem you gain your best insight into how laws operate, and you discover where they might be changed.[31]

Some studies conclude that casework reinforces the "institutionalized suspicion" that administrators and legislators have about each other. To bureaucrats, legislators and their staffs "appear as special pleaders for the narrow interests of their constituents even when these conflict with the 'national welfare,' which bureaucrats tend to equate with the over-all rules and programs of their agency or department to which the senators so often seek exception." Members, in turn, are said to characterize bureaucrats as arbitrary, patronizing, and compulsively attached to their procedures.[32]

These attitudes, while they do exist, are in the minority. Most bureaucrats believe that members of Congress should intervene on behalf of constituents. Casework is accepted as a legitimate and healthy input into the administrative process. Administrators find that casework helps them watch over their subordinates, uncover program flaws, and generate improvements in rules and regulations.[33] Much of the congressional liaison apparatus established in agencies and departments is designed to assist members with casework. Departments that are heavily involved in casework—such as the Veterans Administration, the Office of Personnel Management, and the military services—maintain offices in the Senate and House office buildings.

Nonstatutory Controls

Simple resolutions (adopted by either house) and concurrent resolutions (adopted by both houses) are used to direct administrative action. Although these resolutions are not presented to the president, and therefore escape his veto power, they may be legally binding if sanctioned by a prior statute (see pp. 100-101). Some statutes allow committees, acting by resolutions, to direct an agency to investigate.[34] Without the sanction of a statute, resolutions are advisory only, to be accepted by agencies as a recommended course of action.[35] They express the "sense of Congress" (or of either house) on some aspect of public policy. However, a simple or concurrent resolution that attempts to empower the head of one department to reexamine an action already vested by statute in the head of another department is without force or effect.[36]

In the 1950s, President Eisenhower challenged the constitutionality of "come into agreement" provisions that sought to compel agency officials to seek advance clearance from congressional committees.

Unable to override his vetoes, Congress created an interesting alternative. The new bill provided that before funds could be appropriated for certain real estate actions, contracts had to be approved by separate resolutions adopted by the public works committees. President Eisenhower signed the bill after his attorney general decided that the procedure, based on the authorization-appropriation process, was within the power of Congress.[37] Congress enacted the same procedure in 1972.[38]

Congress directs administrative action through the use of other nonstatutory controls: language placed in committee reports, instructions issued by members during committee hearings, correspondence from committee and subcommittee chairmen to agency officials, and various types of "gentlemen's agreements." Under a philosophy of good-faith efforts by administrators, this system makes sense for both branches. Instead of locking legislative policy into a rigid statutory mold, agency officials are given substantial leeway to adjust programs throughout the year in response to changing circumstances. In return for this latitude, administrators are expected to follow the legislative policy expressed in nonstatutory directives.

In some cases the system fails. In 1975 a conference report adopted by the House and Senate directed the navy to produce as its air combat fighter a derivative of an aircraft to be selected by the air force. Instead of following the directive in the conference report (usually of high priority as legislative history), the navy picked a different type of aircraft. The comptroller general decided that nonstatutory controls are not legally binding on agencies unless there is some ambiguity in a statute that requires recourse to the legislative history. Agencies follow nonstatutory controls for practical, not legal, reasons.[39] To ignore such controls invites Congress to cut agency budgets and add restrictive statutory language.

Two other recent disputes highlight the risk of relying on nonstatutory controls to check delegated power. In 1978 the Supreme Court was asked to allow the Tennessee Valley Authority to complete a dam that threatened the existence of a tiny fish called the snail darter. Opponents of the dam claimed that its operation would violate the Endangered Species Act. The Court declined to allow committee report language, urging completion of the dam, to have precedence over a statute, particularly in the circumstances presented by the case.[40] In another dispute two years later, a lower court rejected the theory that language in a conference report, stating that Congress did not contemplate the use of certain statutory authority, could in any way alter the fact that Congress had granted the authority and had done so with unambiguous language.[41]

Intervention by the GAO and the judiciary generally is not necessary. Most agencies prefer to adhere as best they can to nonstatutory controls rather than risk new limitations placed in a public law. Nonstatutory controls are especially binding in the case of secret budgets for the U.S. intelligence community, composed of the Central Intelligence Agency and several other federal units. A classified "Schedule of Authorization" is prepared, listing the amounts of dollars and personnel ceilings for all the intelligence and intelligence-related programs authorized by Congress. The details in the schedule "are directly incorporated into, and are integral to, the bill itself." [42]

Limitations on Congress

Members of Congress have many legitimate reasons for participating in the administrative process. In some cases, however, the representative function oversteps the legal boundaries and takes on the color of "influence-peddling," leading to indictments in the courts against members who use their legislative and oversight positions for personal gain.

This kind of activity is controlled largely by two statutes. The bribery statute (18 U.S.C. 201) is directed against public officials— including members of Congress—who seek or accept anything of value in return for an official act. The conflict-of-interest statute (18 U.S.C. 203) makes it a criminal offense for members of Congress to receive or seek compensation for services relating to any proceeding, contract, claim, or other activities of the federal government. Depending on the circumstances, members may seek immunity under the Speech or Debate Clause of the Constitution, which prohibits questioning a senator or representative for any legislative act.

The Supreme Court has repeatedly held that members of Congress may not use the Speech or Debate Clause as a shield for contacts with the executive branch. Democratic Representative Thomas Johnson of Maryland, who tried to influence the Justice Department to drop a pending investigation of a savings and loan institution, was accused of receiving more than $20,000 for his efforts. He was found guilty of violating the conflict-of-interest statute. Democratic Representative Bertram Podell of New York pleaded guilty in 1974 to conspiracy and conflict-of-interest charges after he had intervened in several federal agency actions to help an airline company obtain a route between Florida and the Bahamas. His family law firm in Manhattan had been collecting monthly legal fees from the airline's parent company. In another action marking the limits of legislative intervention in agency activities, Democratic Representative Frank Brasco of New York was found guilty of bribery and conspiracy in a scheme to obtain Post Office contracts for a trucking firm. In a more recent action, Democratic

Representative Joshua Eilberg of Pennsylvania was indicted for receiving compensation for helping a Philadelphia hospital win a $14.5 million federal grant. After a federal court held in 1979 that his contacts with the executive branch were not protected by the Speech or Debate Clause, Eilberg pleaded guilty to a conflict of interest charge.[43]

As part of FBI's Abscam operation during the Carter administration, Democratic Representative Michael J. Myers of Pennsylvania was charged with conspiracy, bribery, and traveling in interstate commerce to carry on an unlawful act. In defense, Myers argued that congressional independence would be undermined if government agents could entice members with manufactured opportunities to accept bribes. His charge of entrapment was rejected by an appellate court, which pointed out that Congress may at any time protect itself by redefining the statutory meaning of bribery to exclude a legislator's acceptance of bribes offered by government undercover agents.

Aside from criminal prosecutions, members who interfere in agency proceedings are subject to other limitations. Members immune under the Speech or Debate Clause may face disciplinary action by the House or the Senate. The House Committee on Standards of Official Conduct has issued this guideline: "Direct or implied suggestion of either favoritism or reprisal in advance of, or subsequent to, action taken by the agency contacted is unwarranted abuse of the representative role." However, the committee identified a number of appropriate communications from a member to an executive or independent agency: requesting information or a status report, urging prompt consideration, arranging for interviews or appointments, expressing judgment, and calling for the reconsideration of an administrative response that the member believes is not supported by established law, federal regulation, or legislative intent.[45]

As a result of a Supreme Court decision in 1979, members of Congress who publicize agency waste or abuse by issuing press releases and newsletters to their constituents are not protected by the Speech or Debate Clause. The case arose from a "Golden Fleece Award" announced by Democratic Senator William Proxmire of Wisconsin in 1975. After more than 40 hours of staff research and a hearing by the Senate Appropriations Committee, Proxmire gave the award to the National Science Foundation (NSF), the National Aeronautics and Space Administration (NASA), and the Office of Naval Research for grants they had made to Dr. Ronald Hutchinson for his studies on animal aggression. Proxmire was in a key position to judge agency waste and abuse. He chaired the Senate appropriations subcommittee that funds NSF and NASA and was also a member of the defense and HEW appropriations subcommittees. Hutchinson sued Proxmire, claiming that he had been libelled by Proxmire's press release and newsletter publicizing the award and by Proxmire's appearance on the Mike Douglas television show where he mentioned the award.

Lower courts decided that the press release (almost identical to Proxmire's floor speech) was protected by the Speech or Debate Clause. The newsletter was considered part of the informing function of Congress and therefore immune, while the television appearance was protected by the First Amendment. However, the Supreme Court held that Proxmire's press release and newsletter were not protected by his constitutional function as a legislator. The curious result of this decision is that a member of Congress may disclose the results of agency waste, fraud, and abuse only in official remarks in the *Congressional Record* or in committee hearings. Once the member seeks to publicize the issue, by informing constituents or the press, there is risk of a lawsuit.[46]

THE GROWTH OF FORMAL CONTROLS

Congress pursues a two-pronged strategy: delegating broad grants of power to agencies while insisting on a share in overseeing programs and activities. In the case of appropriations, funds are generally granted to agencies in large, lump-sum accounts, permitting considerable agency discretion throughout the year to withhold spending in some areas (impoundment), shift funds to new programs (reprogramming), and limit the size of the agency workforce (personnel ceilings). In all three areas Congress has begun to abandon its traditional reliance on nonstatutory controls as the instrument for regulating administrative policy. Because of a breakdown in good-faith relations between the branches, Congress over the past decade has increasingly used statutory controls.

Impoundment

Prior to 1974 several administrations resorted to impoundment of funds, justified either on the basis of statutory authority or on the claim that presidents had inherent authority to withhold funds from obligation. Despite confrontations from time to time, the two branches managed to fashion political accommodations that were acceptable to both sides. Rarely was there a stalemate that required the courts to referee the dispute.

This informal system fell apart during the Nixon administration. Funds were withheld in a manner, quantitatively and qualitatively, to threaten Congress's power of the purse. Budgetary priorities established by Congress through the appropriation process were quickly rearranged by administrative officials who refused to spend funds the president did not want. As a result, programs were severely curtailed and in some cases terminated. The administration assumed an adamant, even truculent, position, offering extraordinary and often bizarre legal arguments to justify the impoundments. Although the federal courts handed down decisions against the administration, the lengthy process of litigation meant that program objectives set by Congress could not be achieved.[47]

In response to this unprecedented abuse of presidential power over expenditures, Congress stepped into the administrative process to protect its own prerogatives. The result was the Impoundment Control Act of 1974. When deciding to withhold funds, the president must submit a report to Congress. If the withholding is temporary (a *deferral*), either house of Congress may disapprove it at any time. The funds then must be released for obligation by the agencies. If the withholding is to be permanent (a *rescission*), the president must obtain the support of both houses within 45 days of continuous session. Otherwise, the funds must be released.

A process that traditionally had been part of "budget execution and control," and therefore within the president's realm as administrative chief, is now explicitly tied to congressional review and action. The comptroller general is authorized to reclassify impoundment submissions (changing a rescission to a deferral or vice versa) and to notify Congress of unreported impoundments. This report is accepted as if it had been sent by the president, triggering the congressional procedures for deferrals and rescissions. In the event the administration refuses to release funds for obligation, the comptroller general may file suit in federal court to require that the funds be made available for obligation and expenditure.

The procedures of the Impoundment Control Act eliminated the stark confrontations between the president and Congress that characterized the Nixon years. The statute explicitly recognizes the right of the president to withhold funds but subjects his decision to congressional review and disapproval. Impoundment, however, is only one technique for delaying a program the administration does not want. Members of Congress became aware of "quasi-impoundments" that were not being reported in the deferral and rescission messages. Programs could be delayed because of slow processing of applications, frequent change of agency regulations, rejection of applications for minor technical deficiencies, and many other administrative actions (or inactions). Members could not be certain whether the delays were inherent in the legislation, a deliberate effort by the administration to sabotage a program, or simply the normal course of the bureaucratic process. Whatever the reason, legislators decided that congressional priorities could be protected only by probing ever more deeply into administrative procedures and program implementation.

Reprogramming

It is the practice of Congress to appropriate large, lump-sum amounts for general purposes. For example, the defense appropriation bill for fiscal 1981 contained the following amounts for research, development, test, and evaluation: $3.0 billion for the army, $4.8 billion for the navy, and $6.7 billion for the air force. Other than a few restrictions in each account, the Pentagon is legally free to spend funds for the broad purposes described in the statute. The Defense Department must also adhere to language in authorization bills, but these too are framed in lump-sum amounts.

Administrative discretion of such vast scope is narrowed by the expectation of Congress that agencies will "keep faith" with the itemized material they submit in their budget justifications. Agencies are expected to spend funds for the precise purposes stated in these justifications to Congress. Over the course of a fiscal year, however, officials find it desirable or necessary to depart from their original budget submissions to respond to unforeseen developments, new requirements, incorrect price estimates, wage-rate adjustments, and legislation enacted after appropriations. To allow for these changes, Congress permits agency officials to take funds from one program and "reprogram" them to another within the same appropriation account.

The latitude for reprogramming increased dramatically after 1949 when Congress began to consolidate a number of appropriation accounts. By administering larger accounts, agency officials gained new discretionary authority to reprogram funds. To retain some semblance of control, congressional committees insisted on various types of procedures requiring agencies to notify committees of significant reprogrammings and, in some cases, to seek their prior approval.

The degree of congressional control has gradually become more formalized over the years. At first the appropriations committees asked the Pentagon to keep them advised of major reprogrammings. Next they required semiannual reports. Within a few years the Pentagon had to obtain prior approval from the appropriations committees before proceeding with certain reprogrammings. Shortly thereafter, the armed services committees were added to the system of notification and prior approval for defense reprogrammings.[48]

Similar controls evolved for other agencies. Although these controls were nonstatutory, agencies usually felt bound by them as a means of preserving good relationships with their review committees. As one official told a legislator in 1980: "We are acting under the belief that this is a project of such magnitude that it is necessary for us to appropriately inform the Congress and the committees and to obtain its permission [before reprogramming funds]."[49]

Even with elaborate procedures to govern reprogramming, clearly spelled out in committee reports and agency directives, officials sometimes used reprogramming to bypass congressional control. The next step in legislative supervision was to add statutory controls.

Particularly objectionable to Congress was the Pentagon's practice of requesting funds for a program, being turned down by Congress, and then spending other appropriated funds for the rejected program. Legislation in 1974 specifically prohibited the Pentagon from asking committees for permission to reprogram funds to an item that had been previously submitted to Congress and denied.[50] This language is repeated every year in the defense appropriation bill.

Three new public laws, all signed in 1978, place additional constraints on reprogramming. The provisions came from committees that act on annual authorizations for the Department of Energy and the Department of Justice. The committees did not want to review agency budgets in great detail and pass authorization bills each year for specific programs and activities, only to find their efforts reshaped by subsequent reprogramming agreements worked out by agencies and the appropriations committees. All three laws required notification to the authorization committees of certain categories of reprogramming.[51]

Reprogramming by domestic agencies is now scrutinized with greater care by Congress. The congressional review committees have borrowed some of the controls previously applied to the Defense Department. For example, the House Appropriations Committee published guidelines in its report on the state-justice appropriation bill for 1981 (see box).

These expectations of Congress have been incorporated in agency manuals, supplying additional formality to the understanding between Congress and the executive branch. The financial management manual for the Public Health Service (PHS), for example, identifies circumstances where PHS agencies "must seek congressional approval for reprogramming proposals, and to establish procedures for securing such approval." The Department of Labor and other agencies publish similar manuals on prior approval arrangements with congressional committees.[52]

If presidents and departmental officials object to reprogramming procedures, raising questions about the constitutionality of committee vetoes and the propriety of congressional involvement in administrative matters, they may jeopardize the grant of delegated power. Agencies accept committee-review procedures as a necessary condition for the freedom that Congress gives them. Committee review and agency discretion cannot be separated; they are opposite sides of the same coin.

For example, when the House Committee on Interior and Insular Affairs decided in 1981 to authorize the programs of the Nuclear

Committee Controls on Domestic Reprogramming

The House and Senate reports accompanying the appropriation bills for the Department of State, Justice, and Commerce, the Judiciary, and related agencies for several years have contained sections concerning the reprogramming of funds between programs or activities. Although compliance with these requirements has generally been satisfactory, the Committee is still concerned about the large number of reprogramming requests which have been submitted by several departments and agencies. The number and frequency of such requests appear to reflect a lack of planning and proper management of the resources provided. The Committee, therefore, recommends that each department and agency funded in the accompanying bill review its budget planning and management procedures in a rigorous effort to avoid the necessity for submitting reprogramming requests, except when necessary to meet requirements unforeseen at the time the original budgets were proposed.

With respect to reprogramming requests that are deemed to be necessary, the Committee expects each department and agency to follow closely the reprogramming procedures, listed below, which are the same provisions that applied during fiscal year 1980:

The Committee desires and expects that the Chairman of the Subcommittee on the Departments of State, Justice, and Commerce, the Judiciary, and Related Agencies be notified in writing a minimum of 15 days prior to—

(1) Reprogramming of funds, whether permanent or temporary, in excess of $250,000 or 10 percent, whichever is less, between programs or activities. This provision is also applicable in cases where several activities are involved with each receiving less than $250,000. In addition, the Committee desires to be notified of reprogramming actions which are less than these amounts if such actions would have the effect of committing the agency to significant funding requirements in future years.

(2) Increasing funds or personnel by any means for any project or activity for which funds have been denied or restricted.

(3) Creation of new programs or substantial augmentation of existing programs.

(4) Relocation of offices or employees.

(5) Reorganization of offices, programs, or activities.

The Committee also expects that any items which are subject to interpretation will be reported.

SOURCE: Excerpted from U.S., Congress, House, H. Rept. 96-1091, 96th Cong., 2d sess., 1980, p. 6.

Regulatory Commission on a two-year cycle, rather than the customary one-year grant, it proposed a reprogramming procedure. This enabled the NRC and Congress "to work together to reallocate authorized funds in the event that circumstances change during the authorized period." Reprogramming controls became the instrument for monitoring agency deviations from a two-year authorization. Whenever NRC decides to increase or decrease a program by more than $500,000, it must give the House and Senate authorization committees 30 days to review the proposal. Each committee, before the expiration of that period, must transmit to the commission a written notification that it has no objection to the proposed action.[53]

Personnel Ceilings

To protect legislative priorities, members of Congress have found themselves increasingly involved in monitoring personnel levels. While the Office of Management and Budget (OMB) does not actually withhold funds from agencies, as with impoundment, OMB personnel restrictions prevent agencies from using all the funds. The agencies have the money but lack the manpower to spend it.

Committee studies pointed out that OMB used its personnel ceilings to frustrate congressional additions to the president's budget. Congress found that even when it increased the funding of a program, and funds were not withheld through the deferral-rescission process, the programs augmented by Congress were restricted by OMB ceilings. When the House of Representatives learned in 1980 that OMB had withheld positions from the Immigration and Naturalization Service, Republican Representative Millicent Fenwick of New Jersey asked her colleagues:

> I do not know what is going on in this Congress and in our Government. How is it the business of OMB to decide whether or not the laws we pass are sensible? They are supposed to execute the laws. Have we no right to impeach people? I thought impoundment was ended, that it was no longer legal. How is it that we have a department of the Government that simply defies Congress? What are we doing here? Have we not the right to pass laws and expect that they shall be obeyed?[54]

Committee investigations discovered that OMB ceilings were sometimes adhered to at the cost of hiring thousands of "temporary" employees (on a 39-hour week or 51-week year) to work at what substantially were full-time schedules. Contrivances of this nature led to recruitment difficulties, morale problems, wasteful turnover and retraining, "a watering down in the quality of the staff and the buildup of a caste system with two classes of employees." Another technique of staying within a personnel ceiling was to contract out for services that could have been done less expensively with in-house staff. As part of the "ceiling game," agencies dismissed thousands of employees just before the end of the fiscal year and rehired them when the new year began, thus keeping within end-of-year employment ceilings.

To discourage artificially low personnel ceilings, the House Appropriations Committee began placing the number of authorized permanent positions for each agency in committee reports. Any agency deviations from those figures were to be reported to the committee.[55] The Senate Appropriations Committee insisted that any efforts to restrain agency spending through employment ceilings should be reported to Congress either as a deferral or a rescission.[56]

Nonstatutory directives are usually effective. In the case of the agriculture appropriation bill, however, Congress resorted to *statutory* language to prevent the administration from using personnel ceilings to defeat congressional funding initiatives. The language in a 1977 statute read:

> None of the funds provided in this Act may be used to reduce programs by establishing an end-of-year employment ceiling on permanent positions below the level set herein for the following agencies: Farmers Home Administration, 7,400; Agricultural Stabilization and Conservation Service, 2,473; and Soil Conservation Service, 13,955.[57]

Members of Congress recognize that statutory specifications for personnel and total salary levels can encroach on the executive power of program management. They also realize, however, that legislators bear a responsibility for assuring sound management of the programs they have created and efficient use of taxpayer dollars.[58] The incentive to intervene is all the greater when personnel ceilings become just another form of impoundment.

President Carter took several steps to tighten the policy on personnel ceilings. In 1977 he noted the use of consultant arrangements as a device to bypass or undermine personnel ceilings. He expressed concern that consultants were performing work that should be done by agency officials.[59] Later that year he issued a memo to agency and departmental heads, authorizing an experiment to shift from end-of-year employment ceilings to annual workyears. Part of the purpose was to avoid the various subterfuges by agencies to circumvent employment ceilings.[60]

Congressional efforts to put an end to restrictive personnel ceilings have been unsuccessful partly because of inconsistent legislative policy. When James T. McIntyre, Jr. appeared before the Senate Governmental Affairs Committee in 1978 for his nomination hearing as OMB director, he assured the senators:

> [W]e do not use and will not use personnel ceilings to stop or delay carrying out any program established by the Congress . . . . There are times when it is important to institute some type of personnel ceilings to bring about efficiencies and greater productivity in agencies. . . . But we certainly do not use them to thwart or delay or stop anyone from carrying out the program of the Congress.[61]

This agreement between OMB and Congress was short-lived because of the Civil Service Reform Act that became law later that year. Section 311, known as the "Leach amendment," established a temporary employment limitation on the total federal workforce. Although the language provided some latitude for the president, it also gave OMB a firm statutory foothold to impose personnel ceilings.

Upon assuming office on January 20, 1981, President Reagan ordered a hiring freeze on federal employees. The order was made retroactive to November 5, 1980, the day after his election, and affected thousands of people who had been offered and had accepted a position with the federal government. A district judge upheld the legality of the administration's action, but the National Treasury Employees Union appealed the decision to the D.C. Circuit Court. Since part of Reagan's order affected the staffing of hospitals and clinics administered by the Veterans Administration (VA), he submitted a proposal to defer $31 million in VA funds. The first congressional response came from the comptroller general, who held that the hiring freeze on the VA was illegal because it conflicted with personnel levels mandated by Congress in a previous public law. The Senate promptly passed a resolution that disapproved the deferral and forced the release of the funds.[62]

LEGISLATIVE VETO

The determination of Congress to share in administrative decisions, and to do so through formal statutory controls, is reflected in the recent growth of "legislative vetoes." Legislative vetoes are statutory provisions that delay an administrative action, usually for 60 to 90 days, during which time Congress may vote to approve or disapprove it without further presidential involvement. Congressional action can take several forms: a one-house veto (by simple resolution of either house), a modified one-house veto (the so-called 1½-house veto), a two-house veto (by concurrent resolution), a committee veto, and even a committee chairman's veto. The legislative veto basically originated in the 1930s but proliferated in the 1970s.

In a message to Congress on June 21, 1978, President Carter objected to the growth of legislative vetoes. He charged that they threatened to upset the constitutional balance of responsibility between the executive and legislative branches, representing a "fundamental departure from the way the government has been administered throughout American history." He argued that legislative vetoes (1) infringe on the executive's constitutional duty to carry out the laws faithfully and (2) violate the Presentation Clause of Article I, Section 7 of the Constitution, which requires that every order, resolution, or vote to which the concurrence of the Senate and House of Representatives may be necessary (except on a question of adjournment) must be presented to the president for his signature or veto. By passing a simple resolution, concurrent resolution, or committee veto, Congress denies the president the opportunity to exercise his veto power.

The 'Sole Exception': Reorganization Authority

President Carter recognized the legitimacy of one, and only one, type of legislative veto: the one-house veto that Congress uses to disapprove presidential plans to reorganize the executive branch. This type of legislative veto, Carter stated in his 1978 message to Congress, "does not involve Congressional intrusion into the administration of ongoing substantive programs, and it preserves the President's authority because he decides which proposals to submit to Congress." To Carter, the reorganization act "jeopardizes neither the President's responsibilities nor the prerogatives of Congress."

No amount of rationalization by presidents or the Justice Department can hide the fact that both branches tolerate the aberrant procedure of the reorganization act because it satisfies their interests, regardless of what the Constitution says. It is possible to justify the legislative veto in reorganization statutes, but not on the grounds offered by Carter and not without opening the door to other types of legislative veto. The president's freedom to propose is not a useful criterion for distinguishing the reorganization procedure. The president has discretion to initiate other actions covered by a legislative veto, including arms sales, impoundment deferrals, gasoline rationing plans, and trade agreements.

Carter's acceptance of the reorganization procedure differs from earlier positions of the executive branch. In 1933 Attorney General William Mitchell challenged the constitutionality of the one-house veto attached to reorganization authority, while President Franklin Roosevelt in 1938 insisted that action by concurrent resolution was "only an expression of congressional sentiment" and could not repeal executive action "taken in pursuance of a law."[63] Within the space of a few days, Roosevelt reversed his position after it became clear that the House of Representatives would never delegate reorganization authority to him without retaining for itself the check of a legislative veto. Advocates of reorganization authority had to invent some ingenious theories to justify this 180-degree turnabout in Roosevelt's constitutional principles (see pp. 131-132). Elaborate justifications are still being presented today, but the simple fact is that the president wanted the reorganization authority and was willing, despite serious constitutional misgivings, to accept the conditions that accompanied it.

The legislative veto in reorganization statutes is constitutionally harmless. Disapproval by one house leaves the structure of government unchanged. No new law is produced. If the president has constitutional objections to the process, he may initiate reorganization through the regular legislative route.

The problem with reorganization statutes is that Congress does not formulate a legislative policy. It delegates a major policy issue to the executive branch without first defining it. Nor is there any guarantee that Congress will examine reorganization plans carefully and thoughtfully when they are submitted. Congress becomes a reactive and negative agency, not a creative one.[64] In 1981 both houses were seriously considering the requirement of an *affirmative* vote by Congress before a reorganization plan could take effect.

Other Accommodations

Although the Justice Department and President Carter insisted that all legislative vetoes (other than the one in reorganization statutes) are constitutionally defective, accommodation between Congress and the president runs much deeper. There is no disagreement on the one-house legislative veto of deferrals submitted by presidents under authority of the Impoundment Control Act of 1974. The Nixon, Ford, Carter, and Reagan administrations have never questioned this statute on constitutional grounds.

The president cannot complain that the legislative veto of impoundment deferrals circumvents the executive veto power. Appropriation bills are initially submitted to the president for signature or veto. Once they are enacted into law, Congress has a right to expect that funds will be spent as appropriated. If the president wants to depart from the statutory scheme, Congress should not be forced to go through the entire legislative process another time to tell the president that it wants funds spent in accordance with the appropriation.

Legislative vetoes in arms sales and the War Powers Resolution (despite Nixon's veto of it) are other areas where the two branches have found common ground (see pp. 104-106). Both branches also reconciled their differences regarding a legislative veto for a standby gasoline rationing plan. In a message to Congress on May 7, 1979, Carter recommended that congressional approval take the form of a joint resolution to avoid possible judicial invalidation on constitutional grounds. Since joint resolutions are submitted to the president for signature or veto, there would be no question of violating the Presentation Clause. Within months, however, Carter softened his position, saying he would not object to a one-house veto "if it's done expeditiously. I think only 15 days would elapse. . . . I have no objection to the House, within 2 weeks, either approving the plan that I have tried to put into being, or if either House wants to veto it, they can do that." [65] In 1981 the Reagan administration indicated that it would accept the application of legislative vetoes to regulations issued by the independent agencies (see pp. 168-169).

Committee Vetoes

Ever since 1920, presidents have objected to statutes that delegate to committees final legislative decisionmaking authority. Arguing that the Constitution vests the legislative power in Congress as a whole, presidents have vetoed bills that authorize a committee to share the administration of laws with the executive branch. Yet presidents have signed other bills that permit committee vetoes over real estate transactions, public buildings, watershed projects, small reclamation projects, and river and harbor projects.

Some of the committee vetoes date back to 1867.[66] Most are from World War II and the immediate postwar period. Despite occasional protests from presidents, the two branches have agreed that the committee veto can be an effective and acceptable alternative to having Congress authorize by statute each individual project. It is advantageous to pass a general statute in lump sum and by broad categories without having to identify discrete projects. In return for this broad grant of authority, Congress insists on committee review and approval. It is a quid pro quo, pure and simple.[67]

Committee vetoes also have emerged to protect the integrity of appropriations. In the case of reprogramming, controls can be informal, since the shifting of funds occurs within an appropriation account. But when funds are taken from one account and placed in another, *transfer* authority is required. Congress must grant this authority by statute, and in so doing it has delegated to some committees the responsibility for approving the transfers.

The politics of committee vetoes are brought out vividly in a foreign assistance dispute during the Carter administration. After John Gilligan had been nominated to head the Agency for International Development (AID), he was told by Democratic Senator Daniel Inouye of Hawaii that agency-legislative relationships had deteriorated in the past because of AID's penchant for diverting economic aid to military purposes without ever consulting Congress. Inouye, who chaired the appropriations subcommittee that had jurisdiction over AID, told Gilligan that whenever his agency decided to spend funds for purposes not previously justified to Congress, it would have to seek the approval of the House and Senate appropriations subcommittees responsible for foreign operations. Gilligan agreed to this clearance procedure as a way to improve congressional relations, and when Inouye asked to have the agreement drawn up as a letter he consented to that as well.

As part of the standard procedure within an agency, Gilligan had the draft letter routed through the general counsel's office. Questions were raised there about the legality of allowing congressional committees to participate in administrative decisions. The Justice Department expressly disapproved the arrangement. When Gilligan said he could not send the letter, Inouye countered by placing the agreement in a public law. The foreign assistance appropriation bill for fiscal 1978 contained this language in Section 115: "None of the funds made available by this Act may be obligated under an appropriation account to which they were not appropriated without the written prior approval of the Appropriations Committees of both Houses of the Congress." Carter signed the bill into law without indicating any constitutional misgivings about the clearance procedure, but on that very day he wrote to Secretary of State Cyrus Vance, stating that Attorney General Griffin Bell had challenged the constitutionality of Section 115. Consequently, Vance was to treat the section not as a legally binding requirement for prior approval but rather as a request by the appropriations committees to be notified, after which Vance and AID could spend the funds as they thought best.[68] The appropriations committees did not learn of Carter's letter to Vance until almost two years later.

Had the legislators attached to an appropriation bill a requirement that all agency officials obtain prior approval from designated committees before obligating funds, Congress would have made an unmistakable intrusion into executive responsibilities. But Section 115 did not involve Congress in the execution of a law. It concerned executive *departures* from the law. Congress became a party, and properly so, only when the president wanted to obligate funds for a purpose for which Congress had not appropriated. The president may not redirect budgetary resources in midstream without the legislative control specified by Congress in a public law.

The provision in Section 115 is no different in principle from the one-house veto used for impoundment deferrals. In both cases the administration is free to spend funds as appropriated, without any legislative involvement in the administration of a law. But whenever the executive branch wants to deviate from the statutory schedule, it must secure the support of Congress. Both branches must agree to the departure. The executive cannot act alone. For impoundment, the deferred funds must be released if either house disapproves. In the case of transfers for foreign assistance, the administration needs the support of both appropriations committees. The only difference is the level at which the support (or disapproval) is voiced: one house for deferrals, both committees for transfers.

A president may not accept authority and disregard the condition that goes with it. Administrations do not use impoundment authority while ignoring the one-house veto for deferrals. The presumption must be that Congress would never have delegated the authority in the first place without retaining for itself the right to disapprove deferrals by a simple resolution.

This reasoning is supported by a federal court decision in 1977. A civil servant brought suit to contest the constitutionality of a Senate resolution that had disapproved a pay raise recommended by the president. The court dismissed the complaint after concluding that Congress had delegated the authority for salary adjustments to the president only on the condition that his recommendation be subject to a one-house veto. According to the court, the authority and the condition, as part of a package, are integrally related.[69]

In his letter to Vance, President Carter expressed his unalterable opposition to statutory provisions that permitted Congress (1) to play an "unauthorized role in the execution of the law" in violation of Article II, Section 3 of the Constitution and (2) to control the exercise of administrative discretion "by means short of legislation subject to the veto power of the President" required by Article I, Section 7.

The record, however, is quite the contrary. In both foreign and domestic matters, the executive branch has accommodated a broad range of provisions that permit Congress to share in the administration of laws short of legislation subject to a presidential veto. Participation by congressional committees is tolerated at three levels, descending from statutory conditions to nonstatutory arrangements. These three categories are illustrated in Table 3-1.

In the first category, the Energy Department appropriation act for fiscal 1980 authorized the transfer of up to 5 percent of any appropriation between certain accounts, subject to the approval of the appropriations committees and the authorizing committees.[70] The administration did not question the constitutionality of this procedure. The Department of Energy wanted the authority and acquiesced in the condition.

Second, the Central Intelligence Act of 1949 authorized the CIA to transfer funds from one account to another, both within the agency itself and between the agency and other departments. The statute did not provide for committee approval of these transfers. Nevertheless, the administration submits proposed transfers to the intelligence commit-

Table 3-1 Committee-Approval Provisions

Subject Area	Authority	Condition
Department of Energy Transfers	Statutory	Statutory
Central Intelligence Agency Transfers	Statutory	Nonstatutory
Department of Defense Reprogramming	Nonstatutory	Nonstatutory

SOURCE: Energy Department: P.L. 96-69, 93 Stat. 441 (1979). Central Intelligence Agency: 50 U.S.C. 403 (1976); U.S., Congress, House, H. Rept. 97-101 (Part 1), 97th Cong., 1st sess., 1981, p. 4. Defense Department: Louis Fisher, *Presidential Spending Power* (Princeton: Princeton University Press, 1975), pp. 75-98.

tees and does not proceed unless it first obtains their approval. Here the administration honors a nonstatutory condition while dismissing as legally nonbinding the statutory condition of Section 115 for foreign assistance.[71]

Third, a highly sophisticated and detailed set of controls exists for the reprogramming of funds by the Defense Department. The department is permitted to shift funds within appropriation accounts, subject to various dollar limits and other conditions, including prior approval by appropriations and authorization committees. Both the authority and the conditions are nonstatutory. Executive officials have not challenged this arrangement on constitutional grounds. Since they want the flexibility to shift funds, they accept the conditions imposed by the review committees. The Carter administration tolerated this nonstatutory system but refused to follow the statutory requirement of Section 115.

Carter's letter to Vance suggests that the president successfully repelled a congressional effort to intervene in administrative details. So it was, on the surface. But on the operating level, far below the constitutional principles argued by the White House and the Justice Department, things continued unchanged. Gilligan sought the prior approval of the appropriations committees before diverting funds. Everyone seemed satisfied. The president had defended his prerogatives, Gilligan maintained good relations with Congress, and the review committees continued to exercise their controls.

Agency Regulations

Congress has begun to apply the legislative veto to agency rules and regulations, which number in the thousands each year. Legislative involvement in this area presents novel and complex issues. Agency rulemaking is not discretionary or optional in the same sense as reorganization plans, impoundment deferrals, or other actions covered by legislative vetoes. Agencies must issue regulations to carry out a legislative program and adhere to statutory deadlines. Administrative action cannot proceed in the event of legislative vetoes.

The Administrative Procedure Act was enacted in 1946 to assure fairness and public participation in the rulemaking process. But rulemaking is not an orderly and systematic process. It is essentially political. Agency officials try to formulate a rule that will carry out legislative intent while at the same time satisfying the agency's administrative needs and the interest groups that intervened. There is some danger that legislative vetoes may produce arbitrary and covert actions by Congress, operating through its specialized subcommittees. For example, even if a regulation was completely consistent with legislative intent, Congress might disapprove it for no other reason than a change in the political climate—without bothering to indicate by statute the new mix of public priorities to be pursued.

However, even without the legislative veto, committees are already reviewing proposed regulations and using the regular legislative process either to delay the effective date of a rule or to prevent its implementation. Legislation passed in 1978 requires the Department of Housing and Urban Development (HUD) to submit an agenda of proposed regulations to the banking committees of each house of Congress. Either committee may indicate an intention to review any regulation on the agenda. This review occurs before the regulation is published in the *Federal Register* for notice and comment by the general public. Once the regulation is published in the *Federal Register*, either committee can delay the effective date for 90 additional calendar days by reporting out a joint resolution intended to invalidate or modify the regulation. Use of a joint resolution does not constitute a legislative veto, since it is presented to the president, but the process demonstrates an ability and willingness on the part of congressional committees to evaluate proposed regulations.[72]

Even if the courts would declare unconstitutional all forms of the legislative veto (which is highly unlikely), Congress could always place limitations in appropriation bills to prohibit the use of funds to implement a regulation. On May 9, 1977, HUD issued a regulation that created a furor in Congress. The purpose of the regulation was to define the family groups eligible for public housing. HUD broadly defined "stable family relationships" to include unmarried couples, but because of ambiguities the definition could also cover homosexual couples—a result HUD did not intend. On July 15, 1977, the House voted to nullify the regulation, and shortly thereafter the House amendment became law.[73] Similarly, in 1978 and 1979 Congress attached to an appropriation bill a prohibition on the use of any funds by the Bureau of Alcohol, Tobacco, and Firearms to implement a proposed regulation that members feared would lead to gun control.[74] Whenever legislators sense that their constituents are disturbed by federal regulations, they will intervene by one means or another—including legislative vetoes—to supervise the rulemaking power of agencies.

The Search for Limits

The legislative veto is not a simple instrument, to be justified or repudiated in whole. No single constitutional theory can exonerate or invalidate it. We confront not one element but many different compounds, some easier to justify legally and politically than others.

The courts are unlikely to settle the issue with one sweeping decision. The U.S. Court of Claims, in upholding a one-house veto incorporated in a federal salary act, declined to consider "the general question of whether a one-House veto is valid as an abstract proposition, in all instances, across-the-board, or even in most cases." It dealt with a single mechanism in a specific statute, "not an overarching attempt to cover the entire problem of the so-called legislative veto, or even a large segment of it." The same cautious attitude appeared in a ruling by an appellate court in 1977, after deciding that a one-house veto in a federal elections act was not ripe for judicial consideration. It recommended that the courts treat the question "in a gingerly fashion," avoiding complete reliance on abstract analysis or speculation.[75]

The Presentation Clause of the Constitution means at least this: Congress cannot legislate without participation by the president. Congress may not circumvent the president's veto power simply by calling a bill another name, such as an "order" or a "resolution." However, the situation changes profoundly when the simple or concurrent resolution has been sanctioned by a previous public law. As Attorney General Cushing noted in 1854, a simple resolution cannot coerce a departmental head "unless in some particular in which a law, duly enacted, has subjected him to the direct action of each; and in such case it is to be intended, that, by approving the law, the President has consented to the exercise of such coerciveness on the part of either House." [76]

Although the Constitution requires the president to participate in the creation of a law, the president need not participate in its termination. For example, Congress may decide to delegate emergency authority to the president, subject to termination by concurrent resolution. In the event the president objected to this procedure and the courts agreed, Congress could delegate authority for limited periods—perhaps a year at a time. As the authority was about to expire, the president would have to obtain the support of both houses in order to retain access to the authority. Either house, by withholding support, could cause the authority to terminate. Thus, by objecting to a two-house veto, the president could end up with, in effect, a one-house veto. Programs are terminated whenever Congress fails to renew authority or fails to appropriate funds.

The constitutional scheme is protected by limiting the legislative veto to a yes or no vote by members. Presidential control (and the constitutional process for legislation) would be jeopardized by allowing members to amend a proposal that is not returned to the president. If Congress fails to disapprove an administrative proposal, or if both houses approve, the executive and legislative branches have reached agreement on the law. This procedure is not the one anticipated by the Constitution and certainly deserves the appellation "reverse legislation," but it does not exclude the president. The president signs the enabling statute and initiates all plans and proposals authorized by it. If anything, Congress is at a disadvantage because it cannot amend the president's product.

While presidents traditionally complain that the legislative veto constitutes a congressional usurpation of administrative duties delegated to them, the balance is probably upset in favor of the executive. Congress delegates far greater power with the legislative veto than it would without it. The danger is that legislators, under the illusion that they have retained their authority, will delegate in even broader fashion, permitting the executive branch to decide more of the basic policy questions that should be first hammered out in the course of congressional deliberations.

A wholly different issue arises when Congress *selectively* disapproves a plan or proposal submitted by the president, without returning the altered product to him for signature or veto. In such a case the president would lose control over his submission, allowing Congress to make "new law" without his participation. Any change in the proposal should involve the president. For example, in 1977 Congress authorized the president to submit amendments to the reorganization plans. The president retained control; Congress was limited to a single vote of disapproval.

Selective disapprovals have been used on regulations issued by the General Services Administration (GSA), raising the question whether a regulation, shorn of particular sections or phrases by Congress, would be satisfactory to the GSA in its surviving form.[77] Congress may also selectively disapprove regulations issued by the Federal Election Commission (FEC). In reporting amendments to a statute in 1976, the conference committee stated that Congress could disapprove discrete, self-contained sections of a proposed regulation but not specific words, phrases, or sentences. The public law defines rule or regulation to mean "a provision or series of interrelated provisions stating a single separate rule of law." [78] It has been the practice of the FEC to submit regulations that are interrelated, with interlocking sections, thus forcing Congress to exercise a general rather than an item veto.[79]

In one of the legislative-veto mechanisms, Congress acts as *adjudicator* in deciding deportation cases. Section 244 of the Immigration and Nationality Act authorizes the attorney general to suspend deportation of aliens, subject to a one-house veto. This procedure was adopted decades ago as a compromise arrangement. It gave the attorney general greater discretion to relieve some of the harshness in the immigration law, while at the same time protecting the traditional interest of legislators in this area (generally exercised through private bills).[80]

The contrast between executive and legislative procedures in deportation cases could hardly be more pronounced. The Immigration and Naturalization Service established an adversary hearing procedure, with an opportunity for cross-examination. The attorney general is required by statute to give Congress a complete and detailed statement of the facts and pertinent provision of law in suspension cases, explaining the basis for each suspension. Executive officials are expected to satisfy the requirement of due process.

Congress follows a different course. The judiciary committees do not explain why they recommend the disapproval of suspensions. Reasons are not offered on the floor. In perfunctory manner the House or the Senate agrees to a resolution of disapproval, without a record vote.[81]

An appellate court struck down this procedure in 1980 as a prohibited legislative intrusion upon the executive and judicial branches, particularly the executive authority to execute the laws faithfully and the judicial power to determine cases or controversies. But the decision was narrowly decided and restricted to adjudicatory (trial-like) questions by the agencies. The court expressly put aside the application of legislative vetoes to "a situation in which the unforeseeability of future circumstances" (here the court referred to a two-house legislative veto in the Nuclear Non-Proliferation Act) makes it impractical for Congress to establish specific criteria in the enabling statute. The court also left for another day the application of legislative vetoes to an agency's rulemaking authority.[82]

The one-house veto for deportation cases bears a superficial resemblance to private immigration bills. Certainly Congress has, over the years, reserved for itself a special right of "dispensation" in these matters, but there the similarity ends. Private bills follow the regular legislative course. The initial burden is on Congress to build a record to justify the legislation. Members of Congress call upon the Immigration and Naturalization Service and the State Department to review private immigration bills. If the committee report accompanying a bill shows that an executive agency advises against it, that may be enough cause for any two members (including the "official objectors" appointed to review these bills) to send the bill back to committee. These bills are subjected to the additional check of a presidential veto.

A separate area of dispute is the reliance on legislative vetoes to regulate powers that are not solely legislative in nature and therefore not available for delegation. Congress is not in a position to say to the president: "Here is new authority, subject to these conditions." However, the legislative veto may serve as an acceptable bridge between different and conflicting claims of constitutional power advanced by the two branches. The prime example of a legislative veto that provides a procedural link between conflicting interpretations is the War Powers Resolution of 1973 (see pp. 104-105). This legislative veto has yet to be used. It is possible that a president, under certain circumstances, might decide that the Article II presidential powers have been unconstitutionally abridged by this statutory procedure. The arrangement depends not so much on legal sanctions as on the willingness of the president and administrative officials to respect congressional judgment.

Every new form of legislative control has behind it a specific justification, responding to an agency abuse or a decision by Congress to delegate authority more broadly than in the past. Agencies can check the growth of these controls by limiting arbitrary, bad-faith actions or by accepting more restrictive grants of authority. The first remedy is in the hands of the agency. As for the second, neither branch is eager to return to line-item appropriations and stricter standards of delegation.

FOREIGN AFFAIRS

Presidents especially resist congressional involvement in the administration of foreign affairs and national security. President Ford, who experienced the full force of a resurgent Congress in the post-Vietnam era, tried to resist these congressional initiatives. In an address to Congress on January 15, 1975, he claimed that both by the Constitution and tradition "the execution of foreign policy is the responsibility of the President." While he welcomed the advice and cooperation of the House and the Senate, he warned that Congress "cannot rigidly restrict in legislation the ability of the President to act." The conduct of negotiations is "ill-suited to such limitations." [83] A month later he clarified his view of the division of responsibility between the two branches:

That is not to say that I wish the Congress would keep out of foreign affairs, and that I want to run everything beyond the water's edge in my own way without legislative interference. Under the Constitution, the Congress has a fundamental responsibility in the shaping of all broad matters of public policy, both foreign and domestic. Nobody knows that better than I do. But while the Congress together with the President makes foreign policy, only the Executive can execute it.[84]

In vetoing a foreign assistance bill in 1976, Ford asserted that the measure "would seriously obstruct the exercise of the President's constitutional responsibilities for the conduct of foreign affairs." Shortly before leaving office he urged Congress to reexamine its constitutional role in international affairs to avoid intrusion into the exercise of presidential responsibilities.[85]

A similar theme emerged in the messages and statements of President Carter. In a major address to Congress on June 21, 1978, he warned that "excessive use of legislative vetoes and other devices to restrict foreign policy actions can impede our ability to respond to rapidly changing world conditions." "Reasonable flexibility," he stressed, "is essential to effective government." [86]

Administrative Flexibility

"Flexibility" is often a code word used by executive officials who want to be left alone. Congress has learned that a series of administrative decisions, each relatively innocuous when standing alone, can have an accumulative effect of locking Congress into major commitments—what the Senate Foreign Relations Committee has called "a process of commitment by accretion." [87] Through the use of legislative vetoes, Congress has demonstrated that it understands the need for flexible responses to rapidly changing world conditions, but it does not want the uncertainty and instability of world events to become excuses for preventing or deterring legislative participation.

The War Powers Resolution of 1973 is a case in point. Congress recognized that the president might have legitimate reasons in an emergency situation to use military force pursuant to his own constitutional responsibilities. The Senate wanted to specify by statute the situations where a president could act militarily without advance legislative sanction. The House doubted that it was possible to codify the president's war powers.[88]

During consideration of this legislation in 1973, the problem of congressional control was underscored when a majority in both houses voted to bring the war in Southeast Asia to a halt. Each legislative action was rebuffed by a presidential veto. A federal judge announced that the inability of Congress to override the vetoes should not be taken as legislative authority to continue the war: "It cannot be the rule that the President needs a vote of only one-third plus one of either House in order to conduct a war, but this would be the consequence of holding that Congress must override a Presidential veto in order to terminate hostilities which it has not authorized." [89] To insist that every legislative action must be presented to the president and made subject to his veto power would allow a president to conduct a war with minority backing. No such intention should be read into the Constitution.

The compromise in the War Powers Resolution depends partly on consultation and reporting provisions. Also, if Congress fails to support the president's use of military force in the first 60 to 90 days, he must withdraw the troops. Moreover, Congress may, by concurrent resolution, order the president to withdraw from military activities at any time, thus avoiding the president's veto and the need for an override.

Executive-legislative interests were also reconciled in 1976 with passage of the National Emergencies Act. Emergency proclamations had been issued in the past by presidents, based in part on statutory authority but also on the general executive authority in Article II of the Constitution. In restoring its control, Congress carefully chose a procedure that would terminate emergency powers without disrupting essential operations. The general thrust of the legislation was to terminate existing emergency authority for the president two years from the date the act became law (September 14, 1976). For future national emergencies, the president has to publish his declaration in the *Federal Register*. Congress may terminate a declaration of a national emergency by passing a concurrent resolution. The legislative history of the National Emergencies Act reveals that both branches sought accommodation and were willing to cooperate and negotiate on a bill. Legislation in 1977 applied the legislative veto to the Trading with the Enemy Act, under which presidents have acted in international economic emergencies. [90]

Congress relies on the legislative veto to review pending sales of military arms and services to other nations or international organizations. Any letter of offer to sell U.S. major defense equipment of $7 million or more, or U.S. defense articles or services in the amount of $25 million or more, must be submitted to Congress. The letter cannot be issued if Congress, within 30 calendar days, adopts a concurrent resolution objecting to the proposed sale.

This particular mechanism, while new, is merely the most recent manifestation of a congressional interest in arms sales that has been growing for more than half a century. [91] By 1974 Congress could no longer ignore the fact that foreign military sales had become a major instrument of U.S. foreign policy, allowing the executive branch to involve the country in military situations throughout the world without the knowledge or approval of Congress. The infusion of arms into a particular region of the world, as in the Middle East, can tilt the balance of power and embroil America in a military conflict.

Congress has yet to exercise a veto in arms sales, but the threat of a concurrent resolution of disapproval has produced compromises by the executive branch and ensured a comprehensive justification for controversial sales. In 1975 the House International Relations Committee reported a concurrent resolution to disapprove the transfer of an air defense system to Jordan. Because there appeared to be sufficient votes in each house to disapprove the transaction, President Ford withdrew the letter of offer and agreed to send a communication to Congress placing restrictions on the use of the system. Resistance by the Senate Foreign Relations Committee in 1976 resulted in the reduction in the number of missiles sold to Saudi Arabia, while congressional opposition in 1977 to the sale of AWACS (airborne warning and control system) to Iran prompted President Carter to submit specific assurances to a Senate foreign relations subcommittee. In 1978, to alleviate congressional concerns about the sale of advanced fighter aircraft to Saudi Arabia, it was reported that the Carter administration was willing to sell Israel additional advanced aircraft at a later date.[92] In 1981 the Reagan administration, after encountering substantial opposition from both houses, agreed to delay its plan for selling AWACS to Saudi Arabia until Congress had time to help shape the final package.[93]

During a briefing in 1978, Attorney General Bell was asked whether Carter would consider himself bound if Congress vetoed his Mideast arms sale package. Bell replied that Carter would not be bound, "but we have to have comity between the branches of government, just as we have between nations. And under a spirit of comity, we could abide by it, and there would be nothing wrong with abiding by it. We don't have to have a confrontation every time we can." White House adviser Stuart Eizenstat commented that "with certain of these issues where we think the Congress has a legitimate interest, such as the War Powers Act, as a matter of comity, we are willing to forego the specific legal challenge and abide by that judgment because we think it is such an overriding issue." [94]

The approach by the two branches in war powers, national emergencies, and arms sales has been to leave the arena for presidential action somewhat nebulous, because of inescapable conceptual and philosophical disagreements, while subjecting executive decisions to a two-house veto. This solution narrows, but does not eliminate, the opportunity for conflict between Congress and the president. Even though a legislative veto has the backing of public law, an administration may conclude in a particular instance that Congress has reached too far into the executive domain. In such circumstances a president may decide that a legislative veto is nonbinding. Such outcomes would not wholly discredit the legislative veto. Executive-legislative collisions can help to clarify and highlight the parts of the terrain in foreign affairs that remain in sharp dispute.

Domestic Pressures

The president's preeminence in foreign affairs has been undercut by domestic considerations and the economic and physical interdependence of nations. The Murphy Commission in 1975 noted that "problems of interdependence will sharply affect the domestic economy of this country and therefore merge with domestic political issues, but the processes of our foreign policymaking are still too much designed as though foreign and domestic policy are distinct." [95] In that same year Secretary of State Henry Kissinger acknowledged the new reality in foreign affairs:

> The decade-long struggle in this country over executive dominance in foreign affairs is over. The recognition that the Congress is a coequal branch of government is the dominant fact of national politics today.
> The executive accepts that the Congress must have both the sense and the reality of participation: foreign policy must be a shared enterprise.[96]

Critics of congressional involvement in foreign affairs often point to localism and ethnic group pressures as undesirable elements in the legislative process. But high-sounding and perhaps even high-minded programs pursued by the administration need the support of people at home. Programs must be authorized; they must be funded. As an assistant secretary of state recently observed: "For this we need Congress to refine, to legitimate and to help sell effective international policies." [97]

In this context it is futile to try to exclude local and ethnic interests. The MX missile system presented a major domestic problem for the Reagan administration. The system consists of 200 intercontinental ballistic missiles to be shuttled back and forth between 4,600 underground shelters. Billed as the largest public works project in world history, it threatens to disrupt the land of Utah and Nevada, deplete the water supply, overload public services, and cause irreversible environmental damage. Faced with this prospect, residents of the two states have a legitimate right to protect their interests and natural resources.[98] The Mormon Church, a politically potent force in Utah, announced its opposition to the MX in 1981.

Congress was in a dilemma. It was asked to authorize a program that was being reconsidered by the Reagan administration. As a compromise, the House and Senate armed services committees agreed to authorize funds for the system on the condition that Reagan would (1) submit to Congress the specific design selected by the administration and (2) postpone implementation of the program for 60 days to permit congressional review. The House committee recommended that during the 60-day period Congress adopt a concurrent resolution of approval before the system would receive final authorization. The Senate committee proposed that implementation could begin unless both houses adopted resolutions of disapproval within 60 days. In both cases, however, the legislative veto was recommended to assure some kind of congressional participation in selecting the specific system.[99]

Under the Jackson-Vanik amendment to the Trade Act of 1974, Congress prohibited the president from extending trade concessions to the Soviet Union until he first certified that Russia permitted the emigration of Soviet Jews. American Jews were a prominent ethnic force behind this legislative policy, but other domestic interests coalesced behind this human rights cause.[100]

An administration would benefit by spending more time and energy in understanding these domestic pressures. A former assistant secretary of state for congressional relations said that presidential departmental planning had most often gone astray when it failed to estimate and evaluate developments in Congress. He asked to have someone from the department's policy planning staff assigned to his office, "simply to acquaint that staff with the whole new science upon which future estimates should surely in part be based," but he was unsuccessful.[101]

Congressional review of administrative decisions in foreign affairs and national security is supported by a strong institutional base, within the committee structure, personal staffs, and service organizations of Congress, especially the General Accounting Office, the Congressional Research Service, and the Congressional Budget Office. Instead of periodic and idiosyncratic interventions, Congress now has the institutional capability to monitor major foreign policy decisions on a sustained basis. At least for the present, Congress is composed of younger members, better prepared to challenge assertions and premises from the administration and less willing to show deference to claims of expertise and authority.[102] As a system it is less hierarchical than before, perhaps even more comical in its confusion, but also less likely to enter into commitments abroad for which there is little support at home.

CONCLUSIONS

Despite an accumulation of learned studies and reports that urge Congress to leave administrative duties to the president, the "problem" persists from one decade to the next. The reason has to be found in something more complex than an obstinate desire on the part of members of Congress to overstep constitutional boundaries. Presidents and their supporters face continued frustration because they ignore, or try to overlook, the legitimate stake and interest of Congress in administrative matters.

When executive officials deny Congress the right to add to presidential budgetary estimates, and subsequently withhold funds or restrict programs by various artifices that favor the administration's priorities over those enacted by Congress, they provoke Congress to intervene in the implementation of a statute. Out of frustration, legislators are inclined to place new restrictions in a public law, concluding that flexibility in a statute is used too often by agencies as an excuse for thwarting congressional policy. As Democratic Senator Edmund Muskie of Maine told one official in 1973, after discovering that a broad grant of discretionary authority had been used to cut a legislative program in half:

> Having in mind the devious motives that you pursued to undercut the purposes of Congress, I could now write better language and believe me, I will.
>
> The clear language and debate was what we were giving you, is what we understood to be legitimate administrative discretion to spend the money, not defeat the purposes. Then to have you twist it as you have, is a temptation to this Senator to really handcuff you the next time.[103]

The growth of agency and congressional staff has placed a heavy strain on traditional techniques of legislative oversight and the dependence on good-faith agency efforts. Congress now has the resources to delve more deeply into administration. As the gap between the branches widens, because of staff build-up and turnover, Congress is less able and less willing to rely on customary methods of control. Oral agreements are being replaced by committee report language, which is giving way to statutory directives.

In studies avowedly cynical of the congressional process, scholars have argued that members of Congress and agency bureaucrats have joined forces to produce a system of expensive programs, complex regulations, and legislative intervention in the administrative process— all for the purpose of helping incumbent legislators return to office with larger vote margins. Programs that automatically appropriate and distribute funds, such as revenue sharing, are opposed in Congress because they reduce the need for members to participate in the administration and allocation of federal resources.[104]

Examples can be found to support this scenario, but it is largely contradicted by the legislative record. Recent decades have witnessed the growth of mechanical, automatic formulas that sharply circumscribe the opportunity for members to intervene in agency decisions. What we have instead is a system run on permanent authorizations, permanent appropriations, entitlements, indexing (adjusting benefits to cover inflation), and assorted "uncontrollables." [105] A more telling criticism of Congress is that it has allowed a substantial part of the executive branch to operate without the need for congressional intervention, judgment, or accountability.

NOTES

1. Woodrow Wilson, *Congressional Government* (Boston: Houghton Mifflin Co., 1885), p. 45; *Public Papers of the Presidents,* 1976-77, 2:1483.
2. Philip B. Kurland, *Watergate and the Constitution* (Chicago: University of Chicago Press, 1978), p. 175.
3. Louis Fisher, *President and Congress* (New York: Free Press, 1972), pp. 1-27, 253-270.
4. On Madison, see Max Farrand, ed., *The Records of the Federal Convention of 1787,* 4 vols. (New Haven: Yale University Press, 1937), 2:35. On Wilson, Morris, and Mercer, see ibid., 1:107; 2:52, 298. On Rutledge, see 1:65.
5. On Sherman, see ibid., 1:65; see also Harold C. Syrett, ed., *The Papers of Alexander Hamilton* (New York: Columbia University Press, 1961-   ), 2:404; and Julian P. Boyd, ed., *The Papers of Thomas Jefferson* (Princeton: Princeton University Press, 1950-   ), 11:679.
6. 6 Op. Att'y Gen. 326, 344 (1854); 7 Op. Att'y Gen. 453, 469-470 (1855).
7. Advisory Commission on Intergovernmental Relations, *Citizen Participation in the American Federal System* (Washington, D.C.: Government Printing Office, 1979), pp. 99-179.
8. Louis L. Jaffe, *Judicial Control of Administrative Action* (Boston: Little, Brown & Co., 1965); Martin Shapiro, *The Supreme Court and Administrative Agencies* (New York: Free Press, 1968); Nathan Glazer, "Should Judges Administer Social Services?" *The Public Interest* 50 (Winter 1978):64.
9. Frank C. Neuman and Harry J. Keaton, "Congress and the Faithful Execution of Laws—Should Legislators Supervise Administrators?" *California Law Review* 41 (1953-1954):565, 571.
10. See Title 5 of the U.S. Code; see also Joseph P. Harris, *Congressional Control of Administration* (Garden City, N.Y.: Doubleday, 1965), pp. 180-225.
11. Robert C. Randolph and Daniel C. Smith, "Executive Privilege and the Congressional Right of Inquiry," *Harvard Journal on Legislation* 10 (1973):621, 649.
12. On the Trade Expansion Act, see 76 Stat. 878, sec. 243 (1962). On the Trade Act of 1974, see 19 U.S.C. 2211(a) (1976). On the Secret Service, see U.S., Congress, House, H. Rept. 1196, 96th Cong., 2d sess., 1980, p. 2.
13. P.L. 94-304, 90 Stat. 661 (1976).
14. Watkins v. United States, 354 U.S. 178, 187 (1957); Harris, *Congressional Control of Administration,* p. 1.
15. *Hinds' Precedents of the House of Representatives* (Washington, D.C.: Government Printing Office, 1907), 3:1908-1910.
16. U.S., Congress, House, Committee on Interstate and Foreign Commerce,

Contempt Proceedings against Secretary of Commerce Rogers C. B. Morton (hearings), 94th Cong., 1st sess., 1975; U.S., Congress, *Congressional Record* (daily ed.), 94th Cong., 1st sess., December 16, 1975, 121:H12727; Congressional Quarterly *Weekly Report*, May 17, 1980, pp. 1352-1353.

17. U.S., Congress, Joint Committee on Congressional Operations, *Leading Cases on Congressional Investigatory Power*, 94th Cong., 2d sess., January 1976; Louis Fisher, *The Constitution Between Friends: Congress, the President, and the Law* (New York: St. Martin's Press, 1978), pp. 139-165.
18. Pillsbury Co. v. FTC, 354 F.2d 952, 964 (5th Cir. 1966), emphasis in original. In Koniag, Inc. v. Kleppe, 405 F. Supp. 1360, 1372 (D.D.C. 1975), a federal court characterized hearings by a House committee as "an impermissible congressional interference with the administrative process," but this part of the decision was reversed by Koniag, Inc., Village of Uyak v. Andrus, 580 F.2d 601, 610-611 (D.C. Cir. 1978).
19. D.C. Federation of Civic Associations v. Volpe, 459 F.2d 1231, 1247 (D.C. Cir. 1972), certiorari denied, 405 U.S. 1030 (1972).
20. Gulf Oil Corp. v. FPC, 563 F.2d 588, 610-612 (3d Cir. 1977).
21. United States ex rel. Parco v. Morris, 426 F.Supp. 976, 982 (E.D. Pa. 1977).
22. P.L. 96-68, 93 Stat. 433 (1979).
23. 53 Comp. Gen. 600 (1974).
24. Louis Fisher, *Presidential Spending Power* (Princeton: Princeton University Press, 1975). See also Arthur W. Macmahon, "Congressional Oversight of Administration: The Power of the Purse," *Political Science Quarterly* 58 (1943):161, 380; Lucius Wilmerding, Jr., *The Spending Power* (New Haven: Yale University Press, 1943); and Elias Huzar, *The Purse and the Sword, Control of the Army by Congress through Military Appropriations, 1933-1950* (Ithaca, N.Y.: Cornell University Press, 1950).
25. Clark v. Board of Education of Little Rock Sch. Dist., 374 F.2d 569, 571 (8th Cir. 1967). See also Califano v. Westcott, 443 U.S. 76, 92-93 (1979).
26. United States v. Will (Supreme Court, December 15, 1980), *United States Law Week* 49 (1980):4045; Will v. United States, 478 F.Supp. 621 (N.D. Ill. 1979); Booth v. United States, 291 U.S. 339 (1934); O'Donoghue v. United States, 289 U.S. 516 (1933).
27. 328 U.S. 303 (1946). See also Louis Fisher, "The Spending Power of Congress: A Prerogative Operating Within Boundaries" (Paper presented to the Notre Dame University Law School, March 12, 1981, at Washington, D.C.).
28. Jeffrey M. Glosser, "Congressional Reference Cases in the United States Court of Claims: A Historical and Current Perspective," *American University Law Review* 25 (1976):595. See also G. Lowell Field, "Administration by Statute—The Question of Special Laws," *Public Administration Review* 6 (1946):325; Note, "Private Bills and the Immigration Law," *Harvard Law Review* 69 (1956):1083; Note, "Private Bills in Congress," *Harvard Law Review* 79 (1966):1684.
29. On Cleveland, see James D. Richardson, ed., *A Compilation of the Messages and Papers of the Presidents*, 20 vols. (New York: Bureau of National Literature, 1897-1925), 10:5001-5002 (May 8, 1886), and pp. 5020-5040 (June 21-23, 1886). For statistics on private laws, see Library of Congress, Congressional Research Service, *Private Bills and Federal Charters*, Marc D. Yacker, Report No. 79-110 GOV, p. 22. See also

statement by Representative Boland, *Congressional Record* (daily ed.), 96th Cong., 1st sess., April 9, 1979, 125:H2134.

30. 60 Stat. 831, sec. 131 (1946); 2 U.S.C. 190g (1976), repeated in House Rule XXII, clause 2.

31. Charles L. Clapp, *The Congressman: His Work as He Sees It* (Garden City, N.Y.: Doubleday, 1964), pp. 88-89. On the range of casework and its relationship to legislative duties, see Kenneth E. Gray, "Congressional Interference in Administration," *Cooperation and Conflict,* ed. Daniel J. Elazar (Itasca, Ill.: F. E. Peacock, 1969); and Kenneth G. Olson, "The Service Function of the United States Congress," *Congress: The First Branch of Government,* ed. Alfred de Grazia (Washington, D.C.: American Enterprise Institute, 1966).

32. Donald R. Matthews, *U.S. Senators and Their World* (New York: Vintage Books, 1960), p. 225.

33. John R. Johannes, "Congressional Casework: The Bureaucratic Perspective" (Paper delivered at the annual meeting of the Midwest Political Science Association, Chicago, Ill., April 24-26, 1980). A recent critique of congressional casework is by Robert Klonoff, "The Congressman as Mediator Between Citizens and Government Agencies, Problems and Prospects," *Harvard Journal on Legislation* 16 (1979):701. For a broader and I think more understanding account, see Morris S. Ogul, *Congress Oversees the Bureaucracy* (Pittsburgh: University of Pittsburgh Press, 1976), pp. 162-175; and Frank E. Smith, *Congressman from Mississippi* (New York: Capricorn Books, 1967), pp. 235-257.

34. Under the Trade Act of 1974, resolutions adopted by either tax committee can compel the International Trade Commission to investigate whether an article imported into the United States injures a domestic industry; see 19 U.S.C. 2251(b) (1976).

35. F.H.E. Oil Co. v. Commissioner of Internal Revenue, 150 F.2d 857 (5th Cir. 1945).

36. 19 Op. Att'y Gen. 385 (1889). For more on resolutions, see H. Lee Watson, "Congress Steps Out: A Look at Congressional Control of the Executive," *California Law Review* 63 (1975):983, 1017-1029.

37. 68 Stat. 519, sec. 411(e) (1954); Harris, *Congressional Control of Administration,* pp. 255-258.

38. 86 Stat. 217, sec. 7(a) (1972).

39. 55 Comp. Gen. 319, 325-326 (1975). See also 55 Comp. Gen. 812 (1976).

40. TVA v. Hill, 437 U.S. 153 (1978).

41. National Small Shipments v. Civil Aeronautics Bd., 618 F.2d 819 (D.C. Cir. 1980).

42. U.S., Congress, House, H. Rept. 926 (Part 1), 96th Cong., 2d sess., 1980, p. 3; P.L. 96-450, 94 Stat. 1975 (1980).

43. See *Congressional Ethics* (Washington, D.C.: Congressional Quarterly, 1980), pp. 172-175; United States v. Johnson, 383 U.S. 169 (1966); Gravel v. United States, 408 U.S. 606, 625 (1972); and for the Eilberg case, see *United States Law Week* 47 (1978):2573. Often a legislative act becomes mixed with a member's intervention in an agency. For example, Representative John Dowdy, D-Texas, was indicted for bribery, conspiracy, and perjury stemming from his intervention as subcommittee chairman into a Justice Department investigation. He was charged with accepting $25,000 in return for assisting a home-improvement firm threatened with prosecution. The charges of bribery and conspiracy eventually were dropped

because of the Speech or Debate Clause immunity, particularly in view of his status as subcommittee chairman, but after a new trial he was found guilty of perjury. See United States v. Dowdy, 479 F.2d 213 (4th Cir. 1973).

44. United States v. Myers (2d Cir. August 8, 1980), *United States Law Week* 49 (1980):2160-2161.
45. *Congressional Record,* 91st Cong., 2d sess., 1970, 116:1078.
46. Hutchinson v. Proxmire, 443 U.S. 111 (1979). Proxmire agreed to pay $10,000 from his own funds as an out-of-court settlement; see *Washington Post,* March 25, 1980, p. A3; and *Congressional Record* (daily ed.), 96th Cong., 2d sess., March 24, 1980, 126:S2831-2832.
47. Fisher, *Presidential Spending Power,* pp. 147-201; and James P. Pfiffner, *The President, the Budget, and Congress: Impoundment and the 1974 Budget Act* (Boulder, Colo.: Westview Press, 1979).
48. Fisher, *Presidential Spending Power,* pp. 75-98.
49. U.S., Congress, House, Committee on Appropriations, *Supplemental Appropriation Bill, 1980 (Part 4)* (hearings), 96th Cong., 2d sess., 1980, p. 395.
50. 87 Stat. 1046, sec. 745 (1974).
51. P.L. 95-624, sec. 7, 92 Stat. 3463 (1978); P.L. 95-509, Title II, 92 Stat. 1777-78 (1978); P.L. 95-601, sec. 1(c), 92 Stat. 2948 (1978).
52. PHS Financial Management Manual, Part 2, Budget Formulation, Chapter PHS: 2-6, Request for Reprogramming of Funds, June 19, 1980; Department of Labor Manual Series, DLMS 6 - Financial Management, Manual Transmittal 20, Chapter 400, Section 440, Reprogramming, December 21, 1979.
53. U.S., Congress, House, H. Rept. 97-22 (Part 1), 97th Cong., 1st sess., 1981, pp. 8, 36-37.
54. *Congressional Record* (daily ed.), 96th Cong., 2d sess., July 1, 1980, 126:H5952.
55. U.S., Congress, House, H. Rept. 1218, 94th Cong., 1st sess., 1976, pp. 4-5.
56. U.S., Congress, Senate, S. Rept. 276, 95th Cong., 1st sess., 1977, p. 35. See also U.S., Congress, House, H. Rept. 392, 95th Cong., 1st sess., 1977, p. 13.
57. P.L. 95-97, 91 Stat. 828, sec. 609 (1977).
58. U.S., Congress, Senate, S. Rept. 1058, 95th Cong., 2d sess., 1978, p. 9.
59. *Weekly Compilation of Presidential Documents* 13 (May 12, 1977):718-719.
60. U.S., Congress, House, H. Rept. 932, 95th Cong., 2d sess., 1978, p. 5. For further details on impoundment, reprogramming, and personnel ceilings, see Louis Fisher, "Effect of the Budget Act of 1974 on Agency Operations" (Paper presented to the American Enterprise Institute, Washington, D.C., October 22, 1979, to be published as part of proceedings entitled *The Congressional Budget Process After Five Years).*
61. U.S., Congress, Senate, Committee on Governmental Affairs, *Nomination of James T. McIntyre, Jr.* (hearings), 95th Cong., 2d sess., 1978, pp. 76-77.
62. National Treasury Employees Union v. Reagan, Civil Action No. 81-0195 (D.D.C. February 26, 1981); *Congressional Record* (daily ed.), 97th Cong., 1st sess., May 5, 1981, 127:S4397-4402, and June 2, 1981, pp. S5657-5658.
63. 37 Op. Att'y Gen. 56, 63-64 (1933); *Congressional Record,* 75th Cong., 3d sess., 1938, 83:4487.
64. Louis Fisher and Ronald C. Moe, "Presidential Reorganization Authority: Is It Worth the Cost?" *Political Science Quarterly* (Summer 1981).

65. *Weekly Compilation of Presidential Documents* 15 (May 7, 1979):814; and ibid., July 25, 1979, p. 1310.
66. 14 Stat. 569 (1867).
67. Virginia A. McMurtry, "Legislative Vetoes Relating to Public Works and Buildings," in U.S., Congress, House, Committee on Rules, *Studies on the Legislative Veto,* 96th Cong., 2d sess., February 1980, pp. 432-514. Hereafter cited as *Studies on the Legislative Veto.*
68. P.L. 95-148, 91 Stat. 1235, sec. 115 (1977); letter from President Carter to Secretary of State Vance, October 31, 1977. For testimony on this issue by AID officials, the Senate legal counsel, and Louis Fisher, see U.S., Congress, Senate, Committee on Appropriations, *Foreign Assistance and Related Programs Appropriations, Fiscal Year 1981 (Part 1)* (hearings), 96th Cong., 2d sess., 1980, pp. 53-170.
69. McCorkle v. United States, 559 F.2d 1258, 1261-62 (4th Cir. 1977).
70. P.L. 96-69, 93 Stat. 441 (1979).
71. For the understanding by Congress on CIA transfers and reprogrammings, see U.S., Congress, House, H. Rept. 97-101 (Part 1), 97th Cong., 1st sess., 1981, p. 4.
72. P.L. 95-557, 92 Stat. 2103, sec. 324 (1978). See Grace Milgram, "Legislative Vetoes in Housing," *Studies on the Legislative Veto,* pp. 515-559; and floor statement of Representative Thomas Ashley, *Congressional Record* (daily ed.), 96th Cong., 2d sess., August 21, 1980, 126:H7379.
73. *Congressional Record* (daily ed.), 95th Cong., 1st sess., June 15, 1977, 123:H5931-5932; P.L. 95-119, 91 Stat. 1089, sec. 408 (1977).
74. P.L. 95-429, 92 Stat. 1002 (1978); P.L. 96-74, 93 Stat. 560 (1979). See Frederick M. Kaiser, "Congressional Action to Overturn Agency Rules: Alternatives to the 'Legislative Veto,'" *Administrative Law Review* 32 (1980):667.
75. Atkins v. United States, 556 F.2d 1028, 1059 (Ct. Cl. 1977), certiorari denied, 434 U.S. 1009 (1978); Clark v. Valeo, 559 F.2d 642, 650, note 10 (D.C. Cir. 1977), affirmed by the Supreme Court sub. nom. Clark v. Kimmitt, 431 U.S. 950 (1977).
76. 6 Op. Att'y Gen. 680, 683 (1854).
77. Suzanne Cavanagh, "The General Services Administration and the Legislative Veto: Public Law 93-526," *Studies on the Legislative Veto,* pp. 59-106.
78. U.S., Congress, House, H. Rept. 1057, 94th Cong., 2d sess., 1976, pp. 50-52; P.L. 94-283, 90 Stat. 498-499 (1976).
79. Joseph E. Cantor, "The Federal Election Commission and the Legislative Veto," *Studies on the Legislative Veto,"* pp. 16-58. See also pp. 4-6.
80. Harvey C. Mansfield, "The Legislative Veto and the Deportation of Aliens," *Public Administration Review* 1 (1941):281.
81. For example, see *Congressional Record* (daily ed.), 94th Cong. 1st sess., December 16, 1975, 121:H12609.
82. Chadha v. Immigration and Naturalization Service, 634 F.2d 408, 433 (9th Cir. 1980).
83. *Public Papers of the Presidents,* 1975, Book 1, p. 45.
84. Ibid., p. 251. See also ibid., 1976-77, Book 1, p. 41.
85. Ibid., 1976-77, Book 2, pp. 1481-1485; Book 3, pp. 2920-2921.
86. *Weekly Compilation of Presidential Documents* 14 (June 21, 1978):1148.
87. U.S., Congress, Senate, S. Rept. 129, 91st Cong., 1st sess., 1969, p. 26.
88. Fisher, *The Constitution Between Friends,* pp. 232-246.

89. Holtzman v. Schlesinger, 361 F.Supp. 555, 565 (E.D. N.Y. 1973), reversed by Holtzman v. Schlesinger, 484 F.2d 1307 (2d Cir. 1973), after stays by the Supreme Court, 414 U.S. 1304, 1321 (1973).
90. Harold C. Relyea, "The National Emergencies Act and the Legislative Veto," and "Trading With the Enemy Act Amendments of 1977, National Emergency Power, and the Legislative Veto," *Studies on the Legislative Veto,* pp. 756-802.
91. Christopher J. Deering, "Congressional Control of Arms Transfers: The Evolution of Executive-Legislative Relations" (Paper delivered at the annual meeting of the Midwest Political Science Association, Chicago, Ill., 1979).
92. Richard F. Grimmett, "The Legislative Veto and U.S. Arms Sales," *Studies on the Legislative Veto,* pp. 248-320.
93. "Baker Says U.S. to Delay AWACS Sale," *Washington Post,* April 27, 1981, p. A1.
94. Office of the White House Press Secretary, *Briefing by Attorney General Griffin B. Bell, Stuart E. Eizenstat, Assistant to the President for Domestic Affairs and Policy, and John Harmon, Office of Legal Counsel,* June 21, 1978, p. 4.
95. *Commission on the Organization of the Government for the Conduct of Foreign Policy* (Washington, D.C.: Government Printing Office, June 1975), p. 195.
96. *Department of State Bulletin,* No. 1871, 72 (May 5, 1975):562.
97. Douglas J. Bennett, Jr., "Congress in Foreign Policy: Who Needs It?" *Foreign Affairs* 57 (1978):40, 49.
98. See "The Domestic Impact of the MX Missile," *National Journal,* August 23, 1980, pp. 1400-1402.
99. U.S., Congress, Senate, S. Rept. 97-58, 97th Cong., 1st sess., 1981, pp. 99-101, 193-194; *Congressional Record* (daily ed.), 97th Cong., 1st sess., May 13, 1981, 127:S4933-4945; U.S., Congress, House, H. Rept. 97-71 (Part 1), 97th Cong., 1st sess., 1981, p. 105.
100. Paula Stern, *Water's Edge: Domestic Politics and the Making of American Foreign Policy* (Westport, Conn.: Greenwood Press, 1979).
101. David M. Abshire, *Foreign Policy Makers: President vs. Congress* (Beverly Hills, Calif.: Sage Publications, 1979), p. 7.
102. Thomas M. Franck and Edward Weisband, *Foreign Policy by Congress* (New York: Oxford University Press, 1979), p. 2.
103. U.S., Congress, Senate, Committee on Government Operations and Committee on the Judiciary, *Impoundment of Appropriated Funds by the President* (hearings), 93rd Cong., 1st sess., 1973, p. 411. The official was William D. Ruckelshaus, administrator of the Environmental Protection Agency.
104. Morris P. Fiorina, *Congress: Keystone of the Washington Establishment* (New Haven: Yale University Press, 1977), pp. 71-74. See also R. Douglas Arnold, *Congress and the Bureaucracy* (New Haven: Yale University Press, 1979), and his article, "The Local Roots of Domestic Policy," *The New Congress,* eds. Thomas E. Mann and Norman J. Ornstein (Washington, D.C.: American Enterprise Institute, 1981), pp. 281-284.
105. "How Do You Control the Budget When Benefit Programs Keep Growing?" *National Journal,* August 16, 1980, pp. 1344-1348.

4

Bureaucracy: Agent of Congress or the President?

As a source of executive-legislative friction, it would be difficult to select an issue more deep-rooted than control of the bureaucracy. For almost two centuries, Congress and the president have competed with one another for the power to regulate the activities of departments and agencies. Both branches, while operating within limits, have legitimate claims to a general supervisory power.

According to one constitutional model, the president is the chief administrative officer of a unified and hierarchical executive branch, capable of directing the activities and operations of agency personnel. They serve as the president's agents in seeing that "the Laws be faithfully executed." But another model begins with the premise that Congress creates the departments and may specify how laws are to be implemented. The Constitution empowers Congress to make all laws "which shall be necessary and proper" for carrying into execution the powers vested "in the Government of the United States, or in any Department or Officer thereof."

The issue becomes one of reconciling two competing models of the Constitution. To allow one model to transcend the other would create a concentration of power within one branch that the framers sought to avoid. Some of the precedents established by the First Congress, in creating the executive departments, set the stage for subsequent patterns of bureaucratic control. Much is left to the play of political forces, leaving in doubt whether Congress or the president controls the executive branch. David Truman aptly pointed out that

> a number of key points of decision are established in parallel with no formal, solid basis of hierarchy among them. Informal, extralegal means may provide a measure of superordination and subordination, but the way is always open for an interest group to operate through the Congress or the president alternatively, to play one off against the other, to destroy a fragile hierarchical arrangement and fabricate a transitory substitute.[1]

CREATING THE EXECUTIVE DEPARTMENTS

The Constitution authorized the president to "require the Opinion, in writing, of the principal Officer in each of the executive Departments, upon any Subject relating to the Duties of their respective Offices. . . ." Quite undecided, however, was the relationship between the president and the departmental heads. Were they merely staff advisers to the president, to assist him in carrying out his constitutional responsibilities, or did they also owe allegiance to Congress? Upon entering office as the nation's first chief executive, George Washington suggested that the departments were agents of the president, not Congress:

> . . . I have, however, been taught to believe, that there is, in most polished nations, a system established, with regard to the foreign as well as the other great Departments, which, from the utility, the necessity, and the reason of the thing, provides that business should be digested and prepared by the Heads of those departments.
>
> The impossibility that one man should be able to perform all the great business of the State, I take to have been the reason for instituting the great Departments, and appointing officers therein, to assist the supreme Magistrate in discharging the duties of his trust.[2]

An even stronger statement in support of presidential responsibility was offered by Senator William Maclay of Pennsylvania, after Congress had taken up the question of creating the executive departments:

> . . . There are a number of such bills, and may be many more, tending to direct the most minute particle of the President's conduct. If he is to be directed, how he shall do everything, it follows he must do nothing without direction. To what purpose, then, is the executive power lodged with the President, if he can do nothing without a law directing the mode, manner, and, of course, the thing to be done? May not the two Houses of Congress, on this principle, pass a law depriving him of all powers? You may say it will not get his approbation. But two thirds of both Houses will make it a law without him and the Constitution is undone at once.[3]

The debate on the executive departments began on May 19, 1789, when Elias Boudinot of New Jersey requested that the House of Representatives establish general principles to guide the creation of departments. He believed that the departments under the Articles of Confederation should not be "models for us to form ours upon, by reason of the essential change which has taken place in the Government, and the new distribution of Legislative, Executive, and Judicial powers." [4] Still, the experiences with the departments of foreign affairs, war, and treasury—all of which were created in 1781 by the Continental Congress—had a definite influence on their disposition in 1789. John Jay had taken over as secretary for foreign affairs in 1784 and served throughout the remaining years of the Continental Congress, continuing in that capacity as acting secretary of state in Washington's administration until Jefferson assumed the duties in March 1790. Henry Knox was elected secretary at war in 1785 and remained in that post until the final days of 1794, illustrating vividly the continuity in administrative structures from the confederation to the national government. The treasury, however, had a different history. When Robert Morris retired as superintendent of finance in 1784, financial management returned to the previous board system composed of administrators recruited from outside Congress. [5]

Departmental Heads

Since each department had to be created by statute in 1789, legislators could decide whether to place a department under one individual or establish a board of commissioners. There was some concern that departmental heads might become more important than the legislature, but the experience with the Board of Treasury convinced most members that the board system lacked responsibility, energy, and order. The House voted for single executives to head the departments. [6]

Part of this decision rested on the belief that Congress, by statute, could check and restrain the operations of an executive official. Madison preferred, in all cases of an executive nature, that Congress first consider the powers to be exercised. If the powers were too extensive to be entrusted to a single individual, "proper care should be taken so to regulate and check the exercise, as would give indubitable security for the perfect preservation of the public interest, and to prevent that suspicion which men of integrity were ever desirous of avoiding." [7]

Congress regarded the secretary of foreign affairs and the secretary of war as executive officials, reflecting the experience under the Articles of Confederation. In the words of Representative John Vining of Delaware: "The Departments of Foreign Affairs and War are peculiarly within the powers of the President, and he must be responsible for them."[8] This understanding appears in the statutes creating both departments. On July 27, 1789, Congress established an "Executive department, to be denominated the Department of Foreign Affairs." The secretary of foreign affairs would "perform and execute such duties as shall from time to time be enjoined on or intrusted to him by the President of the United States." The same format and structure was used for the Department of War.[9]

But the House of Representatives regarded the Treasury Department partly as a *legislative* agent, reflecting the mixed record during the Articles of Confederation when the duties shifted back and forth between a superintendent of finance and a Board of Treasury. As a result, the statute creating the Treasury Department in 1789 differed substantially from the statutes for foreign affairs and war. Treasury was not styled an "executive department." Nowhere did the statute direct the secretary of the treasury to perform and execute duties for the president. Instead, the statute included legislative instructions directing the secretary to report and give information to either the House or the Senate, "in person or in writing (as he may be required)," respecting all matters referred to him by Congress.[10]

In practice, however, the treasury secretary performed as an arm of the president, not Congress. No one doubted that Hamilton served as "minister of finance" for President Washington. Senator William Maclay, in a contemporary (if prejudiced) account of Washington's cabinet, voiced his exasperation: "Congress may go home. Mr. Hamilton is all-powerful, and fails in nothing he attempts."[11] As a reaction to Hamilton's influence, Congress eventually drove him from office.

Four decades later, Congress attempted to treat President Andrew Jackson's secretary of the treasury as a legislative agent, delegating to him, rather than the president, the responsibility for placing government money either in the national bank or in state banks. Jackson removed two secretaries of the treasury before finding someone willing to follow his instructions, not those of Congress. A Senate resolution of censure declared that Jackson had assumed "authority and power not conferred by the Constitution and laws, but in derogation of both." In a lengthy and impassioned defense, Jackson answered that the secretary of the treasury was "wholly an executive officer" and could be removed at will by the president. Three years later the Senate ordered its resolution of censure removed from the record.[12]

Hybrid Cases

Treasury matters continue to have a mixed executive-legislative character. In the Budget and Accounting Act of 1921, Congress transferred all powers and duties of the comptroller of the treasury, the six auditors of the Treasury Department, and the division of bookkeeping and warrants of the office of the secretary of the treasury to a newly created General Accounting Office (GAO), generally recognized as part of the legislative branch.[13] A committee established by President Roosevelt in 1937 (the Brownlow Committee) objected to GAO's interference with expenditure responsibilities, which it called "essentially an executive function." A staff study sponsored by the committee recommended (unsuccessfully) that several GAO functions be returned to the Treasury Department.[14] Although GAO functions as an "agent of Congress" when it audits accounts,[15] it carries out "executive" duties by approving payments and settling and adjusting accounts.[16]

Legislative prerogatives in financial matters also prompted Congress to treat the Post Office in unique fashion. The statute creating the Post Office in 1789 did not designate it "executive department," even though the postmaster general was "subject to the direction of the President of the United States in performing the duties of his office. . . ." [17] During the debates on renewing the statute in 1790, members were divided on the question of whether to delegate the power to designate post roads to the president or the postmaster general or to reserve it for Congress. Those who argued against the first option warned that revenue would be centered in the hands of the executive, combining purse and sword and thus leading to the destruction of liberties in America. They also maintained that such delegation was unconstitutional because the power to establish post roads was expressly reserved to Congress by the Constitution.[18]

By 1792, Congress decided to retain for itself the power to specify post roads. The statute authorized the postmaster general (not the president) to enter into contracts and make appointments. It also deleted language making the postmaster general subject to the direction of the president. Financial autonomy was assured by allowing the Post Office to operate from postal revenues, with the balance to be returned to the Treasury.[19]

The location of the Post Office was more than a political struggle between Congress and the executive. Deep divisions existed even within the executive branch. Thomas Jefferson wanted the Post Office in his agency (the Department of State) to keep power away from Alexander Hamilton, his rival who headed the Treasury.[20] Under these circumstances, it was easier for both branches to leave the Post Office floating somewhere outside the executive departments.

Legislation in 1836 put an end to the financial autonomy of the Post Office. All revenues were placed in the Treasury, subject to appropriations by Congress. Beginning with Jackson's administration, the postmaster general became part of the cabinet.[21] By 1935, the

Supreme Court said that a postmaster "is merely one of the units in the executive department and, hence, inherently subject to the exclusive and illimitable power of removal by the Chief Executive, whose subordinate and aid he is."[22]

These "inherent" and "illimitable" powers are not so fixed as the Court implied. In 1970 Congress came full circle by abolishing the Post Office Department and replacing it with the U.S. Postal Service, described in the statute as an "independent establishment of the executive branch...."[23] This reference to the executive branch is exceedingly generous. The president has virtually no control over the Postal Service other than the power to nominate members to the Board of Governors and the Postal Rate Commission, subject to the advice and consent of the Senate. An exception to this general record of autonomy occurred in the first year of the Reagan administration. An executive order issued by Reagan on February 17, 1981, to review the cost-effectiveness of agency regulations, was applied to the Postal Service's proposal for a nine-digit ZIP code.

CONTROL OF FEDERAL PERSONNEL

After creating executive departments and agencies, Congress continues to exercise control by participating in the appointment power, placing conditions and restrictions on the removal power, establishing a civil service system, and mandating the performance of certain duties.

Appointing Officials

The power to appoint agency officals is an essential tool used by both president and Congress to control the bureaucracy. In his report to President John F. Kennedy in 1960, James M. Landis counseled: "The prime key to the improvement of the administrative process is the selection of qualified personnel. Good men can make poor laws workable; poor men will wreak havoc with good laws."[24] The potential of the appointment power has been narrowed by civil service regulations and other restrictions imposed by Congress. Departmental heads are able to appoint only a handful of senior political executives. Michael Blumenthal, Carter's first secretary of the treasury, estimated that out of 120,000 people in his department he was able to select only about 25.[25]

While the power to nominate is the sole act of the president, in creating an office Congress may stipulate in considerable detail the qualifications for appointees. And in practice, if not in theory, the responsibility for recommending nominees often falls to members of Congress. Nominations also depend on recommendations by organizations such as the American Bar Association, farm groups, labor unions, education associations, and professional and scientific organizations. The Senate's advice and consent and "senatorial courtesy" (the power of a single senator to block a nomination) are other counterweights to the president's power to nominate.[26]

The appointment process is taken seriously because it is assumed that "who you get *in* government directly affects what you get *out* of government." [27] The number of Senate rejections cannot be measured by floor votes. Of 40 major nominations rejected from 1961 to 1977, only 4 were rejected by floor vote. Nine were rejected by committee vote, while 27 nominees were forced to withdraw.[28] Ernest Lefever, nominated by President Reagan in 1981 for a top post in the State Department, is a more recent casualty of this process. After the Senate Foreign Relations Committee voted 13-4 to disapprove his nomination, Lefever asked Reagan to withdraw his name. Hundreds of other potential nominees are never even submitted by the White House because of congressional opposition.

Congress has broad powers under the Necessary and Proper Clause of Article I, Section 8, to place restrictions on the president's powers of removal, appointment, organization, and reorganization.[29] But it may not, by law, designate a person to fill an office.[30] Congress tried to do that, in a circuitous way, in 1974. A statute vested in the Commodity Futures Trading Commission the power to nominate its executive director, subject to the advice and consent of the Senate. In signing the bill, President Ford stated that the provision raised "serious constitutional questions, by providing for an executive branch appointment in a manner not contemplated by the Constitution." Recognizing that it had overreached, Congress changed the procedure in 1978 to vest the appointment of the executive director solely in the commission, without submitting the name to the Senate.[31]

This modification followed the Supreme Court's decision two years earlier striking down the method of appointment used by Congress for the Federal Election Commission (FEC). Congress appointed four of the members. All six voting members (including two nominated by the president) required confirmation by the majority of *both* houses. An appellate court justified this procedure by reasoning that Congress possessed adequate authority under the Necessary and Proper Clause, but in 1976 the Supreme Court denied that Congress could appoint members to the FEC, especially since it was created by Congress to discharge more than legislative functions. The FEC, through its duty to exercise an enforcement or prosecutorial power, might have to institute a lawsuit and seek judicial relief. Such actions fell not to Congress but to the president, who is required under the Constitution to "take Care that the laws be faithfully executed." Administrative functions, said the

Court, had to be carried out by "Officers of the United States." The Court limited Congress to one of two constitutional options: letting the president nominate the members, subject to the advice and consent of the Senate, or vesting the appointment power solely in the president, in the courts of law, or in departmental heads.[32] Congress chose the first option when it rewrote the act in 1976.

Removals

Some members of the First Congress believed that the Constitution permitted only one means of removing executive officers: the impeachment process. Others insisted that since the Senate participated in the appointments process, it must consent also to removals. Most of the debate, however, narrowed to two choices: (1) the president, pursuant to constitutional responsibilities, may remove administrators at will, or (2) Congress, since it creates an office, may attach to it any conditions it decides appropriate, including tenure and grounds for removal. This latter position appears in Connecticut Representative Roger Sherman's statement of June 17, 1789:

> As the officer is the mere creature of the Legislature, we may form it under such regulations as we please, with such powers and duration as we think good policy requires. We may say he shall hold his office during good behaviour, or that he shall be annually elected. We may say he shall be displaced for neglect of duty, and point out how he shall be convicted of it; without calling upon the President or Senate.[33]

James Madison led the fight for vesting in the president total discretion to remove executive officials. He maintained that the power is implied in the Constitution and did not belong to Congress to delegate. Statutory limitations, Madison warned, would undermine presidential responsibility and destroy the unity of the executive branch. He forcefully denied that the Senate was entitled to a role in the removal process. To Madison, the Senate's participation in the appointment process represented an exception to the general rule that reserved executive responsibilities for the president. Madison drew support from the president's constitutional duty to "take Care that the Laws be faithfully executed." To fulfill that purpose, the president had to use all necessary means, including the dismissal of incompetent, corrupt, or unreliable administrators. If anything by nature is executive, Madison said, "it must be that power which is employed in superintending and seeing that the laws are faithfully executed." Others pointed out that while the Senate might be acquainted with the record of a nominee, the president was in a better position to judge the person's *performance* in office.[34]

As enacted into law, the statutes governing the executive departments indirectly treated the removal power. The chief clerk of each department would have the responsibility and custody of all records, books, and papers, "whenever the said principal officer shall be removed from office by the President of the United States." This language left unclear whether Congress had acted by declaration (delegating the power) or by implication (acknowledging that the power was inherent or implied by the Constitution).

According to Chief Justice William Howard Taft, the debates of 1789 meant there was not the "slightest doubt" that the power to remove officers appointed by the president and Senate is "vested in the President alone." [35] Taft reached too far; the debates reveal deep divisions among House members and close votes on the Senate side.[36]

Furthermore, the debate on the removal power focused on the president's power to remove the *secretary of foreign affairs*, who members conceded was an agent of the president and executive in nature. It is an error to conclude from that debate that the president's power extends to *all* administrative officials. Much depends on the nature of the office. When the First Congress considered the comptroller's office in the Treasury Department, Madison said that the office "seemed to bear a strong affinity to this branch [the legislature] of the Government." The settlement and adjustment of legal claims "partake too much of the Judicial capacity to be blended with the Executive." To Madison the office was neither executive nor judicial: "I think it rather distinct from both, though it partakes of each...." [37]

The removal power created an explosive issue for the administration of Andrew Johnson. The Tenure of Office Act in 1867 gave the Senate a role in the suspension and removal of executive officials. Johnson vetoed the bill, claiming that it violated the Constitution, but both houses quickly overrode the veto. Johnson decided to suspend Secretary of War Edwin M. Stanton, a disruptive element in his cabinet. Although the Senate refused to concur in the suspension, Johnson removed Stanton, helping set in motion Johnson's impeachment by the House of Representatives. After another executive-legislative confrontation, this time involving Grover Cleveland and the Senate during 1885 and 1886, Congress repealed the Tenure of Office Act.[38]

Congress, however, continued to place statutory limitations on the removal power. It specified causes for removal such as inefficiency, neglect of duty, and malfeasance in office. The Supreme Court has recognized that it is proper for Congress to identify the grounds for removal,[39] especially for independent regulatory commissions (see pp. 163-164). A balance must be struck between the president's removal power and Congress's power under the Necessary and Proper Clause to create an office.[40] The removal power is also limited by procedural rights (sometimes statutory, sometimes adjudicated) that are available to protect employees from arbitrary dismissals.[41]

Three decisions by the Supreme Court in the past decade have kept the boundaries of the removal power in a state of uncertainty. In 1974 the Court decided that a federal employee may be removed prior to a hearing (with recovery of pay if subsequent investigation led to reinstatement), in cases where conduct "hinders efficient operation." Yet in decisions in 1975 and 1980, the Court has used the notion of "efficiency" to *protect* officeholders who are threatened with dismissal solely because of their party affiliation or political beliefs. The Court noted that inefficiency results from the replacement of public employees every time political office changes hands.[42]

Congress is deeply engaged in the process of filling vacancies in the executive branch. Positions are found for former members of Congress and their staff assistants. In fact, Congress is often responsible for *creating* vacancies. One scholar of executive-legislative relationships has estimated that firings and reassignments of executive officials result more from congressional pressure than by presidential action.[43]

Civil Service Reforms

The civil service system, including the reforms of 1978, imposes other restrictions on the president's power to recruit and discipline federal employees. The civil service merit system rests on an elaborate set of procedures to determine the qualifications needed for entry into the federal workforce; specific safeguards are available to employees who face suspension and removal.[44]

Efforts are made periodically to increase the president's power over the civil service. A report commissioned by President Roosevelt recommended in 1937 that the Civil Service Commission be reorganized into a Civil Service Administration, led by a single executive officer. The administrator of this new agency, to be appointed by the president with the advice and consent of the Senate, would serve at the pleasure of the president and act as the president's direct adviser on all personnel matters. The Civil Service Administration was to be "a part and parcel of the Executive Office."[45]

Congress resisted this reform, fearing that presidential control over federal employees would revive political patronage on a grand scale and subvert merit standards and the principle of professionalism. The record of the Nixon administration reinforced this apprehension. The White House personnel operation sought to make the career bureaucracy "responsive" to the president's program. In 1972 the White House created a responsiveness program to improve "Departmental responsiveness in support of the President's re-election." Career employees were screened by the White House for their political philosophy and sense of loyalty to administration goals. Personnel procedures were often manipulated, with the knowledge of the Civil Service Commission, to provide preferential treatment of politically favored candidates for career appointments.[46]

The Civil Service Reform Act of 1978 replaced the Civil Service Commission with an Office of Personnel Management (OPM). Although OPM is identified in the statute as "an independent establishment in the executive branch," the director of OPM is clearly an agent of the president. The legislative history describes the OPM director as "the president's agent" and "the president's chief lieutenant." [47] Independence is suggested by two features: a four-year term for the director and deletion of the Senate's proposed requirement that the term be coterminous with that of the president.[48] However, the director serves at the pleasure of the president and is subject to presidential direction.

The statute also created a new Senior Executive Service (SES) of top-level officials who gave up job security to qualify for substantial bonuses and other benefits. They form an elite corps that can be moved from agency to agency, responding to managerial needs throughout the government. The program, off to a slow start, is still too young for one to know whether the establishment of SES will increase or decrease presidential influence. Presidential appointees can control SES officials through reassignments and pay reductions, but the use of these sanctions can be "a two-edged sword which also cuts away at the initiative and candor of career executives. It will deny to appointees of the new adminstration at crucial points in the decision-making processes substantial knowledge and insights on relevant laws, policies, and programs." [49]

The Civil Service Reform Act of 1978 created two other agencies: the Merit Systems Protection Board (MSPB) and the Federal Labor Relations Authority (FLRA), both of which are independent of the president. The members may be removed by the president only for the specific causes listed in the statute. The FLRA, which establishes policies for federal labor-management relations, may have no more than two of its three members belonging to the same political party; members may be removed only upon notice and hearing; and their terms are staggered, eventually reaching a length of five years.

The MSPB, which investigates and adjudicates federal employee grievances, has three members with no more than two belonging to the same political party. As another means of assuring independence from the president, members are given seven-year terms. Moreover, the statute directs the MSPB to submit its budget requests and legislative recommendations concurrently to the president and Congress. Within the board is a special counsel who is responsible for protecting "whistleblowers" (employees who reveal agency wrongdoing). The special counsel has some autonomy from MSPB, so much in fact that in 1980 the head of MSPB went to court charging that the special counsel had ignored a series of directives from the board. This appeared to be the first instance where one unit of a federal agency sued another unit within the same agency.[50]

Ministerial and Discretionary Duties

The heads of executive departments function only in part as political agents of the president. They also perform legal duties assigned to them by Congress. Even the departments initially labelled as "executive" in character, such as the State and War Departments, have had to serve Congress as well as the president.

This dual role surfaced in the controversy over judicial appointments, precipitating *Marbury* v. *Madison* in 1803. Just before he left office, President John Adams nominated a number of men to serve in the judiciary. The Senate gave its advice and consent, and commissions for the officers were signed by Adams. Even the seal of the United States had been affixed to the commissions to attest to their validity. But after a change in administrations, Jefferson's secretary of state, James Madison, refused to deliver some of the commissions.

Chief Justice John Marshall, writing for the Supreme Court, distinguished between two types of duties for the secretary: ministerial and discretionary. One duty (as a public ministerial officer of the United States) extended to the United States or to its citizens. Here Congress, operating through statutes, could direct the secretary to carry out certain activities. The second duty (as an executive official and adviser) was to the president alone. When the secretary of state performed as an officer of the United States, he was bound to obey the laws:

> He acts, in this respect, as has been very properly stated at the bar, under the authority of law, and not by the instructions of the President. It is a ministerial act which the law enjoins on a particular officer for a particular purpose.[51]

Although in this case Marshall did not issue a writ of mandamus (compelling Madison to deliver the commissions), Marshall's interpretation of a statute opened the door to judicial review of legislation passed by Congress.

The concept of ministerial acts reappears in the case of *Kendall* v. *United States* (1838). Amos Kendall, postmaster general in the Jackson administration, refused to pay the claim of an individual who had contracted to carry the mail and sought compensation for his services. Congress directed that the amount be paid, as did the Circuit Court of the District of Columbia. The Supreme Court affirmed that the postmaster general could not refuse a payment authorized by law. Payment of the claim constituted a "purely ministerial" act for which there could be no discretion. Neither the president nor the postmaster general possessed any authority to deny or control a ministerial act. It would be an "alarming doctrine," said the Court, that Congress could not impose upon any executive officer any duty it thinks proper, "which is not repugnant to any rights secured and protected by the constitution; and in such cases, the duty and responsibility grow out of and are subject to the control of the law, and not to the direction of the president." [52]

Reinforcing this distinction, in 1854 the attorney general stated that when laws "define what is to be done by a given head of department, and how he is to do it, there the President's discretion stops; but if the law require an executive act to be performed, without saying how or by whom, it must be for him to supply the direction...." The courts traditionally defer to the president and executive officials when an executive act demands judgment and discretion.[53]

The courts invoked the ministerial-discretionary distinction on a regular basis during the Nixon administration to force the release of impounded funds. In case after case the judiciary found that the allocation or obligation of funds constituted a ministerial action, permitting no discretion or judgment on the part of an administrator. Some decisions pointed out that discretion existed up to a certain point but no farther. For example, in 1972 Secretary of Agriculture Earl Butz declared that 15 counties in Minnesota were eligible for emergency loans. A federal judge announced that while the act of declaration was discretionary, once the secretary had designated the counties eligible for assistance it was incumbent upon his department to accept loan applications and process them.[54] At that point the statutory purpose of Congress must be carried out. Ministerial duties also apply to the president. In 1974 an appellate court held that President Nixon had violated the law by refusing to carry out a statute on federal pay.[55]

REORGANIZING THE BUREAUCRACY

After Congress creates departments and prescribes specific functions and duties for administrators, it may decide to reorganize the departments and abolish or transfer functions. Congress carried out these changes by statute until it delegated reorganization powers to the president in the 1930s.

"Economy" and "efficiency" became catchwords used by both political parties during the presidential campaign of 1932. Democrats and Republicans alike promised substantial reductions in government spending as one answer to economic depression. A majority in Congress concluded that only a grant of reorganization authority to the president could circumvent the delays created in the legislative branch by private lobbyists and agency resistance. Republican Senator David Reed of Pennsylvania voiced his disillusionment with the congressional process:

> Mr. President, I do not often envy other countries their governments, but I say that if this country ever needed a Mussolini it needs one now. I am not proposing that we make Mr. Hoover our Mussolini, I am not proposing that we should abdicate the authority that is in us, but if we are to get economies made they have to be made by some one who has the power to make the order and stand by it. Leave it to Congress and we will fiddle around here all summer trying to satisfy every lobbyist, and we will get nowhere. The country does not want that. The country wants stern action, and action quickly. . . .[56]

Hoover received statutory authority to reorganize executive departments and independent agencies, but not without raising awkward questions of executive-legislative reponsibilities. The legislation provided that the president could propose a reorganization by an executive order which either house of Congress could disapprove within a 60-day waiting period (the "legislative veto"). Hoover issued 11 executive orders in December 1932, consolidating some 58 governmental activities. By that time, however, he had been overwhelmingly defeated in the general election. It was evident that the Democratic majority in the House, in the closing hours of a lame-duck session, preferred to leave reorganization changes to his successor, Franklin D. Roosevelt. The House of Representatives disapproved all the executive orders.[57]

Before leaving office, President Hoover questioned the constitutionality of the legislative veto. He vetoed one bill that would have required the approval of the Joint Committee on Internal Revenue Taxation for any executive refunds or credits in excess of $20,000. Hoover maintained that it was unconstitutional for Congress to undertake what he considered to be executive and administrative functions.[58] To his veto message he attached an opinion by Attorney General William Mitchell, who challenged not only the tax bill but also the legislative veto procedure for executive reorganization. He did not question the power of Congress to delay execution of an adminstrative order or its power to withdraw the authority to make the order. However, the attempt to give either house, "by action which is not legislation, power to disapprove administrative acts, raises a grave question as to the validity" of the executive reorganization statute of 1932.[59]

When Congress renewed the president's reorganization authority in 1933, it expanded executive power by allowing the president for two years to abolish the "whole or any part of any executive agency and/or the functions thereof." [60] It also eliminated the legislative veto. Legislators had abandoned hope that reductions in federal spending could ever be achieved with congressional involvement. As Republican Senator Arthur Vandenberg of Michigan remarked: "let us confront the precise situation and the realities. We now face the necessity for drastic retrenchment and reorganization of the bureaus, departments, and so forth. We have just witnessed the impossibility of achieving even an incidental step in that direction by presidential order so long as Congress, with its diverse interests, retains the veto."[61]

Roosevelt made only modest use of this two-year grant of reorganization authority. But after two decisions by the Supreme Court in 1935, striking down a delegation of authority to Roosevelt, and a third decision that same year declaring invalid Roosevelt's removal of a commissioner of an independent agency, he turned to administrative reorganization. Roosevelt viewed reorganization "as a possible means of trying to integrate all of the separate independent agencies into major executive departments where they would clearly be subject to the President's administrative supervision." [62]

Roosevelt's request for reorganization authority in 1937 coincided with his attempt to increase the size of the Supreme Court, giving critics the opportunity to warn that he intended to establish a "presidential dictatorship." The Senate passed a reorganization bill in 1938, requiring Congress to disapprove a reorganization by bill or joint resolution. The Senate's action marked a victory for Roosevelt, since both forms of legislation must be presented to the president for his signature or veto. Roosevelt announced that a concurrent resolution (which passes both houses but is not presented to the president) could not be used for congressional disapproval. It was "only an expression of congressional sentiment" and could not repeal "executive action taken in pursuance of a law." [63]

This constitutional position did not have a long life. When Roosevelt realized within a few days that the House of Representatives was adamantly opposed to the requirement of a bill or joint resolution to reject reorganization proposals, he reversed his thinking. In order to attract sufficient votes in the House, he accepted a two-house veto by concurrent resolution. Some imaginative and disingenuous arguments were offered to justify this shift. Supporters explained that after the Senate's action in 1938, Roosevelt had promised to abide by the concurrent *opinion* of Congress if members objected to a reorganization proposal. What was wrong, they reasoned, with abiding by a concurrent *resolution*? Moreover, the president was now described as an "agent" of Congress, exercising legislative rather than executive powers. The legislative veto would be an instrument to announce that the president had violated his power of agency.[64]

By the time the reorganization bill passed in 1939, the White House had surrendered additional ground. The president would now act by reorganization "plan" instead of by executive order, making Roosevelt's request for authority appear less obtrusive. Part of the purpose behind this change was to divest the president's action of "an executive character for constitutional reasons; the theory was that the president submitted the plan as the agent of Congress." [65]

Congress placed other restrictions on the president. The Reorganization Act of 1939 exempted a number of independent agencies, including the Federal Communications Commission, the Federal Power Commission, the Federal Trade Commission, the Interstate Commerce Commission, the National Labor Relations Board, and the Securities and Exchange Commission.[66] Congress removed these restrictions 10 years later, allowing the president to submit reorganization plans for independent commissions as well as for executive agencies.[67] The Reorganization Act of 1977 prohibited the president from proposing to abolish or transfer an independent regulatory agency, or all the functions thereof, and it prohibited the consolidation of two or more such agencies or all the functions thereof.[68]

Some of the major agencies established by reorganization plan include the Office of Management and Budget and the Environmental Protection Agency, both created in 1970. An effort by President Kennedy in 1962 to create by reorganization plan a Department of Urban Affairs and Housing was rejected by Congress. As Presidents Nixon and Carter were later to discover, Congress strongly prefers that executive departments be created by the regular legislative process, rather than by reorganization plan. For example, the Energy Department and Education Department were created by statute during the Carter administration. Of 115 plans submitted since 1939, Congress has rejected 23 (see Table 4-1).

Earlier debates on the periodic renewal of reorganization authority were typically spirited and contentious. Two constitutional issues dominated the debates: (1) was Congress unconstitutionally delegating a legislative function to the president? and (2) could Congress disapprove a reorganization plan without presenting its action to the president for his signature or veto? Members of Congress were uncomfortable about augmenting executive authority; they shared misgivings about the loose standards that accompanied the authority; and they wondered whether the delegation was necessary in the first place.

Throughout this period, from 1932 to the 1970s, Congress debated with great intensity the question: is reorganization a legislative or an executive function?[69] In 1949, as a way of eliminating a string of

Table 4-1 Congressional Action on Reorganization Plans, 1939-1977

Reorganization Act and Extensions	Plans Submitted	Plans Rejected
1939	5	0
1945	7	3
1949	41	12
1953	12	0
1955	3	2
1957	2	1
1961	10	4
1964	5	0
1965	12	1
1969	5	0
1971	3	0
1977	10	0
Totals	115	23

SOURCE: U.S., Congress, House, Committee on Rules, *Studies on the Legislative Veto,* 96th Cong., 2d sess., February 1980, p. 245. Updated by the author.

exemptions in the reorganization act placed there to protect favored agencies, Congress switched from a two-house to a one-house legislative veto. Disapproval by a simple resolution assured members that they could protect the agencies of special interest to them.[70]

The ease with which Congress passed the Reorganization Act of 1977 stands in sharp contrast to the vigor of earlier debates. The bill was approved unanimously in the Senate and encountered only slight opposition in the House. The delegation of reorganization authority to the president rests on shaky premises borrowed from the field of public administration, especially the assumption that reorganization plans submitted by the president will reduce federal spending. The record contradicts this assumption. This grant of authority by Congress, and the motivations behind it, deserves a thorough reexamination by Congress and students of government. There are substantial, often hidden, costs to the reorganization plan process.[71]

AUTONOMY OF AGENCY PROCEEDINGS

The Constitution directs the president to "take Care that the Laws be faithfully executed." However, a long line of opinions by attorneys general have advised presidents of substantial political and legal constraints that limit their ability to intervene in departmental matters.

Even when the president has the *power* to control the decision of a departmental head, such intervention may be inexpedient and of doubtful propriety.[72] While it is theoretically correct that departmental heads shall discharge their administrative duties in such manner as the president may direct, as early as 1863 it was conceded by Attorney General Edward Bates that it is "quite impossible for the president to assume the actual direction of the multifarious business of the departments." [73]

On many occasions an attorney general has advised the president that he had no legal right to interfere with administrative decisions.[74] Congress may distribute ministerial functions of government among various bureau chiefs and executive officials, without regard to hierarchical principles of public administration. Neither the president nor any departmental head "could, by any degree of laborious industry, revise and correct all the acts of his subordinates. And if he could, as the law now stands, it would be as illegal as unwise." [75] If a president agreed to take appeals in one case and to review a subordinate's decision, "it is apparent that it would lie in every case and from all Executive Departments, and soon you would be overwhelmed with the details of administration." [76]

Attorneys general have alerted presidents to other problems. If every dissatisfied claimant had a right to appeal to the president and call upon him to revise and correct the settlement of a lower official, the president "would be constrained to abandon the greater national objects which are committed to his peculiar care, and become the accountant general of the government." [77] The president is responsible for seeing that administrative officers faithfully perform their duties, "but the statutes regulate and prescribe these duties, and he has no more power to add to, or subtract from, the duties imposed upon subordinate executive and administrative officers by the law, than those officers have to add or subtract from his duties." [78]

Departmental officers who discharge quasi-judicial functions have had an independent status from the start, whether they are comptrollers and auditors in the Treasury Department or reviewers of pensions and other claims. In a number of instances Congress lodged these responsibilities in a board operating within an executive agency but later transferred the duties to a "legislative court" (to carry out the responsibilities of Congress under Article I of the Constitution). Still later, Congress converted the legislative court to a "constitutional court," conferring on the judges the protections available under Article III of the Constitution, particularly the privilege of holding office during good behavior and receiving a compensation that may not be diminished during continuance in office. As a result of such changes, the identical function would first travel from the legislative branch to the executive branch and eventually be exercised by the judicial branch.

For example, in 1890 Congress established within the Department of Treasury a Board of General Appraisers to review the acts of appraisers of merchandise and collectors of duties. The board's decision on cases submitted to it was final and conclusive within the department, although appeals could be taken to the circuit courts. Legislation in 1926 created the United States Customs Court to supersede the board. While not changing the powers, duties, or personnel of the board, the statute did establish it as an Article I legislative court. Congress made the Customs Court a constitutional court in 1956. Legislation in 1980 replaced the Customs Court with the Court of International Trade.

A similar evolution followed the handling of claims against the United States. This function belongs "primarily to Congress as an incident of its power to pay the debts," but Congress may exercise it directly or delegate the responsibility to other agents.[80] When the burden of private bills became too great for Congress, it created a Court of Claims in 1855, calling upon it to give advisory decisions but gradually, over the years, establishing for the court a capacity to make binding judgments. Legislation in 1953 made the Court of Claims an Article III constitutional court.[81]

The tax court is another example of functions being placed initially within a department but eventually migrating to a legislative court. Legislation in 1924 created a Board of Tax Appeals. Although the secretary of the treasury was directed to furnish the board with appropriate quarters, staff, and supplies, the board was described in the statute as "an independent agency in the executive branch of the Government." Congress changed the name in 1942 to the Tax Court of the United States and converted it to a legislative court in 1969.[82]

At certain stages of an agency proceeding, intervention by Congress and the president may violate basic principles of administrative law. Particularly sensitive are adjudicatory proceedings and the activities of independent regulatory agencies (pp. 169-170). Agency employees who handle adjudicatory matters have a special right to independence with their decisions. Departmental heads recognize the limitations that prevent them from interfering with decisions by administrative law judges (ALJs).[83] Congressional interference with an adjudicatory proceeding may be of damaging character and constitute an improper intrusion. Questions by a Senate subcommittee in 1955 were so probing that Edward F. Howrey, chairman of the Federal Trade Commission, announced that he would have to disqualify himself from a pending case.[84]

Recent litigation has challenged the right of presidential advisers to contact agency officials in the rulemaking process. One case attacked ex parte (off-the-record) contacts between President Carter's Council of Economic Advisers and officials in the Department of the Interior regarding a proposed rule for strip mining. The contacts were made after the time for public comment had closed but before the rule became final. In this case, a federal judge decided it would be inappropriate for a district court to intercede in a rulemaking proceeding until it had run its course. Another case concerned Carter's legal power to intervene with the Occupational Safety and Health Administration (OSHA is part of the Labor Department) in an effort to modify the agency's proposed rule on cotton dust standards. The administration intervened because it believed that OSHA's decision might undermine the president's anti-inflation program.[86] Objections were also directed against efforts by Carter White House officials, especially from the Council on Wage and Price Stability, to review regulations being developed by the Environmental Protection Agency.[87] Final decisions have not been handed down in these cases, but they do illustrate current efforts to limit intervention by presidential aides in the rulemaking process.

These White House efforts may seem like reasonable initiatives to "coordinate" the activities of the executive branch and carry out the president's program. But ex parte contacts by presidential staffers permit them to gather information privately from the industries or from state officials and to communicate such information in closed-door sessions with agency decisionmakers, without the knowledge of other interested parties in the rulemaking process. Responding to this concern, the Justice Department argued in 1979 that there is no prohibition against communications within the executive branch after the close of the comment period on proposed rules, provided that presidential advisers do not serve as a conduit for persons outside the executive branch to have ex parte communications with agency staff.[88]

The Justice Department's guideline depends too much on self-policing and self-constraint by presidential aides who have a reputation for ignoring procedural niceties that stand in the way of White House objectives. There is a strong tradition—expressed in opinions by attorneys general, statutory language, and decisions by the federal judiciary—for agency autonomy in adjudicatory proceedings. The rulemaking process, while less formal and structured than the adjudicatory model, also must be conducted in a manner that observes standards of openness and fairness.

THE PRESIDENT'S 'INNER CIRCLE'

Fenced in by statutory restrictions and a strong tradition of agency autonomy, presidents turn increasingly to a select "inner circle" for guidance. Political appointments in the departments are made with an eye for controlling the career bureaucracy. A senior adviser in Lyndon Johnson's administration remarked that the separation of power between Congress and the president was not as great "as between a president and those people like subcabinet and bureau officials who become locked into their own special subsystems of self-interested policy concerns." [89]

The Cabinet

Presidents enter office with deep suspicions about the loyalty and motivations of civil servants. Before long they come to distrust even their own cabinet chiefs. After his reelection in 1972, President Nixon commented that "it is inevitable when an individual has been in a Cabinet position or, for that matter, holds any position in Government, after a certain length of time he becomes an advocate of the status quo; rather than running the bureaucracy, the bureaucracy runs him." [90] Carter, in the summer of 1979, asked every member of his cabinet to hand in signed letters of resignation.

In the judgment of a career executive with many years of experience in the White House, presidential aides view cabinet officials as "necessarily living somewhat inflexibly in their worlds of laws, rules, regulations and precedents, and tending to 'go by the books,' whereas in the White House view delicate circumstances often require special sensitivity in interpretation and execution." White House personnel realize that cabinet officials are exposed to substantially greater pressures and entreaties from Congress, interest groups, and independent bureaucrats. They believe that departments have a propensity to leak information that is embarrassing and sometimes politically damaging to the president. Departmental heads are seen as inadequately responsive to the needs of party or campaign officials. In addition to casting the departments in the role of antagonist or protagonist, White House staffers believe that issues of interest to the president cut across so many organizational boundaries that cabinet officials cannot be expected to present well-rounded and comprehensive reports. [91]

Frustration with departmental leaks of agency information resulted in an extraordinary effort in the Carter administration to have top officials sign affidavits saying they were not the source. According to press accounts in 1980, Secretary of State Cyrus Vance, CIA Director Stansfield Turner, and national security adviser Zbigniew Brzezinski signed the affidavits, along with other high-ranking aides. Brzezinski suspected that the State Department was leaking the material; State Department officials were convinced that most leaks came from Brzezinski's National Security Council. [92]

Cabinet officers maintain their own inventory of complaints. They object to White House aides who have the luxury to make policy but need not subject themselves to congressional inquiries. This sours the relationship between protected White House advisers and departmental officials who cannot claim immunity from legislative questions. Cabinet officers find that they have to defend policies, both before the press and the public, that they had vainly argued against within the White House. Moreover, they dismiss the White House claim of superior political judgment, pointing out that departmental employees are regularly in touch with the views of state and local officials, private organizations, local papers, and constituent pressures that are applied to members of Congress.[93]

Thomas Cronin has distinguished between two types of cabinet offices. An "inner cabinet" (state, defense, treasury, and justice) provides the president with counseling and information on broad national topics, acting closely with White House interests and objectives. An "outer cabinet" (agriculture, interior, labor, etc.) pursues a straightforward advocate course, responding to the more specialized needs of their departments.[94]

This is a useful distinction, but some qualifications are needed. The so-called clientele departments (agriculture, labor, etc.) have considerable room to maneuver in responding to White House needs and the demands of specialized interests (see pp. 191-192). Moreover, the recent experiences of Elliot Richardson (attorney general under Nixon), Michael Blumenthal (treasury secretary under Carter), and Cyrus Vance (secretary of state under Carter) provide telling evidence that even members of the inner cabinet are not always trusted by chief executives. All three left office after acrimonious disputes with the White House. In the early months of the Reagan administration, Secretary of State Alexander Haig clashed sharply with White House aides. Secretary of State William Rogers performed more as an outsider in the Nixon administration, unable to compete successfully with the resources and personality of White House adviser Henry Kissinger. President Nixon was not alone in preferring a White House-centered system to the State Department.[95]

It is also interesting that the cabinet "insiders," so closely identified with the White House, are generally excluded from political campaign activities. During hearings in 1979, Republican Senator Strom Thurmond of South Carolina discussed this issue with the nominee for attorney general, Benjamin Civiletti:

> Senator THURMOND. Three Cabinet officials I feel should be all free from political influence especially, [and] not participate in campaigns.

> Last year when I ran for reelection in the U.S. Senate a number of Cabinet officers came down and participated against me in my campaign. Which is all right if they want to do that. On the other hand, the Secretary of State did not come, and the Secretary of Defense did not come. The Attorney General did not come. And those are the three I feel should always be restrained in matters of politics. I presume you would agree with that, would you not?
>
> Mr. CIVILETTI. Yes, sir.[96]

After the Watergate revelations, followed by the resignation of Attorney General John Mitchell, legislation was introduced to make the Justice Department an independent agency and to insulate it from political pressures exerted by the White House. In a private study, a committee of attorneys concluded from their search of historical materials that most of the functions of the Justice Department were not purely and inherently executive in nature, to be placed solely under the president. Even during the early years of the presidency, when the attorney general spent more time as a counselor to the president than as the government's representative in court, "it was recognized that much of what he did had quasi-judicial characteristics. His vastly expanded powers since that time have been largely in various areas of law enforcement." The committee concluded that Congress could place these investigatory and prosecutorial powers in an independent agency while retaining the attorney general's political role as adviser to the president.[97]

President Nixon took a small step in that direction in 1973 by agreeing to establish a special prosecutor in the Justice Department to investigate crimes relating to the Watergate break-in and the 1972 presidential campaign. The Justice Department published a regulation stating that the attorney general would not

> countermand or interfere with the Special Prosecutor's decisions or actions. The Special Prosecutor will determine whether and to what extent he will inform or consult with the Attorney General about the conduct of his duties and responsibilities. The Special Prosecutor will not be removed from his duties except for extraordinary improprieties on his part.[98]

This agreement collapsed later in the year when Special Prosecutor Archibald Cox was fired after insisting that the White House make available the Watergate tapes rather than the tape summaries proposed by Nixon. Attorney General Richardson resigned and Deputy Attorney General William Ruckelshaus was fired for refusing to discharge Cox. That chore fell to Robert Bork as acting attorney general. A district court ruled that Cox had been removed in clear violation of the regulation issued by the Justice Department.[99] The abrupt departures of Cox, Richardson, and Ruckelshaus set in motion a serious effort in

Congress to impeach Nixon. The "firestorm" that followed these dismissals, together with the Supreme Court's decision in *United States* v. *Nixon* (1974) denying Nixon's claim to withhold the tapes, resulted in his release of incriminating information and led to his resignation.

The Ethics Act of 1978 established a mechanism for the court appointment of an independent special prosecutor within the Justice Department to investigate charges against the president, the vice president, and specified high-level executive branch employees—including those in the Executive Office of the President, the Justice Department, the Central Intelligence Agency, and the Commissioner of Internal Revenue. The special prosecutor has "full power and independent authority to exercise all investigative and prosecutorial functions and powers. . . ." The special prosecutor may be removed from office (other than by impeachment and conviction) only by the personal action of the attorney general and only for extraordinary impropriety, physical disability, mental incapacity, "or any other condition that substantially impairs the performance of such special prosecutor's duties." [100]

The Carter administration supported the ethics bill as a necessary step to restore the reputation of the Justice Department. The provision for a special prosecutor, however, implies that the department cannot be trusted to carry out its responsibilities. Some opponents of the bill remarked: "If an Attorney General cannot be trusted to enforce the law against the Executive, the remedy is impeachment and not the cloning of an additional Attorney General to do the job of the first." [101] The Ethics Act attempts to find a middle-level defense short of impeachment.

A special prosecutor was first appointed to investigate charges that Hamilton Jordan, Carter's chief of staff, had used cocaine. Jordan was cleared of the charge in 1980. Another special prosecutor was appointed to look into drug charges against Timothy Kraft, a Carter White House aide. Kraft too was exonerated. The length of these investigations, and the financial cost to both men in defending themselves, has resulted in criticism for this section of the Ethics Act. Moreover, Reagan's attorney general, William French Smith, expressed constitutional objections to the special prosecutor office because it lodges enforcement responsibilities in an officer who is not appointed by or accountable to the president.[102] The office also has been criticized by former Attorney General Civiletti and others for triggering major investigations on the basis of very little evidence.[103]

Executive Office of the President

Under these circumstances presidents are strongly tempted to adopt a fortress mentality, relying on immediate advisers within the

White House for loyalty, support, and understanding. The White House staff expands into a counterbureaucracy to control unruly departments and agencies.[104]

For reasons of comity between the branches, Congress has been reluctant to probe very deeply into the activities of the Executive Office of the President (EOP). An institution of modest size when created in 1939, the EOP is now staffed by almost 2,000 people. At present it consists of the White House Office, the Office of Administration, the Office of Management and Budget, the Office of Policy Development, the Central Intelligence Agency, the National Security Council, the Council of Economic Advisers, the Office of the U.S. Trade Representative, and a number of smaller units.

Science Adviser. Location within the EOP does not assure closeness to the president. For example, the White House staff has often suspected the loyalty of the president's science adviser. Following the launching of the Soviet Sputnik in 1957, President Eisenhower created the office of special assistant to the president for science and technology. After a reorganization plan in 1962, the Office of Science and Technology (OST) was established and placed within the EOP. It had an apolitical reputation in a politically charged environment, producing an "ivory tower," outsider image. The result was arms-length treatment by the White House staff. Since it had been created by reorganization plan rather than by statute, Congress was inclined to treat OST as presidential staff and showed little interest in its functions and responsibilities. OST therefore "fell between two stools and lacked a strong constituency either in the White House or in the Congress." [105]

White House antagonism toward the science unit increased after several former presidential science advisers testified against Nixon's proposal for an antiballistic missile system. Moreover, the chairman of a panel within the President's Science Advisory Committee testified and campaigned publicly against the administration's supersonic transport (SST).[106] Democratic Representative Henry Reuss of Wisconsin asked OST for a copy of a report that evaluated the SST critically, but the Nixon White House refused to release it. White House aide John Ehrlichman said OST had no control over the document because it was a presidential report that was "in the nature of inter- and intra-agency memoranda which contained opinions, conclusions and recommendations prepared for the advice of the President." [107] In amending the Freedom of Information Act (FOIA) in 1974, Congress applied its provisions to the Executive Office of the President except for the president's "immediate personal staff or units in the Executive Office whose sole function is to advise and assist the President."[108]

Two citizens went to court to compel the OST director to release the report. A district judge dismissed the complaint after maintaining that the report was a presidential document and that OST was not an "agency" for purposes of the Freedom of Information Act. Rather, it was part of the president's staff and therefore the report was protected by the doctrine of executive privilege.[109]

An appellate court reached a different conclusion. Classifying OST as an agency, it made the report an agency record available through the FOIA. The legislative history of the OST convinced the appellate court that Congress anticipated that the office would function as an entity distinct from the president's staff. A House committee had noted that, in contrast to previous science advisers to the president, the OST director would be available for questioning by congressional committees.[110]

In 1973, as a result of a reorganization plan submitted by President Nixon, OST was abolished. By returning the advisory function to the National Science Foundation, the administration was able to relieve the science adviser of responsibilities for defense and security issues. A new bureaucratic cycle began in 1976 when Congress established within the EOP an Office of Science and Technology Policy, with a number of functions including national security affairs.[111]

Budget Adviser. The custom of leaving the EOP alone was largely tolerable until a series of misadventures by the Nixon administration provoked Congress to tighten its control. Statutory restrictions in 1978 on confidential White House funds reflect this change in legislative attitudes.[112] Closer controls were also applied to the Office of Management and Budget (OMB), long considered a presidential staff agency. When Congress proposed in 1973 to subject the OMB director and deputy director to Senate confirmation, the Nixon administration insisted that Senate scrutiny of appointees should not extend to the "inner circle" of presidential advisers.[113] OMB Director Roy Ash claimed that the role of the two officers was "clearly that as agents and advisers of the President and therefore clearly inappropriate for Senate confirmation." He described OMB "as an arm—and if he wants to, a physical arm of the President, more eyes, more ears, more heads, and more arms for the President, and to in some way deprive him of their use is to deprive him of his full faculties to do that with which he is charged." [114] Congress enacted legislation in 1974 to apply the confirmation process to future OMB directors and deputy directors.[115]

In his appeal to anthropomorphism, Ash neglected to say that other presidential advisers within EOP had been subject to Senate confirmation, including the director and deputy director of the Central Intelligence Agency and the three members of the Council of Economic Advisers. As for the Budget Bureau (forerunner of OMB), it was never solely an agent of the president. In creating it in 1921, Congress imposed on the agency a duty to advise both branches. The statute directed that the bureau "shall, at the request of any committee of either House of Congress having jurisdiction over revenue or appropriations, furnish the committee such aid and information as it may request." This requirement remains part of the law today.[116] The first circular issued by the Budget Bureau described the director as "an advisor of the President and Congress in the matter of correcting business administration." [117]

Even after President Roosevelt transferred the Budget Bureau from the Treasury Department to the newly formed EOP, statutory ties to Congress remained. By 1970, when Nixon proposed abolishing the bureau and replacing it with OMB, Congress had vested in the bureau at least 58 statutory duties.[118] Sharp opposition materialized in the House to the provision in Nixon's plan that would transfer those statutory functions to the president, who could delegate them to subordinates later. Although the House Government Operations Committee opposed the OMB reorganization plan, the full House favored it by the margin of 193-164. No opposition developed in the Senate.[119]

After the massive impoundments by the Nixon administration, the Senate Government Operations Committee concluded in 1974 that OMB had developed into a "super department with enormous authority over all of the activities of the Federal Government. Its Director has become, in effect, a Deputy President who exercises vital Presidential powers." [120] In addition to the requirement of confirmation for OMB directors and deputy directors, in 1974 Congress created an Office of Federal Procurement Policy (OFPP) within OMB to serve in large part as a staff agency of Congress. The administrator is directed by statute to keep Congress and its "duly authorized committees fully and currently informed of the major activities of the Office, and to submit an annual report to both Houses, and at such other times as may be necessary for this purpose, together with appropriate legislative recommendations." [121] The comptroller general has access to all books, documents, papers, and records of the office.

The administrator of OFPP is appointed by the president, by and with the advice and consent of the Senate. After the first administrator left, Congress was able to replace him with Lester Fettig, at that time a principal staff assistant to Democratic Senator Lawton Chiles of Florida, who had sponsored the OFPP. A few years later Fettig was succeeded by Karen Williams, formerly chief counsel for the Senate Budget Committee and therefore also an assistant to Chiles, who served on that committee.

National Security Adviser. Other parts of the Executive Office of the President have come under congressional scrutiny. Bills have been introduced to make the president's national security adviser subject to Senate confirmation. The adviser serves as staff director of the National Security Council, established by statute to advise the president regarding the integration of domestic, foreign, and military policies. Although presidential advisers are traditionally immune from congressional questioning, greater congressional oversight is invited when presidential staff, including the national security adviser, assume operational responsibilities and compete with the duties of departmental and agency officials. Recent national security advisers, including Henry Kissinger and Zbigniew Brzezinski, have been especially prominent in competing with the secretary of state, producing what Democratic Senator Frank Church of Idaho has called a "mini-State Department." [122]

President Reagan's national security adviser, Richard V. Allen, was given a much lower profile. Allen does not meet alone with the president each morning, as Brzezinski did with Carter, to present a daily intelligence briefing. The briefings still take place, but with others in the room. Allen was also expected to be less visible to the press and to function more as a coordinator than a formulator of policy. Whereas Brzezinski had chaired crisis management in the Carter administration, that assignment was given to Vice President George Bush in the Reagan administration.

When presidential advisers behave as surrogates for departmental heads, it is proper for Congress to call them to account for their actions. The autonomy of White House staff is relative, not absolute. Violations of trust, misapplication of funds, obstruction of legislative programs, and interference with departmental assignments are some of the actions that encourage Congress to circumscribe White House operations.

CONCLUSIONS

Presidents complain about the fragmented nature of the executive branch, which makes it next to impossible for them to carry out a coherent, effective program. The fragmentation is partly their own making. Often they prefer to set up organizational entities outside the regular departments. The Energy Stabilization Corporation, sponsored by President Carter, is a recent example. Even when agencies are located within the regular departments, they may be relatively immune to White House pressures because of adjudicatory functions or political independence. As Harold Seidman has noted, organizations such as the Federal Highway Administration, Army Corps of Engineers, Public Health Service, National Park Service, and Forest Service "constitute the departmental power centers and are quite capable of making it on their own without secretarial help, except when challenged by strong hostile external forces. Often they can do more for the secretary than he can do for them." [123]

Both branches have powerful arguments underlying their efforts to control the bureaucracy. The framers established a single executive for the purpose of assuring responsibility and accountability. They specifically vested in him the duty to take care that the laws be faithfully executed. But these laws often place administrative duties outside the president's immediate control, reflecting not merely a congressional preference but, in the opinion of attorneys general, an appropriate and expedient course of action.

Many of these administrative duties placed outside the president's control are routine ministerial or adjudicatory decisions, concerned with claims, pensions, and other entitlements. But often whole agencies within an executive department are so independent, because of their institutional history and culture, that they can function with a high degree of autonomy from the president and departmental heads. The erosion of presidential control has continued with the application of statutory restrictions to staff within the Executive Office of the President, but the diffusion of executive power is especially conspicuous with the creation of independent regulatory commissions that represent a mix of legislative, executive, and judicial functions.

NOTES

1. David B. Truman, *The Governmental Process* (New York: Alfred A. Knopf, 1964), p. 401.
2. John C. Fitzpatrick, ed., *Writings of Washington,* 39 vols. (Washington, D.C.: Government Printing Office, 1931-1944), 30:334.
3. William Maclay, *Sketches of Debate in the First Senate of the United States, 1789-91* (Harrisburg, Pa.: Lane S. Hart, 1880), p. 107.
4. U.S., Congress, *Annals of Congress,* 1st Cong., May 19, 1789, p. 383.
5. Fisher, *President and Congress* (New York: Free Press, 1972), pp. 14, 16, 275-276.
6. *Annals of Congress,* 1st Cong., May 20, 1789, pp. 384-396.
7. Ibid., p. 392.
8. Ibid., June 17, 1789, p. 512.
9. 1 Stat. 28-29, 49-50.
10. 1 Stat. 65-67.
11. Maclay, *Sketches of Debate in the First Senate,* p. 376.
12. James D. Richardson, ed., *A Compilation of the Messages and Papers of the Presidents,* 20 vols. (New York: Bureau of National Literature, 1897-1925), 3:1288-1312; U.S., Congress, *Register of Debates,* 24th Cong., 2d sess., 1837, pp. 379-418, 427-506; U.S., Congress, *Senate Journal,* 24th Cong., 2d sess., April 15, 1837, pp. 123-124.
13. 42 Stat. 24, sec. 304 (1921).

14. Fisher, *Presidential Spending Power* (Princeton: Princeton University Press, 1975), pp. 41-42.
15. 31 U.S.C. 65(d) (1976).
16. United States ex rel. Brookfield Const. Co., Inc. v. Stewart, 234 F.Supp. 94, 99-100 (D.D.C. 1964), affirmed, 339 F.2d 754 (D.C. Cir. 1964). See also Staats v. Lynn (D.D.C. Civil Action No. 75-0551), "Opposition of Plaintiff to Defendants' Motion to Dismiss," July 28, 1975, pp. 18-48.
17. 1 Stat. 70 (1789).
18. Leonard D. White, *The Federalists* (New York: Macmillan, 1948), pp. 77-78; Henry Barrett Learned, *The President's Cabinet* (New Haven: Yale University Press, 1912), pp. 232-235.
19. 1 Stat. 232-234 (1792).
20. White, *The Federalists,* pp. 226-227. The basic provisions of the statute of 1792 were repeated in 1794; 1 Stat. 354-366.
21. 5 Stat. 80, sec. 1-2 (1836); Learned, *The President's Cabinet,* pp. 220, 244-252. See also Gerald Cullinan, *The United States Postal Service* (New York: Praeger Publishers, 1973), pp. 48-64.
22. Humphrey's Executor v. United States, 295 U.S. 602, 627 (1935).
23. 84 Stat. 720, sec. 201 (1970); 39 U.S.C. 201 (1976).
24. U.S., Congress, Senate, Committee on the Judiciary, *Report on the Regulatory Agencies to the President-Elect,* 86th Cong., 2d sess., 1960, p. 66.
25. W. Michael Blumenthal, "Reflections of a Businessman in Washington," *Fortune* (January 29, 1979).
26. Fisher, *The Constitution Between Friends: Congress, the President, and the Law* (New York: St. Martin's Press, 1978), pp. 111-114, 117-124.
27. G. Calvin MacKenzie, *The Politics of Presidential Appointments* (New York: Free Press, 1981), p. xx.
28. Ibid., p. 177.
29. William W. Van Alstyne, "The Role of Congress in Determining Incidental Powers of the President and of the Federal Courts: A Comment on the Horizontal Effect of the Sweeping Clause," *Law and Contemporary Problems* 40 (1976):102.
30. United States v. Ferreira, 54 U.S. 39, 50-51 (1852).
31. 88 Stat. 1390, sec. 5 (1974); *Public Papers of the Presidents,* 1974, p. 189; 92 Stat. 865, sec. (6) (1978); U.S., Congress, Senate, S. Rept. 850, 95th Cong., 2d sess., 1978, p. 28.
32. Buckley v. Valeo, 424 U.S. 1, 134-143 (1976). See Buckley v. Valeo, 519 F.2d 821, 890-892 (D.C. Cir. 1975); Note, "Congressional Power Under the Appointments Clause After Buckley v. Valeo," *Michigan Law Review* 75 (1977):627.
33. *Annals of Congress,* 1st Cong., June 17, 1789, p. 492.
34. Ibid., pp. 496, 500, 534 (Representative Goodhue).
35. Myers v. United States, 272 U.S. 52, 114 (1926).
36. Fisher, *The Constitution Between Friends,* pp. 51-56.
37. *Annals of Congress,* 1st Cong., June 29, 1789, pp. 613, 614.
38. Fisher, *The Constitution Between Friends,* pp. 58-60; Louis Fisher, "Grover Cleveland Against the Senate," *Congressional Studies* 7 (1979):11.
39. Shurtleff v. United States, 189 U.S. 311 (1903), recognized the potential that Congress has to restrict the president's removal power to specified causes. See also the dissenting opinions by Justices McReynolds and Brandeis in Myers v. United States, 272 U.S. 52, 181-182, 262-264.

40. Edward S. Corwin, *The President's Removal Power Under the Constitution* (New York: National Municipal League, 1927).
41. For example, see 37 Stat. 555, sec. 6 (1912), codified at 5 U.S.C. 7501 (1976). The courts frequently have overturned the removal of federal employees who lacked elementary procedures to challenge assertions that they were disloyal. See Peters v. Hobby, 349 U.S. 331 (1955); Cole v. Young, 351 U.S. 536 (1956); Service v. Dulles, 354 U.S. 363 (1957); Vitarelli v. Seaton, 359 U.S. 535 (1959); Greene v. McElroy, 360 U.S. 474 (1959); and Cafeteria Workers v. McElroy, 367 U.S. 886 (1961).
42. Arnett v. Kennedy, 416 U.S. 134, 168 (1974); Elrod v. Burns, 427 U.S. 347, 364, 372 (1975); Branti v. Finkel (March 31, 1980).
43. Harold Seidman, *Politics, Position, and Power* (New York: Oxford University Press, 1980), p. 54.
44. 64 Stat. 476 (1950), as modified by 80 Stat. 529 (1966) and codified at 5 U.S.C. 7532 (1976); 37 Stat. 555, sec. 6 (1912), as amended by 62 Stat. 354 (1948) and codified at 5 U.S.C. 7501 (1976).
45. The President's Committee on Administrative Management, *Administrative Management in the Government of the United States* (Washington, D.C.: Government Printing Office, 1937), pp. 5-6, 10; see also pp. 7-11.
46. U.S., Congress, House, Committee on Post Office and Civil Service, *Final Report on Violations and Abuses of Merit Principles in Federal Employment,* Committee Print 94-28, 94th Cong., 2d sess., December 30, 1976.
47. U.S., Congress, House, H. Rept. 95-1403, 95th Cong., 2d sess., 1978, p. 6; Senate, S. Rept. 95-969, 95th Cong., 2d sess., 1978, p. 5.
48. U.S., Congress, S. Rept. 95-1272, 95th Cong., 2d sess., 1978, p. 132.
49. Bernard Rosen, "Uncertainty in the Senior Service," *Public Administration Review* 41 (March/April 1981):203, 204.
50. "MSPB Carries Special Counsel Battle to Court," *Federal Times,* December 8, 1980, p. 1. See also statements by Representative Patricia Schroeder, D-Colo., in U.S., Congress, *Congressional Record* (daily ed.), 96th Cong., 2d sess., December 12, 1980, 126:H12388-12389, and December 13, 1980, pp. H12421-12422.
51. 5 U.S. 137, 157, 162.
52. 37 U.S. 522, 610, 613. For other ministerial duties directed by the courts, see United States v. Schurz, 102 U.S. 378 (1880); United States v. Price, 116 U.S. 43 (1885); United States v. Louisville, 169 U.S. 249 (1898); and Clackamus County, Ore. v. McKay, 219 F.2d 479, 496 (D.C. Cir. 1954), vacated as moot, 349 U.S. 909 (1955).
53. 6 Op. Att'y Gen. 326, 341 (1854). See also Decatur v. Paulding, 39 U.S. 497, 516 (1840); Reeside v. Walker, 52 U.S. 272, 290 (1850); United States v. Guthrie, 58 U.S. 284 (1854); and Panama Canal Co. v. Grace Line Inc., 356 U.S. 309, 317-318 (1958).
54. Berends v. Butz, 357 F.Supp. 143, 151 (D. Minn. 1973). See also Bruce Ledewitz, "The Uncertain Power of the President to Execute the Laws," *Tennessee Law Review* 46 (1979):757, 787-793.
55. National Treasury Employees Union v. Nixon, 492 F.2d 587 (D.C. Cir. 1974).
56. *Congressional Record,* 72d Cong., 1st sess., May 5, 1932, 75:9644.
57. 47 Stat. 413-415 (1932). On Hoover's orders, see *Congressional Record,* 72nd Cong., 2d sess., December 9, 1932, 76:233-254. On the House disapproval, see pp. 2125-2126.
58. Ibid., January 24, 1933, 76:2445-2446.

59. 37 Op. Att'y Gen. 63-64 (1933).
60. 47 Stat. 1518, sec. 403(c) (1933).
61. *Congressional Record,* 72d Cong., 2d sess., January 26, 1933, 76:2587.
62. A. J. Wann, *The President as Chief Administrator* (Washington, D.C.: Public Affairs Press, 1968), p. 74.
63. *Congressional Record,* 75th Cong., 3d sess., March 31, 1938, 83:4487.
64. For statement of Representative Knifflin, see ibid., p. 5004; see also statement by Representative Dies, pp. 4602-4603.
65. Louis Brownlow, "Reconversion of the Federal Administrative Machinery from War to Peace," *Public Administration Review* 4 (1944):309, 322.
66. 53 Stat. 561 (1939).
67. 63 Stat. 203 (1949).
68. 91 Stat. 31, sec. 905 (1977).
69. Louis Fisher and Ronald C. Moe, "Delegating with Ambivalence: The Legislative Veto and Reorganization Authority," in U.S., Congress, House, Committee on Rules, *Studies on the Legislative Veto,* 96th Cong., 2d sess., February 1980, pp. 164-247.
70. U.S., Congress, Senate, S. Rept. 232, 81st Cong., 1st sess., 1949, p. 15; *Congressional Record,* 81st Cong., 1st sess., 1949, 95:6227.
71. Louis Fisher and Ronald C. Moe, "Presidential Reorganization Authority: Is it Worth the Cost?" *Political Science Quarterly* (Summer 1981).
72. 10 Op. Att'y Gen. 526 (1863).
73. Id. at 527-528.
74. 1 Op. Att'y Gen. 624 (1823); 1 Op. Att'y Gen. 636 (1824); 1 Op. Att'y Gen. 678 (1824); 1 Op. Att'y Gen. 705 (1825); 1 Op. Att'y Gen. 706 (1825); 2 Op. Att'y Gen. 480 (1831); 2 Op. Att'y Gen. 507 (1832); 2 Op. Att'y Gen. 544 (1832); 4 Op. Att'y Gen. 515 (1846); 5 Op. Att'y Gen. 287 (1851); 11 Op. Att'y Gen. 14 (1864); and 13 Op. Att'y Gen. 28 (1869).
75. 11 Op. Att'y Gen. 14, 15 (1864).
76. 18 Op. Att'y Gen. 31, 32 (1884).
77. 1 Op. Att'y Gen. 624, 629 (1823).
78. 19 Op. Att'y Gen. 685, 686-687 (1890).
79. 26 Stat. 131, 136-138, sec. 12-15 (1890); 44 Stat. 669 (1926); 70 Stat. 532 (1956); P.L. 96-417 (1980).
80. Ex Parte Bakelite Corp., 279 U.S. 438, 452 (1929).
81. 10 Stat. 612 (1855); 12 Stat. 765 (1863); 14 Stat. 9 (1866); 22 Stat. 485 (1883); 23 Stat. 283 (1885); 24 Stat. 505 (1887); 67 Stat. 226 (1953).
82. 43 Stat. 336-338 (1924); 56 Stat. 957 (1942); and 83 Stat. 730 (1969).
83. Nash v. Califano, 613 F.2d 10 (2d Cir. 1980).
84. Pillsbury Company v. FTC, 354 F.2d 952, 954-956, 963-964 (5th Cir. 1966). On also limiting Congress in its contacts with executive officials, see D.C. Federation of Civic Associations v. Volpe, 459 F.2d 1231, 1245-1248 (D.C. Cir. 1971), certiorari denied, 405 U.S. 1030 (1971).
85. Natural Resources Defense Council v. Schultze (D.D.C. No. 79-153, January 26, 1979), *Environmental Law Reporter* 9 (1979):20124. An earlier challenge to communications from the White House to the National Highway Safety Administration was also dismissed because an administrative proceeding was still in progress; Nader v. Volpe, 466 F.2d 261 (D.C. Cir. 1972).
86. AFL-CIO v. Marshall, No. 78-1662 (D.C. Cir. 1979).
87. Paul R. Verkuil, "Jawboning Administrative Agencies: Ex Parte Contacts by the White House," *Columbia Law Review* 80 (1980):943; U.S., Congress,

Senate, Committee on Environment and Public Works, *Executive Branch Review of Environmental Regulations* (hearings), 96th Cong., 1st sess., 1979, pp. 191-230; *Legal Times of Washington,* January 29, 1979, p. 34.
88. *Legal Times of Washington,* January 29, 1979, p. 32.
89. Adviser is quoted in Thomas E. Cronin, *The State of the Presidency* (Boston: Little, Brown & Co., 1980), p. 232.
90. *Public Papers of the Presidents,* 1972, p. 1150.
91. Bradley H. Patterson, Jr., *The President's Cabinet: Issues and Questions* (Washington, D.C.: American Society for Public Administration, 1976), pp. 52-67.
92. "Carter Given Oaths on 'Leaks,'" *Washington Post,* July 16, 1980, p. A1.
93. Patterson, *The President's Cabinet,* pp. 70-72.
94. Cronin, *The State of the Presidency,* pp. 276-286.
95. I. M. Destler, *Presidents, Bureaucrats, and Foreign Policy* (Princeton: Princeton University Press, 1972); Graham Allison and Peter Szanton, *Remaking Foreign Policy: The Organizational Connection* (New York: Basic Books, 1976), pp. 120-140.
96. U.S., Congress, Senate, Committee on the Judiciary, *Confirmation Hearings on Benjamin R. Civiletti, Nominee, Attorney General,* 96th Cong., 1st sess., 1979, p. 16.
97. *The Record,* Association of the Bar of the City of New York, No. 5-6, 29 (1974):492. See also U.S., Congress, Senate, Committee on the Judiciary, *Removing Politics from the Administration of Justice* (hearings), 93d Cong., 2d sess., 1974.
98. *Federal Register* 38 (1973):14688.
99. Nader v. Bork, 366 F.Supp. 104 (D.D.C. 1973).
100. P.L. 95-251, 92 Stat. 1869, sec. 594, 596 (1978).
101. U.S., Congress, House, H. Rept. 1307, 95th Cong., 2d sess., 1978, p. 22.
102. "Attorney General Questions Prosecutor Law," *Washington Post,* April 21, 1981, p. A3; "Attorney General Urges Repeal of Prosecutor Act," ibid., May 22, 1981, p. A4.
103. "Special Prosecutor Investigations Called 'Enormous Waste,'" *Washington Post,* May 21, 1981, p. A20.
104. Richard P. Nathan, *The Plot That Failed: Nixon and the Administrative Presidency* (New York: John Wiley & Sons, 1975).
105. David Z. Beckler, "The Precarious Life of Science in the White House," *Daedalus* (Spring 1974):121.
106. Ibid., p. 124.
107. Soucie v. David, 448 F.2d 1067, 1070 (D.D.C. 1971).
108. U.S., Congress, House, H. Rept. 1380, 93d Cong., 2d sess., 1974, p. 15. See also Sierra Club v. Andrus, 581 F.2d 895, 901-902 (D.C. Cir. 1978).
109. Soucie v. David, 448 F.2d 1067, 1071 (D.D.C. 1971).
110. Id. at 1074-1075.
111. P.L. 94-282, 90 Stat. 459 (1976). See Edward J. Burger, Jr., *Science at the White House: A Political Liability* (Baltimore: Johns Hopkins University Press, 1980).
112. Louis Fisher, "Confidential Spending and Governmental Accountability," *George Washington Law Review* 47 (1979):347, 373-382.
113. U.S., Congress, House, Committee on Government Operations, *Confirmation of the Director and Deputy Director of the Office of Management and Budget* (hearings), 93d Cong., 1st sess., 1973, p. 164.
114. Ibid., pp. 51, 53.

115. P.L. 93-250, 88 Stat. 11 (1974).
116. 42 Stat. 23, sec. 212 (1921); 31 U.S.C. 20 (1976).
117. Bureau of the Budget, Circular No. 1, June 29, 1921, paragraph 2.
118. U.S., Congress, House, H. Rept. 1066, 91st Cong., 2d sess., 1970, p. 6.
119. Fisher, *Presidential Spending Power,* pp. 46-51.
120. U.S., Congress, Senate, S. Rept. 7, 93d Cong., 1st sess., 1973, p. 3.
121. 88 Stat. 798, sec. 8(a) (1974).
122. U.S., Congress, Senate, Committee on Foreign Relations, *The National Security Adviser: Role and Accountability* (hearings), 96th Cong., 2d sess., 1980. See "Beyond the Vance-Brzezinski Clash Lurks an NSC Under Fire," *National Journal,* May 17, 1980, p. 814. For criticism of the national security adviser, see articles by I. M. Destler, "A Job That Doesn't Work," *Foreign Policy* 38 (1980):80, and "Can One Man Do?" *Foreign Policy* 5 (1971-1972):28.
123. Seidman, *Politics, Position, and Power,* p. 135.

5

The Independent Regulatory Commission: Mahomet's Coffin

The independent regulatory commission departs from the conventional administrative model in two ways. It is isolated from the operations of the executive branch, and responsibility falls on a group of administrators with essentially equal power instead of on a single executive. This independent status provoked Professor Corwin to ask, if a commissioner is not in the executive department "where is he? In the legislative department; or is he, forsooth, in the uncomfortable halfway situation of Mahomet's coffin, suspended 'twixt Heaven and Earth?" [1]

The Interstate Commerce Commission (ICC), created by Congress in 1887, is the forerunner and prototype of the independent regulatory commission. Congress modeled the ICC after railroad commissions that had been operating in more than 20 states. It was widely believed that commissions could accumulate more easily than legislators the expert knowledge needed to effectively supervise and control the railroad corporations. With the railroad industry changing rapidly, the commission form seemed a more flexible instrument for regulation than the enactment of fixed statutes. Initially the state railroad commissions were fact-finding and advisory bodies, established as agents of the legislatures. In no sense were they part of the governor or executive branch. Gradually the commissions assumed the character of permanent bodies, discharging duties that might have been entrusted to executive departments.[2]

After the financial panics of 1873 and 1885, many of the small railroad lines went bankrupt. As the lines consolidated they formed interstate, not intrastate, systems. The responsibility for regulation shifted to the national government. The Interstate Commerce Act of 1887, which created the ICC, prohibited railroad practices such as rate discrimination, rebating, pooling, and the charging of unjust and unreasonable rates. Although the ICC had no power to fix railroad rates, it could issue orders against the rates set by railroads and enforce its orders in the courts.

Congress debated two approaches to regulation: allowing the Department of Justice to enforce a specific railroad policy enunciated by Congress or creating a commission to carry out a more general charter. Congress favored the latter approach because it would:

—provide flexible and expert administration of the railroad industry;
—serve as an expert body to aid Congress in formulating a railroad policy;
—protect the public and small shippers against the legal talents of the railroad corporations;
—serve as an arbiter for conflicting interests among the railroads;
—provide valuable expert opinion to the courts; and
—build on the successful model of state commissions.

These arguments prevailed over objections that the commission's "flexibility" would actually dilute the force of statutory policy and that the commission would be powerless to withstand the expertise and political influence of the railroads.[3]

The ICC was followed by the creation of other independent regulatory commissions: the Federal Reserve System (the "Fed") in 1913, the Federal Trade Commission (FTC) in 1914, and the Federal Power Commission (FPC) in 1920. Five other bodies appeared in the 1930s: the Securities and Exchange Commission (SEC), the Federal Communications Commission (FCC), the Civil Aeronautics Board (CAB), the National Labor Relations Board (NLRB), and the Federal Maritime Commission (FMC), although the latter had antecedents dating back several decades. More recent additions include the Consumer Product Safety Commission (CPSC) and the Commodity Futures Trading Commission (CFTC); the latter performs functions previously placed in the Department of Agriculture. The Federal Energy Regulatory Commission (FERC), established in 1977, is successor to the Federal Power Commission. The Nuclear Regulatory Commission (NRC), created in 1974, inherited some of the functions of the now defunct Atomic Energy Commission (see Table 5-1).

CONFLICTING ASSESSMENTS

Ever since their creation, independent regulatory commissions have inspired contradictory evaluations. One of the harshest indictments came from the Brownlow Committee in 1937, which excoriated the commissions as "a headless 'fourth branch' of the Government, a haphazard deposit of irresponsible agencies and uncoordinated powers." According to the committee, the independent agencies violated the "basic theory of the American Constitution that there should be three major branches of the Government and only three." [4]

Far more tolerant was a study by an equally distinguished group, a task force of the 1949 Hoover Commission. It described the independent regulatory commission as a "useful and desirable agency where constant adaptation to changing conditions and delegation of wide discretion in administration are essential to effective regulation." The independent commission provided a means of "insulating regulation from partisan

Table 5-1 Independent Regulatory Commissions*

Agency	*Year Established*
Interstate Commerce Commission	1887
Board of Governors of the Federal Reserve System	1913
Federal Trade Commission	1914
Federal Communications Commission	1934
Securities and Exchange Commission	1934
National Labor Relations Board	1935
Federal Maritime Commission	1936
Civil Aeronautics Board	1938
Board of Governors of the U.S. Postal Service	1970
Consumer Product Safety Commission	1972
Nuclear Regulatory Commission[1]	1974
Commodity Futures Trading Commission	1975
Federal Energy Regulatory Commission[2]	1977

* This table includes only the major independent regulatory commissions. The list could be extended to include the Equal Employment Opportunity Commission, Federal Deposit Insurance Corporation, Federal Home Loan Bank Board, and Occupational Safety and Health Review Commission. Other regulatory bodies are generally considered within the executive branch, such as the Environmental Protection Agency.

[1] Inherited some of the functions of the Atomic Energy Commission, created in 1946.

[2] Successor to the Federal Power Commission, established in 1920.

influence or favoritism, for obtaining deliberation, expertness and continuity of attention, and for combining adaptability of regulation with consistency of policy so far as practical." The task force found that the potential for conflict and inadequate coordination between the commissions and other executive agencies, although a theoretical possibility, had been "limited in extent and generally avoided by cooperation."[5]

These two studies appear to be discussing entirely unrelated organizations. In fact, they focus on different aspects of the same phenomenon, much as two observers might describe a glass as half-full or half-empty. The Brownlow Committee, preoccupied with the *theory and structure* of government, found the commissions repugnant because they did not fit within one of the three branches. The task force of the Hoover Commission concentrated on *functions and administrative experience*. After studying the operations of nine commissions and boards, the task force identified these advantages of the independent commission:

1. *Resistance to pressures.* The extensive powers given to regulatory agencies and the administrative flexibility required for their effective use obviously open the door to favoritism, unfairness, political influence, and even corruption. The independent commission, with its multiple membership, shared responsibility, and security of tenure, is in a favorable position to resist partisan control and to expose pressures and improper actions.

2. *Collective policy formation.* The commission, by requiring collective policymaking and decision, provides a barrier to arbitrary or capricious action and secures decisions based on different points of view and experience. This process has definite advantages where the problems are complex, the relative weight of various factors affecting policy not clear, and the range of choice wide.

3. *Expertness.* Regulated industries are complex and highly technical. Their problems need constant study and continuous attention. While expertness must be supplied in large part by the staff, the commission form is designed to assure expertness or at least familiarity with the problems of the regulated field on the part of the commissioners, who have fixed terms and a good chance of reappointment. Devoting full time to the particular industry, the commissioners become fully familiar with the technical aspects of the industry and its basic problems through day-to-day contacts.

4. *Continuity of policy.* In order to enable private industry to plan ahead, the regulatory agency must seek to achieve as much stability in policy and methods as is consistent with continuous adaptation of regulation to meet changing conditions.[6]

The commissions, as administrative bodies established to carry out a number of judicial duties, required a hybrid form. Adjudicatory decisions are typically made independent from Congress and the White

House. The judicial function also explains why commissions are multi-member (or "collegial") bodies, instead of being headed by a single administrator: "just as we want appellate courts to be made up of plural members, to protect against the idiosyncracies of a single individual, we want agencies that exercise judicial power to be collegial." [7]

Much of the criticism directed at independent commissions is rooted in fundamental misconceptions. Commissions are routinely attacked for being unresponsive to popular pressures, but they were made independent precisely to avoid abrupt policy swings that might otherwise occur from one election to another. It is inconsistent—indeed inconceivable—to expect a commission to be both independent and politically responsive. Moreover, for agencies that decide judicial questions such as licensing and ratemaking, independence from political pressures is entirely compatible with the standards and values we expect for the courts. We do not want commissions to accommodate each political whim and inclination.

Critics argue that the independent commissions have been "captured" by the industries they are charged to regulate. The capture theory does not blend well with the chorus of protests from the regulated community. Agriculture, business, and labor are not monoliths capable of controlling a commission. Truckers and railroads are at cross-purposes in their pleadings before the ICC. The American Telegraph and Telephone Company and smaller segments of the communications industry compete for FCC's favors. Local broadcast stations appeal to the FCC to limit the growth of cable television. Other commissions are faced with similar dissension. The ferocity of this conflict ("cutthroat competition") in the latter half of the nineteenth century created the demand for government regulation in the first place. The private sector tried free enterprise and found the risk and pain unbearable.[8]

Commissions are not created as independent bodies simply because they perform "regulatory" functions. A large number of executive agencies carry out regulatory duties. Consumer protection, for example, is a responsibility not only of the FTC but also of the Food and Drug Administration (located within the Department of Health and Human Services). Antitrust actions are pursued by the FTC as well as by the Department of Justice. The Agricultural Marketing Service, operating within the Agriculture Department, regulates practices in livestock and processed meat markets.[9]

Nor are commissions independent solely because their tasks are complex and technical, requiring expertise and professionalism. Tax and housing issues, exceedingly complex and technical, are left to the Treasury Department and Housing and Urban Development Department in the executive branch.

Independent commissions grow more as a function of happenstance than of logic. Many of the commissions began as part of an executive department, or were closely associated with a department, and only later gained autonomy. The key appears to be shifting statutory sentiment, not constitutional doctrine. For example, when the ICC was established in 1887 it had various ties to the secretary of the interior. The commission could employ and fix the compensation of employees, subject to the approval of the secretary, and expenditures were approved by the chairman of the commission and the secretary of the interior. The commission also reported to the secretary each year. Those ties were severed two years later.[10] The "arm of Congress" concept did not surface until much later, after the ICC had been strengthened by the Hepburn Act of 1906 and the Mann-Elkins Act of 1910.[11]

The Federal Reserve Board was originally composed of seven members, including the secretary of the treasury and the comptroller of the currency as ex officio members. Legislation in 1935 terminated their membership on the board, while the "Accord of 1951" helped free the board from Treasury Department policy demands. When the Department of Commerce and Labor was established in 1903, Congress created within it the Bureau of Corporations to investigate business practices in interstate and foreign commerce. The bureau was abolished in 1914, at which point all pending investigations and proceedings were transferred to the newly created FTC.

Other independent commissions had their start within the executive branch. As established in 1920, the Federal Power Commission (FPC) was composed of the secretary of war, the secretary of the interior, and the secretary of agriculture. The president named the chairman of the commission. A decade later the FPC acquired its independent status. A reorganization act in 1930 changed the FPC to consist of five commissioners with staggered terms. After the original term of the commissioner designated as chairman by the president had expired, future chairmen were to be elected by the commission itself. In 1977 the FPC was renamed the Federal Energy Regulatory Commission (FERC) and located within the newly created Department of Energy. However, FERC retained its status as an independent regulatory organization.

TECHNIQUES OF EXECUTIVE-LEGISLATIVE CONTROL

The "independence" of regulatory commissions is secured by three principal devices: (1) the terms of commissioners are staggered to insulate them from presidential transitions; (2) the president's power to remove commissioners is limited by specific statutory grounds; and (3) restrictions are placed on the number of commissioners who may belong to the same political party. This third restriction may be neutralized to some degree by selecting nominal members of a political party or members who identify their political affiliation as independent.

Regulatory commissions are subject to the control of Congress, the president, and the courts. They have been aptly described as "stepchildren whose custody is contested by both Congress and the executive, but without very much affection from either one." [12] The struggle for influence has been largely defensive, "with each elected branch seeking to prevent the other from exercising active control, but with neither consistently wanting to do so itself." [13]

Congress and the president have at their disposal a number of techniques for controlling the independent commissions. Congress creates the commissions, defines their duties, specifies qualifications for commissioners, votes on appropriations, and exercises the legislative veto in some cases. While presidents designate the chairmen of the commissions, statutory restrictions have severely limited their power to remove commissioners. The president relies on the executive establishment, especially the Justice Department and the Office of Management and Budget, to control the commissions' litigation, review their budget requests and legislative recommendations, and monitor the commissions' requests for information from the business community. The appointment of commissioners is formally shared by the president and the Senate, and yet members of Congress have had impressive influence in designating their own staff to be commissioners.

The Creative Act

Independent commissions are creatures of Congress. Called into existence by statute, they may be modified, circumscribed, or abolished by statute. Congress controls their jurisdiction, purpose, structure, and funding. The standards established by Congress to guide commissions are characteristically more vague than for the executive agencies. The judiciary has been satisfied by general guidelines such as "public convenience, interest, or necessity" for the FCC, "unfair methods of competition" for the FTC, and "public interest" for the ICC.[14]

The Federal Reserve System is often regarded as the very model of independence, autonomous from congressional as well as presidential interference. But the Fed is not legally independent, for this would represent not a delegation but a clear abdication of legislative power. At the time of William McChesney Martin's nomination as chairman of the Fed, Democratic Senator Paul Douglas of Illinois lured the nominee into this dialogue:

Senator DOUGLAS: Let me turn to a general question. Do you regard the Federal Reserve Board as the agent of the Executive or the agent of Congress?

Mr. MARTIN: I regard it as an independent agency of the government.

Senator DOUGLAS: To whom is it responsible? To the executive or the Congress?

Mr. MARTIN: It is responsible to Congress. I will give you my concept as I see it.

Senator DOUGLAS: If you will just say that you regard it as responsible to Congress, that is all I want. . . .

* * * * *

Senator DOUGLAS: Mr. Martin, I have had typed out this little sentence which is a quotation from you: "The Federal Reserve is an agency of the Congress." I will furnish you with scotch tape and ask you to place it on your mirror where you can see it as you shave each morning, so that it may remind you.

Mr. Martin: I will be glad to comply.[15]

Congress has not sustained its interest in monetary policy, although the mere threat of statutory action and the uncertainty about what Congress might do has occasionally caused the Fed to adjust its policy. When Arthur Burns served as Fed chairman during the Nixon administration, he expended considerable time and energy in lobbying Congress—meeting with members for breakfast and testifying before committees.[16] As a result of a concurrent resolution passed in 1975, followed by statutes in 1977 and 1978, the Fed now meets with the House and Senate banking committees twice a year to discuss monetary targets. Members of the Reagan administration announced that they would feel free to advise the Fed on appropriate policies. As a top official in the Treasury Department remarked in 1981: "I think the Federal Reserve has long felt free to advise the administration on what they thought was appropriate fiscal policy. . . . I think the major difference is that we're going to feel free to advise them on what we think is an appropriate monetary policy. . . ." [17]

Although Congress generally treats the regulatory commissions as legislative agents, it has given the president and departmental heads certain responsibilities. In the case of the Civil Aeronautics Board (CAB) and decisions involving overseas or foreign air transportation, Congress inverted the administrative process by subjecting the agency to the president: "Instead of acting independently of executive control, the agency is then subordinated to it. Instead of its order serving as a final disposition of the application, its force is exhausted when it serves as a recommendation to the president." [18]

Appointing Commissioners

Through their power to nominate commissioners, presidents are able to alter the composition and orientation of independent agencies. Within a matter of a couple of years, and in some cases a few months, presidents have used their appointment power to create majorities of their own choosing. By the time of Nixon's resignation in 1974, after five-and-a-half years in office, he had nominated *every* commissioner of these agencies: CAB (5 commissioners), FCC (7), FMC (5), FPC (5), NLRB (5), SEC (5), and CPSC (5).[19]

The opportunity to select commissioners with particular policy orientations gives the president an advantage in the legislative process. During the 1976 presidential campaign, Jimmy Carter committed himself to airline deregulation and, once in office, appointed Alfred Kahn and Elizabeth Bailey to the CAB. Both had made statements favoring deregulation. Under their influence, the agency took several steps to make the industry more competitive. Those initiatives helped build a favorable climate for passing airline deregulation legislation in 1978.[20] Presidents are usually not so purposeful with their appointments. A recent study of the FCC concluded that "the President has never used the appointments power to shape communications policy in any distinctive fashion. The ability to shape policy has been frittered away largely through presidential indifference."[21]

Even though statutes are drafted to protect the nonpartisan nature of commissions, presidents are able to circumvent the restrictions. For example, the six-member Tariff Commission was structured so that no more than three commissioners could be from the same political party. But with Democrats identified nationally as advocates of lower tariffs, and Republicans labeled as protectionists, President Wilson could easily pick a Republican free-trader while Presidents Harding and Coolidge could search for protectionist Democrats. When President Nixon had to name a Democrat to the SEC he chose former Democratic Representative A. Sydney Herlong, Jr., a Florida conservative identified with the business community. When an SEC vacancy appeared in 1981, the replacement was expected to be a Reagan Democrat.[22]

Both branches have received poor marks for their record in appointing high-quality people to the independent commissions.[23] The Senate tended to approve nominations routinely; its rejection of Leland Olds, nominated in 1949 to a third term to the FPC, stands as a rare exception.[24] Floor votes to reject a nominee are rare. Committees prefer to let the White House know that they will not support a candidate, forcing the president to withdraw the nomination.

Recently, though, the Senate has been examining nominations more closely. In 1973 it rejected Robert Morris for the FPC after deciding that the agency was already top-heavy with commissioners oriented toward industry and that Morris, despite his qualifications, could not be counted to represent the consumer's point of view.[25] In 1977 the Senate Environment and Public Works Committee rejected the nomination of Kent F. Hansen to the Nuclear Regulatory Commission. The opposition reflected concern about his limited experience in policy matters and possible conflict of interest questions.[26] Senate committees are examining more carefully the financial backgrounds of nominees to commissions, looking for potential conflicts of interest. They also create a public record of the nominee's depth of knowledge, previous policy commitments, and regulatory philosophy.

Senior staffers from Congress stand a good chance to become commissioners of the independent agencies. John R. Evans, from the Senate banking committee, joined the SEC as commissioner in 1973 and was reappointed to another term in 1979. John Vernon Rainbolt II, after serving as an aide to Democratic Representative Graham Purcell, Jr. of Texas and counsel to the House Agriculture Committee, was named commissioner of the Commodity Futures Trading Commission in 1975. Charles Ferris, for many years director of the Senate Democratic Policy Committee and later general counsel for House Speaker Tip O'Neill, was picked to head the FCC in 1977. Charles B. Curtis, counsel to the House commerce committee from 1971 to 1976, became chairman of the FPC in 1977 and was reappointed in 1979 to chair the successor agency, FERC. President Reagan nominated Charles M. Butler III, an aide to Republican Senator John Tower of Texas, to be a commissioner of FERC. Upon confirmation, Butler was slated to be chairman of the agency.

Some of these staffers have been instrumental in creating the agencies they would later serve on. Stuart Statler was special assistant to the chairman of the National Commission on Product Safety, which had made recommendations leading to the creation of the Consumer Product Safety Commission (CPSC). After serving as chief counsel to the minority for the Senate Permanent Subcommittee on Investigations and counsel to Republican Senator Charles Percy of Illinois, in 1979 Statler was selected to become a commissioner of the CPSC.

The Senate commerce committee has a particularly good record in placing its staff on the independent regulatory commissions. A. Daniel O'Neal, transportation counsel to the committee, became a member of the ICC in 1973 and was designated chairman in 1977. Joseph R. Fogarty, after thirteen years as a committee staffer, joined the FCC as commissioner in 1976. David A. Clanton, after serving eight years as assistant to Republican Senator Robert Griffin of Michigan and as minority staff counsel to the Senate commerce committee, became a commissioner of the FTC in 1976. President Reagan named him acting chairman in 1981. Michael Pertschuk, staff director of the committee, became chairman of the FTC in 1977, while Richard Daschbach, maritime counsel to the committee, was named commissioner of the Federal Maritime Commission that same year. President Reagan selected Mary Ann Weyforth Dawson to be a commissioner of the FCC in 1981. She had previously served with Democratic Representatives James W. Symington and Richard Ichord of Missouri, but during her service as an assistant to Republican Senator Bob Packwood of Oregon she had special responsibility for the Senate commerce committee, chaired by Packwood.

The nomination of a congressional staffer in 1978 created a major embarrassment for the Carter administration. David Gartner, an aide to Democratic Senator Hubert Humphrey of Minnesota, was selected to become a commissioner on the Commodity Futures Trading Commission (CFTC). He told the White House and the Senate agriculture committee that during 1975, 1976, and 1977 he had received, as gifts for his children, stock in the Archer-Daniels-Midland Co. (ADM) valued at approximately $72,000. The gifts were made by Dwayne Andreas, chairman of the board and chief executive officer of ADM, and by his daughter, Sandra McMurtrie, who had also served as secretary to Gartner. ADM, a large corporation engaged in flour milling and soybean processing, was subject to the regulation of the CFTC.

Despite these revelations, Gartner was unanimously supported by the agriculture committee and was confirmed by the Senate on the same day without debate or a dissenting vote. A few days later, however, several members of Congress had second thoughts. Republican Senator Orrin Hatch of Utah remarked:

> I would just like to say that if this was a Republican President and there was the appointment by this Republican President of a Republican staffer, say on the Energy Committee, who had just received $72,000 in a trust account for his children, and an appointment was made to head the Federal Energy Administration, or even appointed to be a member of the Securities and Exchange Commission, or to be a member of the Federal Power Commission, I think all hell would break loose in this society today. And yet hardly a word was said on this Andreas-Gartner affair.[27]

Carter, initially defending the appointment at a news conference, later asked Gartner to resign, as did Vice President Mondale. The Senate agriculture committee brought Gartner back to testify on the legality and propriety of the gifts, the conflict of interest charge, and his ability to function independently as a commissioner of a regulatory agency. Although several senators at these hearings told Gartner that they felt the committee had erred in expediting his nomination, and that upon reflection they believed he had exercised poor judgment in accepting the gifts and had been nominated for the wrong position, Gartner stayed on as commissioner.[28]

Designating Chairmen

When Congress created the Federal Reserve Board in 1913 it gave the president the power to designate the governor. Similarly, the statute creating the Federal Power Commission in 1920 authorized the president to choose the chairman. In other cases, however, the members of the commissions named their chairman. The Interstate Commerce Commission had rotating chairmen, elected annually by the membership.

In 1949 a task force of the Hoover Commission recommended that the chairman of each regulatory commission be designated from among its members by the president, to serve at his pleasure. The task force also recommended that administrative duties be centralized in the chairman.[29] The full commission did not endorse the task force's suggestions and remained noncommittal on the issue.[30]

Beginning in 1950, however, a succession of reorganization plans submitted by presidents implemented the recommendations of the task force.[31] To assure that a new president could appoint his own chairman of the Federal Reserve System, former Fed chairmen Thomas McCabe and William McChesney Martin both favored making the four-year tenure coterminous with the president. The Commission on Money and Credit made the same suggestion in 1961, and President Kennedy included the recommendation in his 1962 economic report.[32] Despite repeated support over the years, this proposal has never been adopted. The political leverage and significance of designating the chairman is well appreciated by Congress. Instead of the president having sole power to designate the chairman and vice chairman of the Fed, Congress passed legislation in 1977 to make those selections subject to the advice and consent of the Senate.[33]

Most of the chairmen of the independent regulatory commissions serve at the pleasure of the president, but upon removal as chairman the individual remains a member of the commission. For example, when President Carter removed NRC Commissioner Joseph Hendrie from his position as chairman, Hendrie retained his seat on the commission.

Despite the commissions' role as "arms of Congress," the chairmen sometimes perform political chores for the White House. During the 1972 presidential campaign, three commission heads campaigned actively for Richard Nixon. The individuals were William Casey of the SEC, Helen Delich Bentley of the FMC, and John Nassikas of the FPC.[34]

Removals

President Franklin D. Roosevelt tested the scope of his removal power by dismissing William Humphrey as an FTC commissioner for policy reasons rather than the statutory grounds for removal (inefficiency, neglect of duty, or malfeasance in office). The Justice Department argued that the statute served to guide but not to limit the president's discretion in exercising the removal power. The grounds were not meant to be exclusive, according to Justice Department officials, unless Congress specified that there were three grounds "and no other." No such language appeared in the FTC statute.[35]

The Justice Department pointed out that if Congress could limit the president to three grounds for removal it could limit him to one, such as malfeasance in office or neglect of duty. The result of such reasoning, said the Justice Department, "would be that the President would have no power, even with the aid of the Senate, to remove an admittedly inefficient officer in the executive branch of the Government." Moreover, the president's faithful execution of the laws "may require more than freedom from inefficiency, neglect of duty, or malfeasance in office."

In a unanimous and remarkably brief opinion for the Supreme Court, Justice Sutherland held that an FTC commissioner could be removed only for one or more of the causes specified in the statute. Sutherland tried to distance the FTC from executive agencies by describing it as "charged with the enforcement of no policy except the policy of the law. Its duties are neither political nor executive, but predominantly quasi-judicial and quasi-legislative." Anticipating this argument, the Justice Department had pointed out that the regular executive departments also performed judicial and legislative functions, as indeed they did.[36]

Sutherland offered a strained and unrealistic view of the doctrine of separated powers: "The fundamental necessity of maintaining each of the three general departments of government entirely free from the control or coercive influence, direct or indirect, of either of the others, has often been stressed and is hardly open to serious question." [37] Yet there is very little that one branch of government can do without being controlled, directly or indirectly, by another branch. To bolster his opinion, Sutherland had to misrepresent the views of James Wilson and Justice Joseph Story, implying that they believed in a strict separation between the branches when in fact they emphasized mutual dependency.[38]

During his last year on the bench, Sutherland expressed uncertainty about the location of independent commissions in the scheme of three branches of government. Upon hearing an argument that the U.S.

Shipping Board (forerunner of the Federal Maritime Commission) was not in the executive branch, he inquired into the legal basis for such an assertion. The counsel replied, "Why, in your Honor's opinion in the Humphrey case." Sutherland pressed further. If not in the executive branch, then where was it? The legislative branch, came the answer. Justice Sutherland "shook his head, as though he disagreed, and seemed to be thinking the question over as the discussion went on to other points." [39]

Although *Humphrey's Executor* has been reinforced by other decisions,[40] we still lack a satisfactory theory on the removal power as applied to the independent commissions. What we have is largely what Sutherland called a "field of doubt" that occupies the territory between *Myers* (for executive officers) and the independent commissions covered by *Humphrey*.[41] The rigid holding in *Humphrey* could have been avoided had Roosevelt based his removal on one of the three statutory grounds specified for FTC commissioners. It is doubtful that the Court would have questioned his judgment, and future commissioners of the independent agencies would have been sensitive to the potential intervention of the president. But even with *Humphrey*, presidents are able to put pressure on commissioners to resign. The Ford White House applied steady pressure on Robert Timm until he finally resigned from the Civil Aeronautics Board. In 1980 the Court of Claims rejected Timm's argument that he had been forced to resign and was entitled to back pay.[42]

Reviewing Budget Estimates

The Budget and Accounting Act of 1921 authorized the president, supported by the Bureau of the Budget, to review and revise budget estimates submitted by all departments and establishments, *including* independent commissions. Despite the clarity of the statutory language, a number of independent regulatory commissions and boards insisted that the provisions for budgetary review did not apply to them. To remove all doubts, Congress had to add Title II to the Reorganization Act of 1939. The reorganization statute amended the Budget and Accounting Act by adding the words "any independent regulatory commission or board" to the list of government agencies whose budgets were subject to review and revision by the Budget Bureau.[43]

Agency budget estimates and supporting material submitted to the Budget Bureau (now Office of Management and Budget) can be disclosed to Congress *after* the president's budget is transmitted.[44] Because of a long train of abuses by the Nixon administration, members of Congress wanted to receive certain agency estimates *before* the president transmitted his budget. In most cases Congress settled on the submission of agency estimates simultaneously to Congress and OMB, but in a few cases the estimates bypassed OMB and the president altogether.

The National Cancer Act of 1971 prohibited the HEW secretary from changing the budget estimates for the national cancer program and required the president and OMB to apportion all funds that Congress appropriated for the National Cancer Institute. A year later Congress adopted the idea of concurrent budget submissions. The Consumer Product Safety Commission, established in 1972, is required to submit its budget concurrently to Congress and to OMB.[45] Congress followed the same approach in 1973 for the National Railroad Passenger Corporation; in 1974 for the U.S. Railway Association, the Federal Election Commission, the Commodity Futures Trading Commission, and the Privacy Protection Study Commission; in 1975 for the National Transportation Safety Board; and in 1976 for the Interstate Commerce Commission.[46] When the secretary of energy seeks funds from Congress, he must show the amount requested by the Federal Energy Regulatory Commission in its budgetary presentation made to the secretary and to OMB.[47] Legislation in 1978 directed the Merit Systems Protection Board to submit its budget concurrently to the president and to Congress.[48]

More serious, from the standpoint of the principles of the Budget and Accounting Act, are prohibitions that deny the president and OMB the right to revise agency estimates. The Senate made a concerted effort in 1972 to have the appropriation requests of independent regulatory agencies submitted directly to Congress rather than to OMB. Commissioners of the agencies complained that OMB review and reductions prevented Congress from appreciating the agency's own assessment of its budgetary needs. As FTC Commisioner Paul Rand Dixon told a Senate committee in 1972: "there is no area more sensitive to formulation of policy than the budget of an agency. You simply cannot do what you cannot afford to do." He complained that five commissioners had their request reviewed by OMB staffers: "here are five presidential appointees, subject to the advice and consent of the Senate, and we go down there and plead with a bunch of low-grade staff people. I have done everything except play the request on a violin." [49]

The Trade Act of 1974 provides that the estimated expenditures and proposed appropriations for the International Trade Commission shall be included in the president's budget "without revision." [50] Also, as a result of legislation passed in 1974, the requests of the Postal Service for "public service costs" (rural delivery) and "foregone revenue" (subsidies for third-class mail) have to be included in the president's budget "with his recommendation but without revision." [51] Other budgets not subject to OMB review include the legislative branch, the judiciary, the Federal Reserve System Board of Governors, the Farm Credit Administration, and the budgets of a number of privately owned, government-sponsored enterprises, including federal land banks, federal intermediate credit banks, and the Federal Home Loan Mortgage Corporation.[52]

Some of the banking institutions are immune from OMB control because they do not depend on appropriations. The Federal Reserve System, for example, generates income in the form of interest on securities held in its investment portfolio. The Board of Governors also levies upon the Federal Reserve banks an assessment sufficient to pay estimated expenses. These funds are not "appropriated moneys," although legislation in 1978 permits the GAO to conduct limited audits of the Federal Reserve Board.[53]

A determined president backed by an electoral mandate to retrench federal programs can cut deeply into agency budgets, including those of the independent commissions. These conditions prevailed in 1981 when President Reagan submitted revisions to Carter's budget. Substantial cuts were made in the budgets of the independent regulatory commissions, particularly CPSC and FTC. The Legal Services Corporation, which had previously enjoyed broad immunity from OMB and presidential control, was slated to be abolished by the Reagan budget.

Reviewing Legislative Recommendations

As part of its central clearance function, OMB reviews legislative recommendations and testimony prepared by the independent commissions, but there are various exceptions to this general principle.[54] CAB's annual recommendations to Congress for additional legislation are not subject to OMB review. Moreover, the ICC had taken the position over the years that it is not required to submit its legislative recommendations and comments for OMB approval.[55]

To strengthen the hand of independent commissions, Congress has recently enacted other exemptions. Whenever the Commodity Futures Trading Commission transmits any legislative recommendations, testimony, or comments on legislation to the president or to OMB, it concurrently forwards copies to the House and Senate agriculture committees.[56] A similar provision in 1974 covers the SEC, the Board of Governors of the Federal Reserve System, the Federal Deposit Insurance Corporation, the Federal Home Loan Bank Board, and the National Credit Union Administration.[57] In 1976 Congress authorized the ICC to transmit to Congress legislative recommendations prepared for congressional hearings, or comments on legislation, at the same time that it sends the information to OMB. Legislation the following year extended the same authority to FERC. The Merit Systems Protection

Board (created in 1978) submits its legislative recommendations concurrently to Congress and to the president. Whenever requested by a committee or subcommittee of Congress, the board may transmit reports, testimony, information, and views "without review, clearance, or approval by any other administrative authority." [58]

Control of Litigation

With certain exceptions, independent agencies must channel their requests for litigation through the Department of Justice when they petition the Supreme Court for review.[59] The ICC has statutory authority to appear independently when its orders are being challenged. Commissioners from other agencies have complained that the review by Justice diminishes their independence and effectiveness.[60]

Congress added another exception in 1973 when it authorized the FTC to appear in court in its own name after formally notifying the attorney general. President Nixon signed the bill reluctantly, stating that FTC's authority "would dangerously decentralize the general control and coordination over federal litigation which has traditionally been exercised by the Department of Justice." [61] In 1974 the Department of Justice opposed legislation designed to authorize the independent commissions in any civil action, including appeals to the Supreme Court, to act in their own names and through their own attorneys.[62] Congress did not pass this legislation.

Federal Reports

During World War II, as part of a campaign to reduce the burden of excessive paperwork on business enterprises, Congress passed the Federal Reports Act of 1942. The responsibility for implementing this statute fell to the Budget Bureau. Federal agencies, including the independent regulatory commissions, were required to seek approval from BOB (later OMB) before collecting information from the private sector. The commissions objected that their investigative functions were being hampered by this procedure, adversely affecting their independence and their ability to carry out statutory missions.[63]

In 1973, at the height of congressional furor over presidential and OMB arrogance, Democratic Senator Philip Hart of Michigan successfully offered an amendment to the trans-Alaska oil pipeline bill to exempt the independent regulatory agencies from OMB review under the Federal Reports Act. The responsibility for reviewing these agencies was transferred to the General Accounting Office, although the agencies would make the final determination as to what information they needed to carry out statutory duties.[64]

When President Nixon signed the bill, he remarked that the

provision "will unfortunately eliminate present safeguards against bureaucratic harassment of business and industry by permitting endless duplication of requests by regulatory agencies." GAO was not happy about its new assignment and three years later admitted its limited success in stemming the paperwork requirements imposed on the public by the regulatory agencies. In 1980, following GAO's recommendation, Congress returned the responsibility for information clearance to OMB. In a peculiar "agency veto," a majority of commissioners can vote to override OMB's decision.[65]

Legislative Vetoes

Of all the independent commissions, none fared quite so badly in the 1970s as the Federal Trade Commission. It became a lightning rod for the frustrations, complaints, and lamentations directed at federal regulation. Some of its proposed rules—on mobile homes, the cereal industry, insurance businesses, children's television advertising, and the funeral industry—helped trigger a counterattack from the private sector and from within Congress. For several years it had to survive without an authorization by Congress, kept alive by continuing resolutions and special appropriations.

Much of the delay in authorizing the FTC resulted from members of the House of Representatives who wanted a legislative veto over FTC rules and the reluctance of senators to support this form of congressional control. The deadlock was eventually broken by the Federal Trade Commission Improvements Act of 1980. The statute requires the FTC, after promulgating a final rule, to submit the rule to Congress, where it is referred to the Senate and House commerce committees. The rule becomes effective after 90 days unless both houses adopt a concurrent resolution of disapproval. The statute also provides for expedited treatment in the federal courts to handle challenges to the constitutionality of this procedure.[66]

President Carter objected to the two-house legislative veto of FTC rules, saying the provision was "unwise and unconstitutional." He signed the bill, despite the presence of the legislative veto provision, "because the very existence of this agency is at stake." He looked forward to an early court challenge, but a year later there had been no initiative by private parties or the Justice Department to test the constitutionality of this legislative veto.[67]

James C. Miller III, one of President Reagan's top regulatory advisers, suggested in a speech in 1981 that the administration would not object to legislative vetoes aimed at the independent regulatory commissions, although it would continue to oppose such interference with the executive departments. Because the president has limited control over the independent agencies, Miller concluded that a legislative veto might serve to curb unnecessary federal regulations. In a more formal presentation to the House Judiciary Committee, he confirmed the administration's support for a legislative veto over regulations issued by the independent commissions, provided the veto assumed the form of a concurrent resolution of disapproval rather than a one-house veto.[68]

Ex Parte Contacts

Members of Congress are invited to offer their views about issues that fall within a commission's responsibility. However, an off-the-record (ex parte) contact about a particular case pending before a commission, when it involves an adjudicatory proceeding or formal rulemaking, may fall into the category of an ex parte communication prohibited by law.

Ex parte communications are prohibited to insure that the formal decisions of agencies will not be tainted or unfairly influenced by private, off-the-record contacts with those having a personal interest in the outcome. Sherman Adams, President Eisenhower's assistant, had to resign in 1958 after congressional investigations publicized his frequent interventions with the FTC, the SEC, and the CAB.[69]

The Government in the Sunshine Act of 1976 established new restrictions on ex parte contacts in the commissions. After a proceeding is "noticed" for hearing, an interested person outside the agency shall not make an ex parte communication with any agency employee expected to be involved in the decision. Nor may the employee make an ex parte communication with an interested person outside the agency. If the employee receives or makes a forbidden communication, the public record must contain all written communications, memoranda stating the substance of oral communications, and all written responses and memoranda relating to the oral responses. These requirements apply only to formal rulemaking proceedings.

The CAB established a special file in 1977 that contained letters and memoranda of ex parte contacts between individuals outside the board and staff members on the board with regard to any pending case.[70] In 1979 the ICC issued a memorandum explaining the different proceedings before the commission and distinguishing between appropriate and inappropriate contacts. Letters or contacts from members of Congress inquiring about the status of a proceeding are not ex parte communications. However, letters or contacts addressing the *merits* of a proceeding are prohibited from the time an on-the-record proceeding is noticed for oral hearing. Ex parte communications are not shown to the chairman, to other members of the commission, or to decisionmakers at lower levels. Communications received after the record is closed are answered by ICC's congressional relations office. When a member of Congress becomes a party to a commission proceeding, that information is made public "in case the member has other constituents who may want him or her to participate in favor of the other side of the issue." [71]

Various rulings by the judiciary have limited the right of agency officials to meet privately with groups or individuals in off-the-record sessions. Basic fairness requires that agency proceedings be carried on in the open. Ex parte meetings exclude the public from following agency proceedings and also frustrate judicial review by keeping crucial deliberations from the courts. [72]

The primary control that Congress exercises over the independent commissions is *structural*. The statutory framework is designed to provide decisionmaking by a multi-member (collegial) body, terms of five to seven years that exceed the president's, staggered terms to promote continuity of policy, and restrictions on the president's power to remove commissioners.

Other forms of control have been spotty and episodic. Neither branch has developed a systematic approach to selecting and nominating commissioners or defining a broad framework for regulatory policy. Congress intervenes occasionally to offer protection for the budget estimates and legislative recommendations of commissions, but generally recognizes the need for centralized review by OMB. This staccato record is most visible in the control over federal reports, a task assigned to the Budget Bureau in 1942, taken away from its successor agency (OMB) in 1973, and then returned to OMB seven years later. Moreover, Congress acknowledges the need for placing within the Justice Department a coordinating responsibility for litigation, despite occasional pleas from the commissions for unimpeded access to the court.

The structure that Congress has created for the independent commissions has protected the autonomy and continuity of their operations, except for scandals or overriding political pressures. The next section explores proposals to shift greater control to the president.

MORE POWER TO THE PRESIDENT?

For more than four decades we have been advised to place the independent commissions under the control of the president. In 1937 the Brownlow Committee recommended that the commissions be placed within the regular executive departments, with their work divided into an administrative section and a judicial section. The chief of the administrative section would be directly responsible to the departmental secretary, while the judicial section would be wholly independent of the secretary and the president. The Hoover Commission in 1949 proposed that the "purely executive functions of quasi-legislative and quasi-judicial agencies" be brought within the regular executive departments. The Ash Council in 1971 recommended that rulemaking functions of the independent commissions be placed directly under the president and their adjudicatory functions transferred to a new institution called the Administrative Court of the United States.[73]

To those fascinated by organizational neatness, these proposals have a certain appeal. Upon closer examination, however, the attractiveness fades. The basic problem is that the work of independent commissions does not divide so crisply between "rulemaking" and "adjudicatory." In a 1960 study, Emmette Redford doubted that the "regulatory scrambled egg can be cleanly separated into an executive-policy determining yellow and a quasi-judicial white."[74] Indeed, agencies have substantial discretion in choosing between rulemaking and adjudication.[75] When rules are required by statute to be made on the record after opportunity for an agency hearing, rulemaking follows a process described in the courts as "essentially rulemaking using adjudicatory procedures."[76]

Federal judges and specialists in administrative law have not been comfortable with the dichotomy between rulemaking and adjudication. "Unhappily," Chief Judge David Bazelon has remarked, "no such bright line can be drawn between rulemaking and adjudicatory proceedings."[77] Agencies, discovering that adjudication of each case results in huge backlogs, turn increasingly to rulemaking in order to expedite their operations.[78] To further complicate matters, Congress and the courts have developed a hybrid type of administrative proceeding that combines some adjudicatory safeguards with informal rulemaking. In 1978 the Supreme Court stepped back from its involvement in this process, holding that the decision to elaborate on informal rulemaking lay with Congress and the agencies, not the courts.[79]

Placing independent commissions within the executive departments appears to be neither practical nor desirable. Less drastic reforms, however, are available to subject the commissions to presidential review and direction. Beginning in 1961, after Kennedy entered the White House, all regulatory commissions were requested to send monthly reports on their activities to the president. The reports, about two pages long, covered general policy and administrative actions, not specific decisions pending before the commissions.[80] Presidents may also submit to Congress specific proposals to monitor the activities of the regulatory agencies. Kennedy's message to Congress on April 13, 1961, is a notable example.[81]

Presidents have met with the heads of independent commissions to describe administration goals and seek the commissions' support. In one such meeting Lyndon Johnson summed up the curious relationship between the president and the commissions with this tantalizing sentence, suggesting that the commissions are agents carrying out presidential duties: "I want to convey my deep sense of reliance upon you and your agencies in discharging the responsibilities which have been thrust upon me." [82]

President Ford met with commissioners from the independent regulatory agencies in 1975 and urged them to scale down their activities. At a news conference a few days later he told reporters that he expected to make headway with regulatory reform: "If we don't we will change some of the commissions." However, neither Ford nor his White House staff followed through by calling other conferences or proposing specific recommendations. [83]

In 1977, regarding a proposed executive order to improve government regulations, President Carter asked for public comment on the question of whether the procedures outlined in the order should apply to the independent regulatory agencies. Thirteen senators wrote to him a month later, stating their "unqualified view" that the order could not cover the independent agencies without an express statutory basis. When the final order was published on March 24, 1978, it exempted the independent regulatory agencies. [84] Although the Justice Department had advised Carter that most of the order could bind the independent agencies, he decided that a confrontation with Congress "would only detract from the important reform steps being taken" and therefore asked the chairmen of the independent agencies to apply on a voluntary basis the policies and procedures of the order. [85]

Carter's executive order was revoked in 1981 by President Reagan, who issued his own order covering federal regulation. The purpose was to reduce the burdens of existing and future regulations, increase agency accountability for their regulatory decisions, minimize duplication and conflict of regulations, and provide for presidential oversight of the regulatory process. However, the order specifically excludes the following agencies: the Board of Governors of the Federal Reserve System, CAB, CFTC, CPSC, FCC, FERC, FMC, FTC, ICC, NLRB, NRC, SEC, and several other banking corporations and safety commissions. [86]

An influential study by Lloyd Cutler and David Johnson in 1975 advocated legislation authorizing the president to modify or direct certain actions by the regulatory agencies, subject to a one-house legislative veto and to expedited judicial review. [87] A study commission of the American Bar Association (ABA) considered this proposal and suggested a similar approach, but without the legislative veto. The commission recommended that Congress enact a statute authorizing the president to direct certain regulatory agencies, "both within and outside the executive branch," to consider or reconsider the issuance of "critical regulations." Before the presidential order became effective, Congress would have a specified number of days to react to the order. Based on this reaction, the president could modify or withdraw the order and issue a new one. The commission preferred this approach over legislative vetoes, which it believed were constitutionally suspect and politically inefficient.[88]

The commission's recommendation did not cover agency actions that were "adjudicatory" or "quasi-judicial." A majority of the commission believed that presidential orders should apply to the regulations of most independent agencies. On the question of excessive participation by presidential staff, the commission anticipated that issues critical enough to justify presidential intervention would arise only three to four times a year, assuring his personal participation in each decision.[89]

Delegating additional powers to the president will not necessarily yield greater expertise and coordination of regulatory policy, nor will it assure freedom from the "special interests" that supposedly dominate Congress. Organized groups from the private sector are not fastidious about their source of assistance. They influence whatever branch of government, including executive, is in a position to help. Unless the decisions are kept to a bare minimum, power transferred to the president will slide past him and be exercised by various assistants of uncertain experience, skill, and judgment. An observation by Judge Henry J. Friendly, offered two decades ago, is still on target:

> . . . it is indulging in fantasy to speak of "the President" as formulating policy pronouncements for the agencies himself. The spectacle of a chief executive, burdened to the limit of endurance with decisions on which the very existence of mankind may depend, personally taking on the added task of determining to what extent newspapers should be allowed to own television stations or whether railroads should be allowed to reduce rates only to or somewhat below the truck level, is pure mirage.[90]

Writing in 1979, however, Judge Friendly supported the ABA commission's recommendation for closer presidential control over regulatory activities, including those in the independent agencies. ABA's proposed grant of power to the president seemed to Friendly narrow in scope and highly structured. If abused, Congress could withdraw the authority.[91]

There is considerable doubt how the process would work. The initial task of identifying issues and bringing them to the attention of the president must fall to the White House staff. They have no unique claim to be operating in the "national interest." Like the executive agencies and independent commissions, they too have a special interest: protecting the president. As has been demonstrated on more than one occasion in recent decades, the political interests of the president are not necessarily synonymous with the national interest. Those who have contributed financially to the president or to his party will have greater access to the White House staff, able at that point to specify the regulations they want overturned or modified. Requirements can be established for a public record of such ex parte contacts, but the peculiar status of White House staff does not allow Congress or the courts the same degree of review they can exercise over executive agencies or independent commissions.

NOTES

1. Edward S. Corwin, *The President: Office and Powers, 1787-1957* (New York: New York University Press, 1957), p. 93.
2. Robert E. Cushman, *The Independent Regulatory Commissions* (New York: Oxford University Press, 1941), pp. 21-34.
3. Ibid., pp. 45-54.
4. The President's Committee on Administrative Management, *Administrative Management in the Government of the United States* (Washington, D.C.: Government Printing Office, 1937), p. 36.
5. Commission on Organization of the Executive Branch of the Government (Hoover Commission), *Task Force Report on Regulatory Commissions* [Appendix N] (Government Printing Office, 1949), p. viii.
6. C. Herman Pritchett, "The Regulatory Commissions Revisited," *American Political Science Review* 43 (1949):978, 982.
7. Kenneth Culp Davis, *Administrative Law of the Seventies* (Rochester, N.Y.: Lawyers Co-operative Publishing Co., 1976), p. 15.
8. Richard A. Posner, "Theories of Economic Regulation," *The Bell Journal of Economics and Management Science* 5 (1974):335.
9. For an inventory of federal regulatory organizations, see *The Challenge of Regulatory Reform*, a report to the president from the Domestic Council Review Group on Regulatory Reform (Washington, D.C.: Government Printing Office, 1977), pp. 50-57.
10. 24 Stat. 386, 387, sec. 18, 21 (1887); 25 Stat. 861-862, sec. 7, 8 (1889).
11. Cushman, *The Independent Regulatory Commissions*, pp. 100-102.
12. William L. Cary, *Politics and the Regulatory Agencies* (New York: McGraw-Hill, 1967), p. 4.
13. Lloyd N. Cutler and David R. Johnson, "Regulation and the Political Process," *Yale Law Journal* 84 (1975):1395, 1410.
14. Henry J. Friendly, *The Federal Administrative Agencies: The Need for Better Definition of Standards* (Cambridge: Harvard University Press, 1962); Federal Comm'n v. Broadcasting Co., 309 U.S. 134, 137-138 (1940); Federal Trade Comm. v. Gratz, 253 U.S. 421, 427, 436-437 (1920); N.Y. Central Securities Co. v. United States, 287 U.S. 12, 24-25 (1932).
15. Ralph K. Huitt, "Congressional Organization and Operation in the Field of Money and Credit," *Fiscal and Debt Management Policies* (Englewood Cliffs, N.J.: Prentice-Hall, 1963), pp. 470-471.
16. John T. Woolley, "Congress and the Conduct of Monetary Policy in the 1970s" (Paper delivered at the annual meeting of the Midwest Political Science Association, Chicago, Ill., April 22-24, 1980), pp. 1, 14.
17. *Washington Post,* February 4, 1981, p. E1:4.
18. C.&S. Air Lines v. Waterman Corp., 333 U.S. 103, 109 (1948); 49 U.S.C. 1461

(1976); and 52 Stat. 1014, sec. 801 (1938).

19. *Guide to Congress* (Washington, D.C.: Congressional Quarterly, 1976), p. 186. See also David M. Welborn, "Presidents, Regulatory Commissioners and Regulatory Policy," *Journal of Politics* 15 (1966):3; Glen O. Robinson, "On Reorganizing the Independent Regulatory Agencies," *Virginia Law Review* 57 (1971):947, 951, note 14. For individual studies see Seymour Scher, "Regulatory Agency Control Through Appointment: The Case of the Eisenhower Administration and the NLRB," *Journal of Politics* 23 (1961):667.

20. Bradley Behrman, "Civil Aeronautics Board," *The Politics of Regulation,* ed. James Q. Wilson (New York: Basic Books, 1980), pp. 110-120.

21. Glen O. Robinson, "The Federal Communications Commission: An Essay on Regulatory Watchdogs," *Virginia Law Review* 64 (1978):169, 184.

22. On the Tariff Commission, see Philip G. Wright, *Tariff-Making by Commission* (Washington, D.C.: The Rawleigh Tariff Bureau, 1930), pp. 17-29; Catherine Hackett, "The Failure of the Flexible Tariff: 1922-1927," *The New Republic* (July 27, 1927):244-247; E. Pendleton Herring, "The Political Context of the Tariff Commission," *Political Science Quarterly* 49 (1934):421. On Nixon, see *New York Times,* January 14, 1970, p. 26. On Reagan, see "SEC's Mystery Woman Busy Learning the Ropes," *National Law Journal* (March 16, 1981):16.

23. U.S., Congress, Senate, Committee on Commerce, *Appointments to the Regulatory Agencies,* 94th Cong., 2d sess., April 1976; Senate, Committee on Government Operations, *Study on Federal Regulations: The Regulatory Appointments Process* (Volume 1), 95th Cong., 1st sess., January 1977.

24. Joseph P. Harris, "The Senatorial Rejection of Leland Olds: A Case Study," *American Political Science Review* 45 (1951):674.

25. U.S., Congress, *Congressional Record,* 93d Cong., 1st sess., 1973, 119:19492-19508.

26. *Congressional Quarterly Almanac 1977* (Washington, D.C.: Congressional Quarterly, 1977), p. 48-A.

27. *Congressional Record* (daily ed.), 95th Cong., 2d sess., May 22, 1978, 124:S7958.

28. *Weekly Compilation of Presidential Documents* 14 (June 14, 1978):1096; and ibid., June 26, 1978, p. 1182.

29. Hoover Commission, *Task Force Report on Regulatory Commissions* [Appendix N], pp. 31-32, 46-49.

30. Hoover Commission, *Concluding Report* (May 1949), p. 72; C. Herman Pritchett, "The Regulatory Commissions Revisited," *American Political Science Review* 43 (1949):978.

31. On the FTC, see Reorganization Plan No. 8 of 1950, 64 Stat. 1264, 15 U.S.C. 41 (1976). On the FPC, see Reorganization Plan No. 9 of 1950, 64 Stat. 1265; see also the provisions for its successor, the Federal Energy Regulatory Commission (FERC), 91 Stat. 582, sec. 401(b) (c), which authorizes the president to designate the chairman and makes the chairman responsible for executive and administrative operations. On the SEC, see Reorganization Plan No. 10 of 1950, 64 Stat. 1265, 15 U.S.C. 78d (1976). On the CAB, see Reorganization Plan No. 13 of 1950, 64 Stat. 1266, 49 U.S.C. 1321(a) (1976); and Reorganization Plan No. 3. of 1961, 75 Stat. 837, 49 U.S.C. 1324 (1976). On the FMC, see Reorganization Plan No. 7 of 1961, 75 Stat. 840, 46 U.S.C. 1111 (1976). On the ICC, see Reorganization Plan No. 1 of 1969, 83 Stat. 859, 49 U.S.C. 11 (1976). On the FCC, see 48 Stat. 1066, sec. 4(a)

(1934), 47 U.S.C. 154(a) (1976). On the NLRB, see 29 U.S.C. 153(a) (1976).

32. Commission on Money and Credit, *Money and Credit: Their Influence on Jobs, Prices, and Growth* (Englewood Cliffs, N.J.: Prentice-Hall, 1961), pp. 85-87.

33. P.L. 95-188, sec. 204, 91 Stat. 1388 (1977).

34. " 'Impartial' Regulators Stump for Nixon," *Washington Star-News*, October 8, 1972, p. C5.

35. Humphrey's Executor v. United States, 295 U.S. 602, 612-613 (1935).

36. Id. at 624, 617.

37. Id. at 629.

38. Id. at 630. See J. D. Andrew, ed., *The Works of James Wilson*, 2 vols. (Chicago: Callaghan & Co., 1896), 1:367-368; and Joseph Story, *Commentaries on the Constitution of the United States*, 4th ed., 2 vols. (Boston: Little, Brown & Co.), 1:525.

39. Cushman, *The Independent Regulatory Commissions,* pp. 447-448.

40. Morgan v. Tennessee Valley Authority, 28 F.Supp. 732 (E.D. Tenn. 1939); Morgan v. Tennessee Valley Authority, 115 F.2d 990 (6th Cir. 1940), certiorari denied, 312 U.S. 701 (1941); Wiener v. United States, 357 U.S. 349 (1958); Nader v. Bork, 366 F.Supp. 104 (D.D.C. 1973).

41. Humphrey's Executor v. United States, 295 U.S. 602, 632 (1935).

42. Louis Fisher, *The Constitution Between Friends* (New York: St. Martin's Press, 1978), pp. 79-80; *Washington Star*, March 17, 1980, p. A9.

43. 42 Stat. 20, sec. 2 (1921); 53 Stat. 565, sec. 201 (1939). See also U.S., Congress, House, H. Rept. 120, 76th Cong., 1st sess., 1939, p. 3.

44. OMB Circular No. A-10, November 12, 1976, paragraph 3.

45. 85 Stat. 780, sec. 407(b)(9) (1971); 86 Stat. 1229, sec. 27(k)(1) (1972).

46. In order of listing: for 1973, 87 Stat. 553, sec. 601(b)(1); for 1974, 87 Stat. 992, sec. 202(g)(2), 88 Stat. 1283, sec. 311(d)(1), 88 Stat. 1390-1391, sec. 101(9)(A), and 88 Stat. 1906, sec. 5(a)(5)(A); for 1975, 88 Stat. 2170, sec. 304(b)(7); and for 1976, 90 Stat. 60, sec. 311.

47. 91 Stat. 583, sec. 401(j).

48. 92 Stat. 1125, sec. 1205(j).

49. U.S., Congress, Senate, Committee on Government Operations, *Regulatory Agency Budgets* (Part 2) (hearings), 92d Cong., 2d sess., 1972, pp. 299, 301.

50. 88 Stat. 2011, sec. 175(a)(1). See U.S., Congress, House, H. Rept. 62, 96th Cong., 1st sess., 1979, p. 4.

51. 88 Stat. 288, sec. 3.

52. OMB Circular No. A-11, May 25, 1978, sec. 11.1.

53. 12 U.S.C. 244 (1976); P.L. 95-320 (1978).

54. OMB Circular No. A-19, September 20, 1979, p. 2 (definition of agency).

55. On the CAB, see 49 U.S.C. 1325 (1976). On the ICC, see U.S., Congress, Senate, Committee on Government Operations, Subcommittee on Budgeting Management, and Expenditures, *Regulatory Commissions' Independence Act, S. 704: Compendium of Materials,* 93rd Cong., 2d sess., September 1974, p. 9.

56. 7 U.S.C. 4a(h)(2) (1976). In signing the bill with this provision, Ford objected that the extension of the procedure "would make it difficult for me to develop and present to the Congress a coherent, coordinated legislative program." See *Public Papers of the Presidents,* 1974, p. 462.

57. 88 Stat. 1506, sec. 111 (1974).

58. 90 Stat. 60, sec. 311 (1976); 91 Stat. 583, sec. 401(j) (1977); 92 Stat. 1125, sec. 1205(k), 1209 (1978).

59. 28 U.S.C. 518 (1976). For exceptions to centralizing litigation in the Department of Justice, see Robert G. Dixon, Jr., "The Independent Commissions and Political Responsibility," *Administrative Law Review* 27 (1975):1, 7-8, note 26. On the litigation issue, see also U.S., Congress, Senate, Committee on Governmental Affairs, *Study on Federal Regulation* (Volume 5), 95th Cong., 1st sess., December 1977, pp. 54-67.

60. For the ICC, see 28 U.S.C. 2323 (1976). For other agencies, see A. Everette MacIntyre, "The Status of Regulatory Independence," *Federal Bar Journal* 29 (1969):1, 6-9.

61. 87 Stat. 592, sec. 408(d) (1973); *Public Papers of the Presidents,* 1973, pp. 945-946.

62. See *Regulatory Commissions' Independence Act, S. 704: Compendium of Materials,* pp. 135-137.

63. MacIntyre, "The Status of Regulatory Independence," pp. 10-12.

64. 87 Stat. 576, 593-594 (1973), 44 U.S.C. 3501-3512 (1976). See *Congressional Record* (daily ed.), July 14, 1973, 119:13441-13446.

65. *Public Papers of the Presidents,* 1973, p. 946; U.S., Congress, General Accounting Office, *Status of GAO's Responsibilities Under the Federal Reports Act: Independent Federal Regulatory Agencies,* OSP-76-14, May 28, 1976; P.L. 96-511, sec. 3507, 94 Stat. 2820 (1980).

66. P.L. 96-252, sec. 21, 94 Stat. 393-396.

67. *Weekly Compilation of Presidential Documents* 16 (May 28, 1980):982-983.

68. "White House Unopposed to Proposed Rule Veto," *Washington Star,* April 2, 1981, p. C1; and "Administration Backs Some Legislative Veto," *Washington Post,* May 8, 1981, p. D1.

69. Cary, *Politics and the Regulatory Agencies,* pp. 13-15; *Congressional Quarterly Almanac 1958* (Washington, D.C.: Congressional Quarterly, 1958), pp. 687-692; William R. McIntyre, "Pressures on Federal Regulatory Commissions," *Editorial Research Reports* (April 2, 1958):241-260; and Leon I. Salomon, ed., *The Independent Federal Regulatory Agencies* (New York: H. W. Wilson Co., 1959).

70. "CAB Sets Up 'Ex Parte' File," *Washington Star,* Jan. 26, 1977, p. B5.

71. *Congressional Record* (daily ed.), 96th Cong., 1st sess., March 6, 1979, 125:E902-904.

72. Sangamon Valley Television Corp. v. United States, 269 F.2d 221 (D.C. Cir. 1959); Moss v. CAB, 430 F.2d 891, 893 (D.C. Cir. 1970). For the unsettled nature of the law on ex parte contacts, compare Home Box Office, Inc. v. FCC, 567 F.2d 9, 57 (D.C. Cir. 1977), certiorari denied, 434 U.S. 829 (1977), with Action for Children's Television v. FCC, 564 F.2d 458 (D.C. Cir. 1977).

73. *Administrative Management in the Government of the United States,* p. 37; Hoover Commission, *Concluding Report,* pp. 9, 72; President's Advisory Council on Executive Reorganization, *A New Regulatory Framework: Report on Selected Independent Regulatory Agencies* (Washington, D.C.: Government Printing Office, January 1971). This report was widely criticized for reaching conclusions and making generalizations in the absence of factual and analytical evidence. See Glen O. Robinson, "On Reorganizing the Independent Regulatory Agencies," *Virginia Law Review* 57 (1971):947; and Roger G. Noll, *Reforming Regulation: An Evaluation of the Ash Council Proposal* (Washington, D.C.: Brookings Institution, 1971), pp. 12-13.

74. Emmette S. Redford, *The President and the Regulatory Commissions* (Unpublished report prepared for the President's Advisory Committee on Government Organization, 1960), p. 2. See also his article, "The President

and the Regulatory Commissions," *Texas Law Review* 44 (1965):288.

75. Securities Comm'n v. Chenery Corp., 332 U.S. 194, 203 (1946); Securities Comm'n v. Chenery Corp., 318 U.S. 80 (1943); David L. Shapiro, "The Choice of Rulemaking or Adjudication in the Development of Administrative Policy," *Harvard Law Review* 78 (1965):921; NLRB v. Bell Aerospace, 416 U.S. 267, 294 (1974).

76. Mobil Oil Corporation v. Federal Power Commission, 483 F.2d 1238, 1249 (D.C. Cir. 1973).

77. Nat. Res. Def. Council v. U.S. Nuclear Reg. Com'n, 547 F. 2d 633, 655 (D.C. Cir. 1976), footnote omitted.

78. Phillips Petroleum Co. v. Federal Power Com'n, 475 F.2d 842, 844-845 (10th Cir. 1973), certiorari denied, 414 U.S. 1146 (1974); National Petroleum Refiners Association v. FTC, 482 F.2d 672 (D.C. Cir. 1973), certiorari denied, 415 U.S. 951 (1974).

79. Vermont Yankee Nuclear Power Corp. v. Natural Resources Defense Council, 435 U.S. 519 (1978). See Stephen F. William, " 'Hybrid Rulemaking' Under the Administrative Procedure Act: A Legal and Empirical Analysis," *University of Chicago Law Review* 42 (1975):401; and J. Skelly Wright, "The Courts and the Rulemaking Process: The Limits of Judicial Review," *Cornell Law Review* 59 (1974):375, 388.

80. *Congressional Record*, 87th Cong., 1st sess., 1961, 107:3927-3933. See Hugh M. Hall, Jr., "Responsibility of President and Congress for Regulatory Policy Development," *Law and Contemporary Problems* 26 (1961):261.

81. *Public Papers of the Presidents,* 1961, pp. 267-276.

82. *Public Papers of the Presidents,* 1963-64, p. 18.

83. *Public Papers of the Presidents,* 1975, Book 1, pp. 949-954, 976; Glen O. Robinson, "The Federal Communications Commission: An Essay on Regulatory Watchdogs," *Virginia Law Review* 64 (1978):169, 211-212.

84. *Federal Register* 42 (1977):59741; *Congressional Record* (daily ed.), 95th Cong., 2d sess., April 5, 1978, 124:S4863-4864; *Federal Register* 43 (1978):12664, sec. 6(b) (5).

85. *Federal Register* 43 (1978):12670. The exempted agencies include the CAB, CFTC, CPSC, FCC, FDIC, FEC, FERC, FHLBB, FMC, FRB, FTC, ICC, NLRB, NRC, SEC, the Federal Mine Safety and Health Review Commission, the Occupational Safety and Health Review Commission, and the Postal Rate Commission.

86. *Weekly Compilation of Presidential Documents* 17 (February 17, 1981):124, sec. 1(d); see P.L. 96-511, sec. 3502 (10) (1980).

87. Cutler and Johnson, "Regulation and the Political Process," pp. 1395, 1414-1417.

88. Commission on Law and the Economy of the American Bar Association, *Federal Regulation: Roads to Reform*, Final Report 1979, With Recommendations, pp. 79-82, 88-91.

89. Ibid., pp. 82-84. See also Harold H. Bruff, "Presidential Power and Administrative Rulemaking," *Yale Law Journal* 88 (1979):451. This article supports greater involvement by the president in the proceedings of regulatory agencies. This proposed delegation of power to the president is challenged by "Delegation and Regulatory Reform: Letting the President Change the Rules," *Yale Law Journal* 89 (1980):561.

90. Friendly, *The Federal Administrative Agencies*, p. 154.

91. *Federal Regulation: Roads to Reform*, pp. 163-164.

6

Representing the Public Interest

In the midst of polemics and conflict, members of the three branches sometimes forget that they share a common task: representing the public interest. While each branch of government must remain alert to transgressions of its boundaries, a dogmatic insistence on prerogatives can lead to a breakdown of government. The public is not served when each branch adopts fixed, nonnegotiable positions. Former Attorney General Edward Levi wrote that the framers "did not envision a government in which each branch seeks out confrontation; they hoped the system of checks and balances would achieve a harmony of purposes differently fulfilled. The branches of government were not designed to be at war with one another. The relationship was not to be an adversary one, though to think of it that way has become fashionable." [1] Deadlock and stalemate are easy to accomplish; more valuable is the search for accommodations and intermediate positions that permit government to operate effectively without sacrificing or compromising constitutional values.

Congress and the executive have an ongoing contest over which branch best represents the nation. Ever since the American colonists broke with England and delivered their protest against "taxation without representation," we have entertained different theories and meanings of representative government. While Congress deserves the title "First Branch of Government" because of the extensive powers assigned to it by the Constitution, the responsibility for representing the people is shared with the president, the courts, and the bureaucracy.

CONGRESS

Under the constitutional principle of federalism, Congress consists of two distinct centers of power. The House of Representatives is chosen every two years by the people of the states. Senators are chosen for six-year terms to represent the states. The legislatures of the states, not the people, originally selected senators, until the Seventeenth Amendment (added in 1913) provided for direct election of senators by the people. This change broadened the Senate's popular mandate, but it did not alter the vast disparity among the states in population. Each state, regardless of its population—ranging from less than one-half million for Alaska and Wyoming to more than 23 million for California—is entitled to two senators.

In contrast, the House is supposed to be composed of legislators from districts of roughly equal size. This equality is upset from one census to the next. Because of the migration of people from the Northeast to the Sun Belt from 1970 to 1980, congressional districts in 1981 ranged from 233,787 for Democratic Representative Robert Garcia of the South Bronx, New York, to 890,000 for Republican Representative Bill McCollum of Florida's Fifth District. With the 1980 census results in, state legislatures will have to draw new district lines to achieve populations of substantially equal size.[2] The sheer size of congressional districts makes it difficult for members of the House to carry out their representative function. Instead of each member representing 30,000 constituents, as in 1789, congressional districts have now increased to an average of about 519,000.

Representation is further complicated by the fact that members of Congress represent the interests of a particular constituency and yet also respond to interests outside their district. Indeed, most legislators look both within and beyond their districts for guidance.[3] Rather than evaluating members solely in terms of their constituency relationships, we should judge how well Congress reflects the country as a whole. For example, disenfranchised southern blacks were "represented" by northern black and liberal white members of Congress who pushed for civil rights legislation during the 1950s and 1960s.[4]

Delegate and Trustee

Within their own constituencies, legislators have selected different models of representation: that of a *delegate* (voting the majority's desires even when contrary to their own) and of a *trustee* (voting in accordance with what they consider to be best for their constituents and the country). The trustee concept is exemplified by Edmund Burke's speech to the electors of Bristol in 1774, upon his election to the British Parliament. While remaining attentive to their advice and wishes, he was determined to vote his own conscience:

> Certainly, Gentlemen, it ought to be the happiness and glory of a representative to live in the strictest union, the closest correspondence, and the most unreserved communication with his constituents. Their wishes ought to have great weight with him; their opinions high respect; their business unremitted attention....
>
> But his unbiased opinion, his mature judgment, his enlightened conscience, he ought not to sacrifice to you, to any man, or to any set of men living. These he does not derive from your pleasure,—no, nor from the law and the Constitution. They are a trust from Providence, for the abuse of which he is deeply answerable. Your representative owes you, not his industry only, but his judgment; and he betrays you, instead of serving you, if he sacrifices it to your opinion.[5]

Burke argued that Parliament was not a *"congress* of ambassadors from different and hostile interests," obligating members to advocate the particular interests of their districts. Parliament was a *"deliberative* assembly of *one* nation, with *one* interest, that of the whole—where not local purposes, not local prejudices, ought to guide, but the general good, resulting from the general reason of the whole." [6]

The delegate theory is expressed in the "doctrine of instruction," offered in the First Congress as part of the Bill of Rights. To language that already protected "the right of the people peaceably to assemble and consult for their common good, and to apply to the Government for redress of grievances," Representative Thomas Tucker of South Carolina moved to add "to instruct their representatives." Tucker wanted a mandatory and enforceable voice for the people.

Representative Thomas Hartley of Pennsylvania objected to the motion, arguing that it was contrary to constitutional principles to permit a constituency to send binding instructions to a legislator. Said Hartley: "Representation is the principle of our Government; the people ought to have confidence in the honor and integrity of those they send forward to transact their business...." [7] According to Hartley, instructions that embody a local or partial view could never be assimilated to form a national policy. The power of legislation requires volition, free agency, and judgment—the right to make law as legislators deem expedient. If members of Congress were instructed by their constituents, they could find themselves torn between their constituents' voice and their oath to defend the Constitution. The House voted against Tucker's motion to add the doctrine of instruction to the Bill of Rights; 10 members were in favor and 41 opposed.[8]

The doctrine of instruction survived for a few decades in the

Senate. Members of that body considered themselves responsible to the state legislatures, which regularly instructed them how to vote on specific issues. Few senators felt bound by instructions after the Civil War, although the custom did not formally end until the Seventeenth Amendment severed the electoral connection between state legislatures and U.S. senators.[9]

For the most part, members of Congress must function as trustees, not as delegates (or as a combination of the two, called "politico").[10] The majority in a constituency does not express an opinion on every issue a legislator confronts. When the constituency does speak, it is generally with a muffled or divided voice. On most issues a member must chart a course with little guidance from the voting public. One senator advised his colleague: "Look—if you try to figure out what your constituents want on each issue and vote accordingly, you will soon have grey hair and be a one-termer, too." [11]

A legislator's vote depends on many factors: (1) the intensity of local interests, (2) how challengers might exploit a particular vote, (3) what a successor might do in office, (4) obligations toward minority interests, political parties, and organized interest groups, (5) how a trusted colleague votes, and (6) appeals by the president or party leaders. One member recalled:

> ... a congressman can do pretty much what he decides to do and he doesn't have to bother too much about criticism. I've seen plenty of cases since I've been up here where a guy will hold one economic or political position and get along all right; and then he'll die or resign and a guy comes in who holds quite a different economic or political position and he gets along all right too. That's the fact of the matter.[12]

The representativeness of Congress was sharply attacked in the years following World War II. Malapportionment, concentration of power in a handful of committee chairmen (seniority rule), and dilatory tactics (filibusters) by southern legislators were among the major objections raised. Scholars linked the decline of Congress directly to its defects as a representative body.[13]

Committee Reforms

Court decisions striking down malapportionment have improved the reputation of Congress as a representative body. Major reforms were adopted in the 1970s to dilute the power of committee chairmen and to make it easier to stop filibusters. From the standpoint of representation, the principal structural defect of Congress continues to be the composition of committees.

The relationship between Congress and its committees was much different during the first few decades of the nation. Members debated issues on the floor before assigning them to select (temporary) committees. In this way general principles were established by the full body to guide committee deliberations.[14] Once Congress completed action on a committee's recommendation, the committee—acting solely as an agent of the House or Senate—would disband.

The creation of standing (permanent) committees has aggravated the problem of ideological and geographical biases. In a sentimental impulse we sometimes call congressional committees "little legislatures," but they misrepresent the membership of Congress as a whole. Standing committees, organized to promote the specific interests of clients, create the very factions that Madison warned against in *Federalist 10*.

Clientele committees are now established to attend to such discrete interests as veterans' affairs, the aged, small business, and the merchant marine. Committees and subcommittees are "stacked" with members who want to satisfy the needs of specific economic and social interests.[15] These biases can be corrected by floor amendments (which increased in the 1970s), but the custom of reciprocity among committees and members still goes a long way toward protecting a committee's product. This means that a member's effectiveness, and hence the opportunity to represent a constituency, is largely restricted to the work of a few committees on which the legislator sits.

In 1973-1974, the House Select Committee on Committees (the Bolling Committee, named after Democratic Chairman Richard Bolling of Missouri) considered some far-reaching changes designed to produce a better balance in the committees. Rotation of committee members was considered but not recommended. Special attention was also directed to add new subject matter to narrow-based committees or to merge competing interests, such as energy and environment, in one committee. Little change resulted from this effort or from the counterpart exercise in the Senate by the Stevenson Committee (named for Democratic Chairman Adlai Stevenson of Illinois).[16]

The representative function of Congress has also been upset by the shift from short-term assignments available to citizens of the nineteenth century (who served as "citizen legislators") to the career perspective of legislators of the twentieth century.[17] This trend is compounded by legislators' dependence on large sums of money from private interests to finance reelection campaigns. Members express concern about their freedom to vote after accepting contributions from political action committees (PACs) that advocate specific positions on issues.

The representative function has also been affected by the build-up of congressional staff during the 1970s. Members have become overly dependent on their staffs, delegating to them some of the policy decisions that should be made directly by representatives. Staffs undercut the opportunity for direct communications from member to member, which give legislators a chance to appreciate each other's feelings about public issues and to develop a base for effective compromises. Because of the increased dependence on staff, this deliberative process in forging broad positions is being replaced by staff negotiations on more narrow, technocratic issues.[18]

THE PRESIDENT

During the colonial period, with resentment running high against the British king, American citizens assumed that their interests were automatically enhanced whenever legislators gained new powers from the royal governors. After the break with England, however, the state legislatures showed themselves just as capable of violating individual rights and acting in a capricious and arbitrary manner. They also demonstrated a talent for usurping executive and judicial powers. At the national level, the Continental Congress proved itself so ineffectual that delegates at the Philadelphia Convention readily agreed upon the need for a separate and strengthened executive.

At the Convention, Gouverneur Morris wanted to make the president capable of providing protection for "the mass of the people" and resisting the influence of the wealthy classes. James Madison looked to the president as a national officer, "acting for and equally sympathising with" every part of the nation. Uneasy with this optimism, Edmund Randolph favored a three-membered executive, to be drawn from different parts of the country.[19] His position was in the minority, however, and the Convention agreed on a single executive to promote unity.

To protect the president's independence, the delegates rejected the Virginia Plan that authorized the legislature to select the president. Still, the delegates were reluctant to rely on direct election by the people. Finally they decided on a system of electors who would meet in their respective states and vote for two persons, "of whom one at least shall not be an Inhabitant of the same State with themselves." The latter restriction was added to avoid a long list of local favorites, with no one meriting a national backing. In the event that no one attracted a majority of electors, or in case of a tie vote, the House of Representatives would choose the president.[20] The Twelfth Amendment, ratified in 1804, required electors to designate on their ballots the person voted for as president, and on separate ballots the person voted for as vice president, to minimize the possibility of a tie vote for president.

For several decades the congressional caucus of each party selected the nominees for president. By the 1820s, with the development of nominating conventions in the states, presidents could legitimately claim that they served as the direct representative of the people rather than as the hand-picked choice of congressional factions. President James Polk advanced this theory in 1848:

> If it be said that the Representatives in the popular branch of Congress are chosen directly by the people, it is answered, the people elect the President. If both Houses represent the States and the people, so does the President. The President represents in the executive department the whole people of the United States, as each member of the legislative department represents portions of them.[21]

With minor variations, the same theme has been repeated over the years by scholars and presidents. In 1908 Woodrow Wilson offered this description of the chief executive: "He is the representative of no constituency, but of the whole people." After leaving the Oval Office, Harry Truman said that the only lobbyist the whole people had in Washington was the president.[22]

In what has degenerated into a tiresome and trite ritual, presidents try to score points by calling Congress the servant of special interests. When the House of Representatives rejected a standby gasoline rationing plan in 1979, President Carter announced that a majority of the House had followed local or parochial interests, allowing "political timidity [to] prevent their taking action in the interests of our Nation." In a subsequent address he charged that Congress "has yielded to the narrow interest on energy issues time and time again." [23]

Special interest groups, however, do not spend all their time and resources on Capitol Hill. They also seek representation inside the administration. In fact, the White House has been organized for some time to respond to special interests. Beginning after World War II, White House assistants have been recruited to represent the aged, youth, women, blacks, Jews, labor, Hispanic-Americans, the business community, governors and mayors, artists, and citizens of the District of Columbia. As one scholar noted: "Where once the White House had been a mediator of interests, it now had become a collection of interests." [24]

Presidential candidates enter into bargains and understandings with special interests. During the campaign of 1976, Jimmy Carter promised the National Education Association (NEA) that he would create a cabinet-level Department of Education. Carter kept his promise, and in 1980 the NEA board of directors returned the favor by giving him their backing for his renomination.[25] Veteran analysts in the Office of Management and Budget were astonished by the financial commitments that Carter had made to special groups. In 1979, speaking before an Italian-American organization, President Carter assured the audience that "all of us, from the President, the Vice President on down, attempt every day accurately to mirror the interest of ethnic Americans." [26]

The cabinet, from the very beginning, has represented different economic, political, and social interests. Geographical balance has always been an important consideration. To President James Monroe, the cabinet "should be taken from the four sections of the Union, the East, the Middle, the South and the West." [27] The banking community must be comfortable with the secretary of the treasury; businessmen want suitable appointments to the Department of Commerce. Although the executive departments were initially created to serve general interests (state, war, and treasury), departments were gradually added to represent the interests of specialized groups, such as agriculture and labor. The creation of a separate Education Department in 1979 was only the latest in a long line of presidential efforts to respond to special interest demands.

THE COURTS

As the only branch of the federal government not elected by the people, the Supreme Court is routinely criticized for its undemocratic character. To critics, judicial policymaking is wholly incompatible with democratic theory and representative government. Members of the judiciary sometimes acknowledge the gap between their institution and representative government. When Associate Justice Potter Stewart resigned from the Supreme Court in 1981, he said there was "nothing more antithetical" in the process of appointing a successor than "to think it has something to do with representative democracy." [28] In its own way, however, the Supreme Court often represents individual rights that are poorly served by the volatile and impulsive politics of majority rule.[29]

Even if not subject to popular election, judges have many explicit ties to the public. Often they have held public office, sometimes in the legislative branch. The appointment process allows members of the executive and legislative branches to evaluate the fitness of a candidate. Once on the bench, judges make frequent appearances before public groups, and their decisions are closely examined and analyzed by law reviews and other publications. Most important, judges have a duty to uphold a Constitution that has been ratified by the people's representatives. To permit judges to execute that task, Article III of the Constitution provides for an independent judiciary, in terms of both tenure and compensation. Broad support for this institutional autonomy was evident in the public outcry against Franklin Roosevelt's plan to increase the size of the Supreme Court to make room for new appointees.

When courts stray too far from what the public will tolerate, the Constitution can be amended to override unpopular decisions. Four amendments (the Eleventh, Fourteenth, Sixteenth, and Twenty-sixth) have been added to nullify earlier decisions by the Supreme Court.[30] There have been an assortment of other proposals designed to curb the courts, including congressional control over the appellate jurisdiction of federal courts.[31]

To protect the legitimacy and acceptability of judicial review, presidents use their appointment power to maintain geographical and ideological balance. While sectionalism has declined as a qualification, religious affiliation and ethnicity have emerged as important considerations in the nomination of judges. For many years it was customary to preserve a "Catholic seat" and a "Jewish seat" on the Supreme Court. With the elevation of Thurgood Marshall to the Court in 1967, pressure will be strong to perpetuate a "Black seat." [32] To further the representative nature of the Court and to broaden its popular appeal, various groups urged President Carter to appoint a woman. During the 1980 campaign, Ronald Reagan declared his intention to place a woman on the Supreme Court. He fulfilled that promise in 1981 by nominating Sandra D. O'Connor.

The Omnibus Judgeship Act of 1978 took note of the fact that "only 1 percent of Federal judges are women and only 4 percent are blacks." Although President Carter had no opportunity to select a member of the Supreme Court, he made striking gains in appointing blacks, Hispanics, and females to district and appellate courts. These steps are important in building within a pluralistic society confidence in the courts.[33]

Once on the Court, justices assume a responsibility to protect interests that are neglected by the political branches. In a famous footnote to a decision in 1938, Justice Stone urged that the Court had a special responsibility to intervene for the protection of "discrete and insular minorities." [34] Justice Jackson, in a powerful opinion in the flag-salute case of 1943, insisted that individual rights (in this case, those of a minority religious sect) could not be left to majority rule. The purpose of the Bill of Rights was to withdraw certain subjects from

> the vicissitudes of political controversy, to place them beyond the reach of majorities and officials. . . . One's right to life, liberty, and property, to free speech, a free press, freedom of worship and assembly, and other fundamental rights may not be submitted to vote; they depend on the outcome of no elections.[35]

The Court has intervened to protect citizens living in malapportioned districts[36] and offered support to individuals and groups who were at a decided disadvantage when pitted against the interests of the state. In particular, the Court has declared invalid vague loyalty oaths and protected employees dismissed for alleged security reasons.[37]

THE BUREAUCRACY

Representation within the bureaucracy became an issue during the early days of the Republic. The Jeffersonians protested that the Federalists had positioned their supporters throughout the executive branch. Once elected to the White House, however, Jefferson used his removal power sparingly. He directed it chiefly against John Adams's midnight appointments of federal judges (*Marbury* v. *Madison*), against certain classes such as marshals, collectors of customs, and some postmasters, and a few cases of moral delinquency.[38]

Not until the administration of Andrew Jackson did the "theory of rotation" lead to a large number of turnovers in the executive establishment. Congress had paved the way for this development in 1820 by passing legislation that limited a number of federal officers to terms of four years, "removable from office at pleasure." [39] Jackson used this statutory authority to advance his idea of wide participation by citizens in federal office. Regular exchange of people in the federal service was one way to avoid the corruption that Jackson feared was inevitable with tenure:

> There are, perhaps, few men who can for any great length of time enjoy office and power without being more or less under the influence of feelings unfavorable to the faithful discharge of their public duties. Their integrity may be proof against improper considerations immediately addressed to themselves, but they are apt to acquire a habit of looking with indifference upon the public interests and of tolerating conduct from which an unpracticed man would revolt.[40]

Scholars of the twentieth century have argued that the federal bureaucracy is as representative of the country as Congress, if not more so.[41] Indeed, executive programs, such as the county committees that help the Department of Agriculture carry out soil conservation policies, are often organized to permit direct and ongoing participation by private citizens.[42] The popular description of bureaucrats as "faceless" and "remote" is a caricature of actual operations. Through the use of field offices, the federal government operates directly with local citizens, often more closely than state governments. In fact, critics maintain that some federal agencies represent constituencies so well, and operate with such autonomy from the three branches of government, that they threaten the constitutional system of checks and balances.[43]

Public participation in agency rulemaking includes notice of the proposed rule, agency hearings, and an opportunity for the public to comment on the rule. Since public participation in rulemaking is generally restricted to a select few who have the training, time, and money to monitor complex regulations, federal funds are available to encourage more members of the private sector to intervene in agency proceedings. The Magnuson-Moss Act of 1975 authorized the Federal Trade Commission to provide compensation for reasonable attorney fees, expert witness fees, and other costs of participating in a rulemaking proceeding.

Federal courts have pointed out in a number of cases that the right of effective participation in the political process "is of the essence of a democratic society, and any restrictions on that right strike at the heart of representative government." [44] The theory that agencies can always effectively represent the public interest is an assumption the courts abandon when the facts show otherwise.[45] Agency advisory committees sometimes improve the representative nature of the departments, but advisers and agency officials can also form a narrow and closed circle of interests, especially when a "revolving door" brings advisers into the government and returns agency officials to the industry being regulated.[46]

Congress attempts to build representation into the structure of agencies. For example, it directs that no more than one of the members of the Federal Reserve Board shall be selected from any one federal reserve district. Moreover, in selecting the members, the president "shall have due regard to a fair representation of the financial, agricultural, industrial, and commercial interests, and geographic divisions of the country." [47] Appointments come mainly from the East Coast, however, since presidents pick nominees on the basis of where they were born regardless of where they have lived or worked.[48]

Agency responsiveness to the public has been improved by a number of recent actions, including the Federal Advisory Committee Act of 1972 (opening up advisory committee meetings to public observation), the Legal Services Corporation Act of 1974 (providing legal assistance to low-income citizens), the Freedom of Information Act Amendments of 1974 (strengthening the "people's right to know" about governmental activities), and the Government in the Sunshine Act of 1976 (permitting greater public observation of agency decisionmaking).

The higher ranks of the civil service are less representative of the country than the lower ranks. With each increase in rank the unrepresentativeness becomes more pronounced.[49] At times these biases are encouraged and supported by Congress, as when it grants preference to veterans seeking federal employment. "Affirmative action" programs have been designed to increase minority and female employment in the federal government. As originally conceived, these programs were intended to utilize more fully the availability of minority talent. In 1978, however, with passage of Section 310 of the Civil Service Reform Act, Congress shifted the focus from *underutilization* to *underrepresentation*. The concept of "affirmative action" was replaced by numerical targets to make the percentages of minority and female federal employees in specific grades and occupational categories conform to their percentages in the civilian labor force. A minority recruitment program has been established to achieve full representation of minority groups and women in every category of civil service employment.[50]

Bureaucratic reforms do not alter the plain and simple fact that Congress is the agency authorized to formulate public policies. Legislators are the elected representatives; they retain their legitimacy by subjecting themselves to periodic public control through free elections. Agencies are not, like legislators, representative instruments. They are not created to formulate and express a will. Their essential duty is to carry out the will of the legislative body.[51]

SUBSYSTEMS

Thus far, representation has been discussed in terms of discrete institutions: Congress, the president, the courts, and the bureaucracy. Parts of these institutions also combine to form subsystems called "iron triangles," "subgovernments," or "policy whirlpools." It is conventional to define these subsystems as a coalition of congressional committees, agency personnel, and interest groups, all devoted to a common and narrow objective. There is particular danger that representation will be distorted when a subsystem is not effectively counterbalanced by a rival subsystem.

Important qualifications need to be added to this simple model of subsystems. The iron triangle is not a fixed and permanent institution. In the first place, the "cozy triangle" can be interrupted by outside political events. The overlapping and competing jurisdictions of congressional committees permit one subcommittee to take the initiative on an issue when another subcommittee is noncommittal. For example, in 1975 Senator Edward Kennedy's Subcommittee on Administrative Practice and Procedure (Judiciary Committee) held hearings on airline deregulation, an issue usually within the jurisdiction of the Subcommittee on Aviation (Commerce Committee). Kennedy's initiative in publicizing the issue and dramatizing the need for reform helped build political support for what eventually became the Airline Deregulation Act of 1978.

Second, when an issue is adjudicated the iron triangle changes shape to form a different coalition: the agency, interest group, and federal court.[52] This triangle is further complicated by the emergence of "public interest groups," such as the Sierra Club, Ralph Nader's Congress Watch, the Environmental Defense Fund, and Common Cause, all of which litigate federal policy issues. Moreover, law firms engaged in this process hire agency or committee staffers who then litigate in their areas of expertise.[53]

As Hugh Heclo notes in a perceptive essay, the iron triangle concept "is not so much wrong as it is disastrously incomplete." [54] Instead of closed triangles of control, he finds fairly open networks of policy specialists who float in and out of agencies, committees, private organizations, and law firms. In the words of Heclo:

> The notion of iron triangles and subgovernments presumes small circles of participants who have succeeded in becoming largely autonomous. Issue networks, on the other hand, comprise a large number of participants with quite variable degrees of mutual commitment or of dependence on others in their environment; in fact it is almost impossible to say where a network leaves off and its environment begins. Iron triangles and subgovernments suggest a stable set of participants coalesced to control fairly narrow public programs which are in the direct economic interest of each party to the alliance. Issue networks are almost the reverse image in each respect. Participants move in and out of the networks constantly.[55]

Third, the notion of an iron triangle ignores the freedom that executive departments have in piecing together their own coalitions with interest groups. A standard criticism of departmental heads is that they go "native," aligning themselves with congressional committees and interest groups against the White House.

However, a study by Graham Wilson in 1977 explicitly rejects this idea. Wilson deliberately studied an agency noted for its attachment to specific interests: the Department of Agriculture. Instead of finding a farm bloc that controls the secretary of agriculture, Wilson discovered a number of farm pressure groups that do not agree on a national agriculture policy. The secretary therefore has a choice of interest groups to listen to and freedom to shape a policy satisfactory to the White House.

Wilson examined the records of two secretaries of agriculture who served for eight continuous years while their parties controlled the White House. Ezra Taft Benson served President Eisenhower from 1953 to 1961, while Orville Freeman remained in the post throughout the Kennedy and Johnson administrations. Eight years should be sufficient time to become captive of the agriculture interests, but Benson waged war on the farm subsidy system, created antagonism with the agriculture committees, and retained an extremely close relationship with the president. Indeed, Eisenhower thought Benson was *too* loyal to White House policies. Freeman enjoyed better relations with Congress, but sustained a strong allegiance to presidential programs.

Wilson suggests that the American labor movement, also fragmented, produces a similar freedom of choice for the secretary of labor. It is difficult to be "captured" by one labor interest without offending another. Secretaries are free to piece together a consensus. Furthermore, the secretaries rarely come from unions. Most of them have been recruited from universities or the legal profession.[56]

The question of whether a departmental head is a political assistant of the president, an ally of Congress, or an instrument of special interests cannot be decided in the abstract or derived from general principles. The answer in each case depends on the particular department, statutory language, the interests and motivations of members of Congress, established customs and traditions, and the political climate that prevails at a given moment. The configurations are too complex and variable to warrant shorthand descriptions of "iron triangles." To understand representation and the system of shared power, there is no substitute for investigating the total political system, especially as it operates and adjusts over time. This investigation will be more successful by remaining alert to the conceptual and rhetorical problems discussed in the epilogue.

NOTES

1. Edward H. Levi, "Some Aspects of Separation of Powers," *Columbia Law Review* 76 (1976):371, 391.
2. "Congressional Districts Out of Balance," *Washington Post,* June 10, 1981, p. A6.
3. Roger H. Davidson, "Congress and the Executive: The Race for Representation," *Congress: The First Branch of Government,* ed. Alfred De Grazia (Washington, D.C.: American Enterprise Institute, 1967), p. 382; and Roger H. Davidson, *The Role of the Congressman* (New York: Pegasus, 1969), pp. 121-126.
4. Robert Weissberg, "Collective vs. Dyadic Representation in Congress," *American Political Science Review* 72 (1978):535, 536.
5. *The Works of the Right Honorable Edmund Burke* (Boston: Little, Brown & Co., 1871), 2:95.
6. Ibid., p. 96.
7. U.S., Congress, *Annals of Congress,* 1st Cong., August 15, 1789, p. 733.
8. Ibid., p. 747.
9. William H. Riker, "The Senate and American Federalism," *American Political Science Review* 49 (1955):452.
10. Donald A. Gross, "Representative Styles and Legislative Behavior," *Western Political Quarterly* 31 (1978):359.
11. Donald R. Matthews, *U.S. Senators and Their World* (New York: Vintage Books, 1960), p. 224, note 15.
12. Lewis Anthony Dexter, "The Representative and His District," *New Perspectives on the House of Representatives,* eds. Robert L. Peabody and Nelson W. Polsby (Chicago: Rand McNally, 1969), pp. 4-5.

13. Samuel P. Huntington, "Congressional Responses to the Twentieth Century," *The Congress and America's Future,* ed. David B. Truman (Englewood Cliffs, N.J.: Prentice-Hall, 1965), pp. 16-17.
14. See the explanation by Representative Boudinot in *Annals of Congress,* 1st Cong., May 19, 1789, p. 380.
15. Roger H. Davidson, "Representation and Congressional Committees," *The Annals* 411 (1974):48.
16. See Roger H. Davidson and Walter J. Oleszek, *Congress Against Itself* (Bloomington: Indiana University Press, 1977); and Judith H. Parris, "The Senate Reorganizes Its Committees, 1977," *Political Science Quarterly* 94 (1979):319.
17. For proposals to limit congressional tenure and thereby increase the representativeness of Congress, see U.S., Congress, *Congressional Record* (daily ed.), 96th Cong., 1st sess., January 24, 1979, 125:S551, S594-595, S597-598; ibid., January 31, 1979, pp. H343-344; ibid., February 1, 1979, p. H407; ibid., 96th Cong., 2d sess., August 27, 1980, 126:E4051; and ibid., 97th Cong., 1st sess., May 20, 1981, 127:H2353-2360.
18. Michael J. Malbin, *Unelected Representatives: Congressional Staff and the Future of Representative Government* (New York: Basic Books, 1980).
19. Max Farrand, ed., *The Records of the Federal Convention of 1787,* 4 vols. (New Haven: Yale University Press, 1937), 2:52, 81; see also 1:88.
20. Lucius Wilmerding, Jr., *The Electoral College* (New Brunswick, N.J.: Rutgers University Press, 1958), pp. 3-22.
21. James D. Richardson, ed., *A Compilation of the Messages and Papers of the Presidents,* 20 vols. (New York: Bureau of National Literature, 1897-1925), 6:2515 (Dec. 5, 1848).
22. Woodrow Wilson, *Constitutional Government in the United States* (New York: Columbia University Press, 1908), p. 68. Truman's speech of May 8, 1954, is reprinted in *The Presidency,* eds. John P. Roche and Leonard W. Levy (New York: Harcourt, Brace & World, 1964), pp. 30-31.
23. *Weekly Compilation of Presidential Documents* 15 (May 11, 1979):840; and ibid., August 7, 1979, p. 1410.
24. Stephen Hess, *Organizing the Presidency* (Washington, D.C.: Brookings Institution, 1976), pp. 9-10.
25. "Teachers' Union: Vital Bloc for Carter," *Washington Post,* July 2, 1980, p. A1:4.
26. *Weekly Compilation of Prsidential Documents* 15 (August 7, 1979):1412.
27. Richard F. Fenno, Jr., *The President's Cabinet* (New York: Vintage Books, 1959), p. 71, but see also pp. 67-81; and Leonard D. White, *The Jeffersonians* (New York: Free Press, 1951), pp. 360-362.
28. *Washington Post,* June 20, 1981, p. A1.
29. For a recent review of this issue, see Jesse H. Choper, "The Supreme Court and the Political Branches: Democratic Theory and Practice," *University of Pennsylvania Law Review* 122 (1974):810.
30. Chisholm v. Georgia, 2 U.S. 419 (1793); Scott v. Sandford, 60 U.S. 393 (1857); Pollock v. Farmers' Loan and Trust Co., 157 U.S. 429 (1895); and Oregon v. Mitchell, 400 U.S. 112 (1970). See Laurence H. Tribe, *The Constitutional Structure of American Government: Separation and Division of Powers* (Mineola, N.Y.: Foundation Press, 1978), p. 51, footnote 8.
31. Walter F. Murphy, *Congress and the Court* (Chicago: University of Chicago Press, 1962), pp. 127-241. There are current efforts to strip from federal courts the issues of busing, school prayer, and abortion.

32. Joel Grossman, *Lawyers and Judges* (New York: John Wiley & Sons, 1965); and Robert Scigliano, *The Supreme Court and the Presidency* (New York: Free Press, 1971), pp. 110-115.
33. P.L. 95-486, 92 Stat. 1633, sec. 8 (1978); Judith H. Parris, "The President, the Senate, and the Judges: Innovation in the Federal Judicial Selection Process, 1977-1980" (Paper presented at the annual meeting of the Midwest Political Science Association, Chicago, Ill., April 22-24, 1980), pp. 21-22; Robert J. Lipshutz and Douglas B. Huron, "Achieving a More Representative Federal Judiciary," *Judicature* 62 (May 1979).
34. United States v. Carolene Products, 304 U.S. 144, 152, n. 4 (1938). For recent analyses of the Court's function in protecting minority rights and assuring broad participation in the governmental process, see John Hart Ely, *Democracy and Distrust: A Theory of Judicial Review* (Cambridge: Harvard University Press, 1980), and Jesse H. Choper, *Judicial Review and the National Political Process* (Chicago: University of Chicago Press, 1980).
35. West Virginia State Board of Education v. Barnette, 319 U.S. 624, 638 (1943).
36. Baker v. Carr, 369 U.S. 186 (1962); Reynolds v. Sims, 377 U.S. 533 (1964).
37. E.g., Keyishian v. Board of Regents, 385 U.S. 589 (1967), and Greene v. McElroy, 360 U.S. 474 (1959). See Louis Fisher, *President and Congress* (New York: Free Press, 1972), pp. 200-204, 319-321.
38. White, *The Jeffersonians,* pp. 379-381.
39. 3 Stat. 582 (1820).
40. Richardson, *Messages and Papers of the Presidents,* 3:1011 (Dec. 8, 1829). See also Leonard D. White, *The Jacksonians* (New York: Free Press, 1954), pp. 300-346. While Jackson's removals were large in number compared to his predecessors, he did not make a "clean sweep" of the bureaucracy; see Erik McKinley Eriksson, "The Federal Civil Service Under President Jackson," *Mississippi Valley Historical Review* 13 (1927):517.
41. Norton Long, "Bureaucracy and Constitutionalism," *American Political Science Review* 46 (1952):808.
42. 16 U.S.C. 590h (1976).
43. Grant McConnell, *Private. Power and American Democracy* (New York: Alfred A. Knopf, 1967), p. 164; Charles M. Wiltse, "The Representative Function of Bureaucracy," *American Political Science Review* 43 (1941):510.
44. D.C. Federation of Civic Associations, Inc. v. Volpe, 434 F.2d 436, 441 (D.C. Cir. 1970), citing Reynolds v. Sims, 377 U.S. 533, 555 (1964).
45. Office of Communication of United Church of Christ v. FCC, 359 F.2d 994, 1003-1004 (D.C. Cir. 1969).
46. Joseph P. Witherspoon, "The Bureaucracy as Representatives," *Representation,* eds. J. Roland Pennock and W. Chapman (New York: Atherton Press, 1968), pp. 229-256; Roger C. Cramton, "The Why, Where and How of Broadened Public Participation in the Administrative Process," *Georgia Law Journal* 60 (1972):525; Ernest Gellhorn, "Public Participation in Administrative Proceedings," *Yale Law Journal* 81 (1972):359.
47. 12 U.S.C. 241 (1976).
48. U.S., Congress, Senate, Committee on Banking, Housing, and Urban Affairs, *Nomination of Lyle E. Gramley* (hearings), 96th Cong., 2d sess., 1980, p. 4. Statement by Republican Senator Edwin Jacob Garn.
49. Kenneth John Meier, "Representative Bureaucracy: An Empirical Analysis," *American Political Science Review* 69 (1975):526, 534. See Samuel

Krislov, *Representative Bureaucracy* (Englewood Cliffs, N.J.: Prentice-Hall, 1974).

50. For background on this issue, see Harry Kranz, *The Participatory Bureaucracy: Women and Minorities in a More Representative Public Service* (Lexington, Mass.: D. C. Heath, 1976).

51. *Administrative Procedure in Government Agencies,* report on Administrative Procedure, appointed by the Attorney General, originally reproduced as U.S., Congress, Senate, Senate Doc. No. 8, 77th Cong., 1st sess., 1941; reprinted in 1968 by the University Press of Virginia, see pp. 101-102.

52. Martin M. Shapiro, "The Presidency and the Federal Court," *Politics of the Oval Office,* ed. Arnold J. Meltsner (San Francisco: Institute for Contemporary Studies, 1981).

53. Hugh Heclo, "Issue Networks and the Executive Establishment," *The New American Political System,* ed. Anthony King (Washington, D.C.: American Enterprise Institute, 1978), pp. 100-101.

54. Ibid., p. 88.

55. Ibid., p. 102.

56. Graham K. Wilson, "Are Department Secretaries Really a President's Natural Enemies?" *British Journal of Political Science* 7 (1977):273.

Epilogue

Words are instruments for communicating thought. They serve as vehicles for clarification, refinement, and enrichment. Some words, however, obscure thought and discourage inquiry. Instead of aiding investigation they form a barrier. Objects then become imprisoned by our preconceptions.

Much of the vocabulary used to discuss Congress and the executive is an impediment to learning and exploration. Abstract concepts, especially when derogatory, prevent us from appreciating the subtle interactions between the branches, the prerogatives available to them, and the opportunities present for constructive compromise.

Slogans, always tempting, can backfire in unexpected ways. In 1959 President Eisenhower admonished legislators for calling foreign aid a "giveaway" program. It would be tragic, he said, "to allow a valuable program to be shot down by a slogan!" Later, however, he resorted to the term "pork barrel" to justify his veto of a public works appropriation bill. Members of Congress were quick to point out the administration's inconsistency in championing dams and reclamation projects abroad while deploring similar efforts at home. Both houses overrode the veto, the first time in seven years that an Eisenhower veto had not been sustained.[1]

In recent years political scientists have pointed out in rich detail the defects and liabilities of Congress. The federal bureaucracy receives

197

harsh treatment as well, criticized for being "unresponsive" and "resistant to change." Yet despite the failings of individual occupants of the Oval Office, there appears to be a different standard for the presidency. Legislators seem to travel the low road of "localism" while the president is associated with lofty qualities such as rationality, accountability, and a commitment to the public interest.

High principles, as Willmoore Kendall suggested some years ago, can be a euphemism for empty platitudes. He believed that as a constituency increased in size, from the congressional district to the national forum for a president, "there is greater and greater danger that the persons concerned will find themselves talking about *nothing*, not *something*, and will also find themselves talking about situations and problems that are too large, too complicated, for them to understand." Presidents are not more rational than legislators. They simply draw from different sources, and different levels, of information.[2]

In 1975 I participated in an all-day conference held in Washington, D.C., to analyze the tension between the executive and legislative branches. Throughout the morning and the afternoon, we were joined by members of Congress while senior editors and writers from a national magazine observed. That evening, at the Kennedy Center, we continued the conference over cocktails and dinner. Again the writers and editors listened. After I finished a conversation with one senator, several senior staffers from the magazine approached me and asked, visibly shaken, "Are *other* members of Congress this bright?" I wondered what stereotypes about Congress they had harbored over the years, how much they had miseducated their readers, and whether this experience with members who were demonstrably informed, thoughtful, and articulate would change their image of Congress.

The literature on Congress and the executive is filled with words that are a stumbling block to careful analysis and deeper probing. Why say that Congress, in the legislative process, practices "delay" instead of "deliberation" or "conscientious review"? Is the delay justified? Is there, in fact, a need for the legislation at all? Honest answers would require careful investigation into an individual case, but this kind of search takes time, homework, and persistence beyond the appetite of most analysts.

On a particular issue was Congress "obstructive" or did it merely reject an unworthy presidential proposal? Did Congress "gut," "mangle," "cripple," "mutilate," or "emasculate" a president's bill, or was it necessary to add amendments to a bill imperfectly drafted by the administration? Answers to these questions do not come easily. A researcher must master the original bill and its motivations, anticipate its impact on the public sector, comprehend the purpose behind the amendments, and take into account other considerations of a social, economic, and political nature.

Studies accuse Congress of "parochialism," "localism," and the pursuit of "particularistic" goals, all of which supposedly differentiate Congress from the president. But surely the White House is receptive to special interests. Indeed, it is inconceivable to think of a genuinely democratic political system that would prohibit intervention by special or local interests. What is gained by calling Congress an "assembly of special interests," instead of an institution that allows access, expression, and participation by the voters?

At each point along the legislative journey a bill is exposed to delay and adjustment as it passes through executive agencies, subcommittees, committees, the House and Senate, and conference committee. The complexity of this process has been criticized as "open season" for lobbyists and special interests to work their will. Would we find greater comfort in a more closed system, or would that give rise to complaints about autocracy and centralization? At least with the present system we have an opportunity to see interests at work. And since legislation has a major impact on society, we should encourage a process that permits intervention by affected parties.

"Parochialism" can be attributed to any group: Congress, the White House, the bureaucracy, or the judiciary. While it is true that members of Congress are more likely than executive officials to be recruited from small towns and local politics, this background enables Congress to perform its representational role and to offset the particular perspective of federal agencies. As one study notes, parochialism "may exist in various forms. If the experiences of congressmen incline them toward local parochialism, those of bureaucrats may incline them toward functional and agency parochialisms." [3]

Specialists in the agencies may attach undue importance to their areas of responsibility. Francis Wilcox recalled that during his service in the State Department the assistant secretary in charge of European affairs "vigorously defended the interests of his clients in Western Europe, often presenting their views with greater clarity and conviction than the Europeans themselves." And reflecting on his own responsibilities for United Nations affairs, Wilcox conceded that he "probably attached more significance to the role of the United Nations in American foreign policy than it merited." [4]

The different "parochialisms" of Congress and the president are essential to checks and balances. Proposals to have members of Congress elected at large in the nation, for the purpose of bringing the two branches closer, would jeopardize the constitutional system. Checks and balances are not negative instruments designed to frustrate government. They exist because of the propensity of public officials (like the rest of us) to make mistakes and abuse privileges. Checks and balances allow these mistakes to surface so they can be corrected before the damage becomes too great.

Commonly we hear of "fragmentation" within Congress. Unity seems preferable, and yet it is obvious that every organization, public or private, legislative or executive, depends on a division of labor and allocation of responsibilities to subgroups. Congress cannot decide everything on the floor in general assembly. Nor can it create, with any success, supercommittees to represent every interest. It tried that in 1946 with a joint budget committee consisting of 102 members from the taxing and appropriations committees of each house. After three ineffectual efforts the committee disbanded in 1949.

Recent proposals for a joint committee on national security encounter the same problems. If all of the legislative interests were represented the committee would be far too large, suffer poor attendance, and eventually delegate authority to subunits, defeating the original objective of comprehensiveness. An administration must be willing to work with ad hoc legislative groups of shifting memberships, varying with the particular issue. Committee realignment has its limits. It is impossible to include within a single committee total control over energy, national security, or other overarching issues that cut across Congress and the departments. Basic reliance must be on shared jurisdiction, referral of bills to more than one committee in each house, and special arrangements to deal with unique circumstances.

Criticism of Congress and the executive will not always be tempered, balanced, and fair. However, we can at least recognize when it is contradictory and even irrational. A recent newspaper account referred to an "ossified bureaucracy." Yet the same article managed to describe agency employees who somehow possessed the energy and skills to work assiduously in their schemes to sabotage the White House.[5] "Entrenched bureaucracy" is a sensational label that covers what would otherwise be quite ordinary: civil servants protected from political dismissals. White House officials complain about bureaucrats "blocking" programs, but investigation usually reveals that bureaucrats simply carry out the laws enacted by Congress rather than presidential proposals that are not yet public law. Do we really want bureaucrats to behave differently?

Presidents are criticized first for one thing and then another: Lyndon Johnson for wheeling and dealing, Jimmy Carter for failing to compromise and bargain. If legislators do not act quickly enough they are condemned for delay. If they act too quickly they are called a rubber stamp. For such criticism the only defense—aside from a sense of balance and humor—is an ability on the part of Congress and the president to articulate coherent policy, inspire public consensus, and cooperate effectively on emerging issues.

NOTES

1. Congressman Jim Wright, *You and Your Congressman* (New York: Capricorn Books, 1976), pp. 60-63; statement by Senator Mike Mansfield in U.S., Congress, *Congressional Record*, 86th Cong., 1st sess., September 10, 1959, 105:18873-18874.
2. Willmoore Kendall, "The Two Majorities," *Midwest Journal of Political Science* 4 (1960):317.
3. Joel D. Aberbach and Bert A. Rockman, "The Overlapping Worlds of American Federal Executives and Congressmen," *British Journal of Political Science* 7 (1977):23, 33.
4. Francis O. Wilcox, *Congress, the Executive, and Foreign Policy* (New York: Harper & Row, 1971), p. 61.
5. "Reagan Has Power to Remold Bureaucracy," *Washington Post,* November 19, 1980, p. A1.

Selected Bibliography

Books

Abshire, David M. *Foreign Policy Makers: President vs. Congress.* Beverly Hills, Calif.: Sage Publications, 1979.

Arnold, R. Douglas. *Congress and the Bureaucracy.* New Haven: Yale University Press, 1979.

Barber, Sotirios A. *The Constitution and the Delegation of Congressional Power.* Chicago: University of Chicago Press, 1975.

Berger, Raoul. *Executive Privilege: A Constitutional Myth.* Cambridge: Harvard University Press, 1974.

Binkley, Wilfred E. *President and Congress.* New York: Vintage Books, 1962.

Burnham, James. *Congress and the American Tradition.* Chicago: Henry Regnery Co., 1959.

Chamberlain, Lawrence H. *The President, Congress and Legislation.* New York: Columbia University Press, 1946.

Cohen, Benjamin V., et al. *The Prospect for Presidential-Congressional Government.* Berkeley, Calif.: Institute of Governmental Studies, 1977.

Conaway, O. B., Jr., ed. *Legislative-Executive Relationships in the Government of the United States.* Washington, D.C.: The Graduate School of the U.S. Department of Agriculture, 1954.

Crabb, Cecil V., Jr., and Holt, Pat M. *Invitation to Struggle: Congress, the President and Foreign Policy.* Washington, D.C.: Congressional Quarterly Press, 1980.

Dahl, Robert A. *Congress and Foreign Policy.* New York: Harcourt, Brace and Co., 1950.

Davis, James W., and Ringquist, Delbert. *The President and Congress: Toward a New Power Balance.* Woodbury, N.Y.: Barron's Educational Series, 1975.

De Grazia, Alfred. *Republic in Crisis: Congress Against the Executive Force.* New York: Federal Legal Publications, 1965.

Dodd, Lawrence C., and Schott, Richard L. *Congress and the Administrative State.* New York: John Wiley & Sons, 1979.

Edwards, George C. III. *Presidential Influence in Congress.* San Francisco: W. H. Freeman & Co., 1978.

Egger, Rowland, and Harris, Joseph P. *The President and Congress.* New York: McGraw-Hill, 1963.

Fisher, Louis. *President and Congress: Power and Policy.* New York: Free Press, 1972.

_____. *Presidential Spending Power.* Princeton: Princeton University Press, 1975.

_____. *The Constitution Between Friends: Congress, the President, and the Law.* New York: St. Martin's Press, 1978.

Franck, Thomas M., and Weisband, Edward. *Foreign Policy By Congress.* New York: Oxford University Press, 1979.

Freeman, J. Leiper. *The Political Process: Executive Bureau-Legislative Committee Relations.* New York: Random House, 1965.

Gwyn, W. B. *The Meaning of the Separation of Powers: An Analysis of the Doctrine from its Origin to the Adoption of the United States Constitution.* New Orleans: Tulane University Press, 1965.

Hamilton, James. *The Power to Probe: A Study in Congressional Investigations.* New York: Random House, 1976.

Harris, Joseph P. *Congressional Control of Administration.* Washington, D.C.: Brookings Institution, 1964.

Horn, Stephen. *The Cabinet and Congress.* New York: Columbia University Press, 1960.

Jackson, Carlton. *Presidential Vetoes, 1792-1945.* Athens: University of Georgia Press, 1967.

Koenig, Louis W. *Congress and the President.* Glenview, Ill.: Scott, Foresman & Co., 1965.

Kurland, Philip B. *Watergate and the Constitution.* Chicago: University of Chicago Press, 1978.

Lehman, John F. *The Executive, Congress and Foreign Policy: Studies of the Nixon Administration.* New York: Praeger Publishers, 1976.

Livingston, William S., et al., eds. *The Presidency and the Congress: A Shifting Balance of Power?* Austin: University of Texas Press, 1979.

Malbin, Michael J. *Unelected Representatives: Congressional Staff and the Future of Representative Government.* New York: Basic Books, 1980.

Mansfield, Harvey C., Sr., ed. *Congress Against the President.* New York: Praeger Publishers, 1975.

Merry, Henry J. *Constitutional Function of Presidential-Administrative Separation.* Washington, D.C.: University Press of America, 1978.

_____. *Five-Branch Government: The Full Measure of Constitutional Checks and Balances.* Urbana: University of Illinois Press, 1980.

Moe, Ronald C., ed. *Congress and the President: Allies and Adversaries.* Pacific Palisades, Calif.: Goodyear Publishing Co., Inc., 1971.

Ogul, Morris S. *Congress Oversees the Bureaucracy.* Pittsburgh: University of Pittsburgh Press, 1976.

Polsby, Nelson W. *Congress and the Presidency.* Englewood Cliffs, N.J.: Prentice-Hall, 1976.

Rhode, William E. *Committee Clearance of Administrative Decisions.* East Lansing, Mich.: Michigan State University Press, 1959.

Ripley, Randall B., and Franklin, Grace A. *Congress, the Bureaucracy, and Public Policy.* Homewood, Ill.: Dorsey Press, 1976.

Robinson, James A. *Congress and Foreign Policy-Making.* Homewood, Ill.: Dorsey Press, 1967.

Schlesinger, Arthur M., Jr., and De Grazia, Alfred. *Congress and the Presidency: Their Role in Modern Times.* Washington, D.C.: American Enterprise Institute, 1967.

Travis, Walter Earl, ed. *Congress and the President: Readings in Executive-Legislative Relations.* New York: Teachers College Press, 1967.

Vile, M. J. C. *Constitutionalism and the Separation of Powers.* Oxford: Oxford University Press, 1967.

Wayne, Stephen J. *The Legislative Presidency.* New York: Harper & Row, 1978.

Wilcox, Francis O. *Congress, the Executive, and Foreign Policy.* New York: Harper & Row, 1971.

Articles

Bestor, Arthur. "Separation of Powers in the Domain of Foreign Affairs: The Original Intent of the Constitution Historically Examined." *Seton Hall Law Review* 5 (1974):529.

Bruff, Harold H., and Gellhorn, Ernest. "Congressional Control of Administrative Regulation: A Study of Legislative Vetoes." *Harvard Law Review* 90 (1977):1369.

Cash, Robert B. "Presidential Power: Use and Enforcement of Executive Orders." *Notre Dame Lawyer* 39 (1963):44.

Cotter, Cornelius P., and Smith, J. Malcolm. "Administrative Accountability to Congress: The Concurrent Resolution." *Western Political Quarterly* 9 (1956):955.

Davis, Eric L. "Legislative Liaison in the Carter Administration." *Political Science Quarterly* 94 (1979):287.

――――. "The President and Congress." In *Politics and the Oval Office,* edited by Arnold J. Meltsner. San Francisco: Institute for Contemporary Studies, 1981.

Dodd, Lawrence C. "Congress, the Constitution, and the Crisis of Legitimation." In *Congress Reconsidered,* 2d ed., edited by Lawrence C. Dodd and Bruce I. Oppenheimer. Washington, D.C.: Congressional Quarterly Press, 1981.

Dry, Murray. "The Separation of Powers and Representative Government." *Political Science Review* 3 (1973):43.

Engstrom, Richard L., and Walker, Thomas G. "Statutory Restraints on Administrative Lobbying—'Legal Fiction'." *Journal of Public Law* 19 (1970):89.

Fisher, Louis. "Congress, the Executive and the Budget." *The Annals* 411 (1974):102.

———. "A Political Context for Legislative Vetoes." *Political Science Quarterly* 93 (1978):241.

Ginnane, Robert W. "The Control of Federal Administration by Congressional Resolutions and Committees." *Harvard Law Review* 66 (1953):569.

Heaphy, Maura E. "Executive Legislative Liaison." *Presidential Studies Quarterly* 5 (1975):43.

Hebe, William. "Executive Orders and the Development of Presidential Power." *Villanova Law Review* 17 (1972):688.

Jones, Charles O. "Congress and the Presidency." In *The New Congress,* edited by Thomas E. Mann and Norman J. Ornstein. Washington, D.C.: American Enterprise Institute, 1981.

Hilsman, Roger. "Congressional-Executive Relations and the Foreign Policy Consensus." *American Political Science Review* 52 (1978):725.

Jenkins, Gerald. "The War Powers Resolution: Statutory Limitation on the Commander in Chief." *Harvard Journal on Legislation* 11 (1974):181.

Kelley, Stanley, Jr. "Patronage and Presidential Legislative Leadership." In *The Presidency,* edited by Aaron Wildavsky. Boston: Little, Brown, & Co., 1969.

Manley, John F. "Presidential Power and White House Lobbying." *Political Science Quarterly* 93 (1978):255.

Manning, Bayless. "The Congress, the Executive and Intermestic Affairs: Three Proposals." *Foreign Affairs* 55 (1977):306.

McGowan, Carl. "Congress, Court and Control of Delegated Power." *Columbia Law Review* 77 (1977):1119.

Murphy, John F. "Knowledge is Power: Foreign Policy and Information Interchange Among Congress, the Executive Branch, and the Public." *Tulane Law Review* 49 (1975):505.

Neighbors, William D. "Presidential Legislation by Executive Order." *University of Colorado Law Review* 37 (1964):105.

Nelsen, Ancher. "Lobbying by the Administration." In *We Propose: A Modern Congress,* edited by Mary McInnis. New York: McGraw-Hill, 1966.

Parnell, Archie. "Congressional Interference in Agency Enforcement: The IRS Experience." *Yale Law Journal* 89 (1980):1360.

Pipe, G. Russell. "Congressional Liaison: The Executive Consolidates Its Relations With Congress." *Public Administration Review* 26 (1966):14.

Stevens, Charles J. "The Use and Control of Executive Agreements: Recent Congressional Initiatives." *Orbis* 20 (1977):905.

Sundquist, James L. "Congress, the President, and the Crisis of Competence in Government." In *Congress Reconsidered,* 2d. ed., edited by Lawrence C. Dodd and Bruce I. Oppenheimer. Washington, D.C.: Congressional Quarterly Press, 1981.

Younger, Irving. "Congressional Investigations and Executive Secrecy: A Study in the Separation of Powers." *University of Pittsburgh Law Review* 20 (1959):755.

White, Howard. "Executive Responsibility to Congress via Concurrent Resolution." *American Political Science Review* 36 (1942):895.

Zeidenstein, Harvey G. "The Reassertion of Congressional Power: New Curbs on the President." *Political Science Quarterly* 93 (1978):393.

Index of Cases

Index